COOKING WITHOUT BORDERS

The Cookbook of Atlanta International School

Cover Food Photography: Steve Pelosi   Food Stylists: Donna Creel and Peg Blackley

Atlanta International School
Ecole Internationale d'Atlanta
Colegio Internacional de Atlanta
Internationale Schule Atlanta

Atlanta International School invites you to enjoy culinary treasures from our parents, friends and students. Like our school, the strength of this cookbook is its diversity. You will find recipes from around the world to relish and to enjoy. I am happy to see this project move from our home and the homes of many of our families into yours.

In addition to the pleasure that you will get from preparing the dishes and savoring the results of your work, your investment in this cookbook will help us fulfill part of our school's mission. We believe that a cohesive community of students and faculty from a variety of backgrounds is a particularly rich culture for growing the heart and mind of every student. Such diversity best prepares students for life-long learning in a diverse, interdependent world. A portion of the proceeds from this cookbook will go towards our endowment. This endowment allows us to provide scholarships to students who can benefit from and contribute to our rigorous international program of study but need financial assistance to attend.

At Atlanta International School, we believe in the intrinsic joy of learning and hope, sustained and nurtured in a diverse school community, united in its commitment to mutual respect and purposeful effort to set and achieve high standards.

We also believe that great food, like human potential, has no borders.

Enjoy,

David B. Hawley
David B. Hawley
Headmaster

For additional copies use the order form in the back or send a check for $19.95 plus $3.50 shipping and handling (Georgia residents add 7% sales tax per book) to:

Cooking Without Borders
Atlanta International School
2890 North Fulton Drive
Atlanta, Georgia 30305
404-841-3845
www.aischool.org

First Printing   September 1999   5,000

Copyright © 1999
Atlanta International School
Parents Association
Atlanta, Georgia
All Rights Reserved

ISBN   0-966-37320-0

Printed in the USA by
WIMMER
The Wimmer Companies
Memphis
1-800-548-2537

Cooking Without Borders is a true international community cookbook, consisting of the favorite recipes of the families and friends of Atlanta International School, who represent over 55 countries.

Interestingly, as the book progressed, we discovered many similarities as well as the expected diversity of foods from around the world. We enjoyed pancakes from Lithuania, Russia and Holland; meatballs from Greece, India and Germany; and noodles from the Philippines, Indonesia, Thailand, Vietnam and Italy.

Many of the recipe contributors have been cooking without borders for years as they traveled and lived in various countries; enjoying the flavors and culture of their new homes and incorporating them with their native cuisine; creating deliciously exotic flavor combinations that can be attributed to no one country. The Indian version of the Swiss dish, Rösti, is a good example along with many others throughout the book, which demonstrate how recipes evolve and grow.

We tried to include a good distribution of recipes with regard to both country and food categories. Some are very simple to make, while others are more complex. Most are made with commonly found ingredients, while a few require special ingredients. In both cases, the results are well worth any extra effort.

This book has been a labor of love from an entire team of dedicated people, and a totally enjoyable project. Literally thousands of hours have been given by a wide variety of talented volunteers to bring you *Cooking Without Borders*. Hundreds of recipes were contributed. Volunteers spent a year and a half testing each recipe three or more times. Many people opened their homes for the tastings. The word processors and proofreaders worked endless hours, along with the metric conversion volunteers, and many many others.

On behalf of all the people who created *Cooking Without Borders*:

Bon Appetit, **BUON APPETITO**, 𝕾makelijk, Buen Provecho
Guten Appetit, *Pritnovo Apetita*, **Dobir Tek**

Jane Harwood   Leisa Weld   3

Cooking Without Borders
Cookbook Committee 1997-1999

Co-Chairpersons
Jane Harwood   Leisa Weld

Testing Coordinators
Suzanne Clark   Julie Audibert

Art Director and Designer
Lisa Cannon Taylor

Public Relations
Judith Moen Stanley

Section Editor Chair
Sharon Hermann

Metric Conversion and Glossary
Agnes Morrell   Jane Joyce

Recipe Consultants
Cathie Touhy Wattles   Leisa Weld

Chairperson Elect
Leonie Ley-Mitchell

Section Editors
Maggie Bethel
Trinkett Clark
Jane Joyce
Michèle Taylor
Margarietta Vranicar

Word Processing
Dianna Bowen
Rose Bredy
My Dam
Ruthann Fellows
Kathy Gerkin
Wendy Kendrick
Cathy Lacy
Camille Oladele
Catalina Scott

Marketing and Sales
Sabine Bickert
Anke Fischer
Kathy Gerkin
Wendi McAfee
Jennifer Monopoli-Tailhardat
Yolanta Melamed
Fariba Teimorabadi

Divider Art Work
Penelope Smith

Cover Photo Set Dressing
Susan Pritchett

Children's Cover Photo
Don Dory

Sidebars
Jane Harwood

Sidebar Contributors
Recipe Contributors
Luba Bland
Jane Harwood
Paul Tastenhoye
Michèle Taylor
Leisa Weld

Special Mention
Clarice Bricteux
Mary Ann Carbonell
Beryl Dover
Susan Mack
Olga Plaut

Special thanks are due to the many people who helped test these recipes as each recipe was tested three or more times. Some people tested over 100 recipes, tried them on their families and brought them to testing parties. Without their work this cookbook could not have been written.

Recipe Testers

Zahra Akhavan
Julie Audibert
Surinder Bal
Maggie Bethel
Luba Bland
Clarice Bricteux
Suzanne Clark
Kathy Collura
Alexandra Curry
Julie Davis
Diane Dear
Victoria Denson
Jan Douglas
Beryl Dover
Helga Engmann
Anke Fischer
Joseph Funk
Kathleen Funk
Dee Gill
Molly Griffin
Jane Harwood
Leigh Haynie
Regina Imbsweiler
Jane Joyce
Jaques Le Mouel
Debra Leff
Stan Levitt
Leonie Ley-Mitchell

Rosemary Lynn
Susan Mack
Laurie Martin
Lisa Marx
Yolanta Melamed
Judith Moen
Agnes Morrell
Anne-Catherine Mulliez
Lori Novak
Lisa Olens
Hima Patel
Lone Pederson
Olga Plaut
Kelli Potts
Gillian Quille
Diana Silverman
Thierry Tailhardat
Paul Tastenhoye
Michele Taylor
Arthur Douglas Thayer
Frans Van Eysinga
John Varner
Lynn Varner
Sigrid Vorwerk
Cathie Tuohy Wattles
Leisa Weld
Clayton Wheatley
Sarah Woelz

Many thanks to those who generously contributed recipes. Our only regret in producing Cooking Without Borders *is that space, duplication, similarities and the availability of ingredients would not allow for all the wonderful recipes to be included.*

R e c i p e   C o n t r i b u t o r s

Zarah Ahkavan
Nora Arenas
Philippe Audibert
Julie Audibert
Pascale Audibert
Joan Awai
Surinder Bal
Martina Berent
Alicia Bertera
Maggie Bethel
Luba Bland
Barbara Blumberg
JB Booth
Brigitte Brake
Rose Bredy
Clarice Bricteux
Lana Bueno
Tracy Bulostin
Lisa Cannon Taylor
Giordano Checchi
Marisa Checchi
Yung Clancy
Suzanne Clark
Trinkett Clark
Pauline Coetzee
Stef Coetzee
Chi Colberg
Alexandra Curry
My Dam
Julie Davis
Diane Dear
Keiko Doi
Gail Dougherty
Beryl Dover
Mary Dowdy
Martha Dubbert
Juergen Engert
Helga Engmann
Ruth Anne Fellows
Virginia Ferandel
Thierry Flamant
Annouska Frey
Karen Geiger
Petra Gentsch
Dean Gill
Olga C. de Goizueta
Esther Gordon
George Hammond
Jane Harwood
Melita Easters Hayes

Leigh Haynie
Rona Hernandez
Marie-Claire Hunn
Regina Imbsweiler
Susanna Jenny
Jane Joyce
Stefanie Karacic
Cigdem Kilic
Cathy Lacy
Maguy LaRochelle
Marcia Levitt
Stan Levitt
Leonie Ley-Mitchell
Rosana Lima
Rosemary Lynn
Ute Machat
Karin Manidis
Lisa Marx
Sam Massell
Marti Matthews
Natasha Maus
Nicolette Maus
Teodoro Maus
Heike McNally
Judith Medinilla
Claire Millous
Parke Simpson Mock
Judith Moen
Agnes Morrell
Ann Muromachi
Ava Navin
Pia Nilsson
Larry North
Lori Novak
Cirila Nunez-Rumaguera
Enid Palmer
Hima Patel
Tatiana Peeters
Starr Pellerin
Pauline Pellerin
Rebecca Perez
Alice Pettway
Cecile Peyronnet
Olga Gomez Plaut
Remedios Polo
Olga Popkova
Gillian Quille
Ayleen Ramirez
Elisabetta Rebuffi
Brooke Reeve III

Marika Reither
Reinierte Rietmeijer
Brigitte Rose
Firouzeh Rouhani
Behzad Rozei
Jann Rubio
Michaela Rueckel
Jill Sare
Brigitte Schoene
Monique Seefried
Anastasia Simos
Penelope Smith
Annette Stilwell
Christine Stock
Tomoko Takeo
Paul Tastenhoye
Michèle Taylor
Fariba Teimorabadi
Arthur Douglas Thayer
Sarah Thomas
Ruth Ellen Todd
Cindy Tracy
Marlene Tucker
Frans Van Eysinga
Rasamy Vanijcharoenkarn
Marianne Viberg
Catherine Vigouroux
Uberto Visconti di Modrone
Sigrid Vorwerk
Margareta Vranicar
Mary Ward
Amy Waterman
Cathie Touhy Wattles
Katja Weber
Leisa Weld
Cynthia Westergaard
Clayton Wheatley
Theresia Widmer
Emily Wilingham-Adair
Aileen & Steve Williams
Suzanne Wilner
Carol Ann Wilson
Father George Wiltz, S.J.
Annette Witte
Sarah Woelz
Tomer Woelz
Andrew Young

Table of Contents

Know Your Ingredients

Bacon is usually streaked with fat in the US, while in Europe it is often made from the tenderloin, is leaner, less salty and can be bought in thick pieces. Many of the recipes in this book call for lean, thick cut bacon as the closest approximation to European bacon or look for Irish bacon in international markets. When using fatty bacon, the bacon fat needs to be drained off before cooking the recipe further.

Cheese:
Chèvre is French goat cheese, from the French word for goat. The cheese has a tart flavor and can be moist and creamy or dry and fairly firm. It comes in different shapes and can also be bought crumbled, which is useful in salads and sauces.

Edam is a popular Dutch cheese covered in a red waxy layer. It varies in size and can be bought as miniatures that are convenient for children.

Emmentaler cheese is named after Switzerland's Emmental valley in the canton of Bern. A cow's milk cheese, it is hard in texture and has many holes. It is often used in fondue.

Feta cheese is a classic Greek cheese traditionally made from sheep or goat's milk. It has a rich tangy flavor and goes well in salads.

Fontina comes from the Val d'Aosta in Italy. It is made from cow's milk and has a semi-firm creamy texture. The pale yellow cheese is dotted with small holes and the whole is covered in a golden brown rind. It melts very smoothly.

Gorgonzola is named after a town outside Milan where it was originally made. It has a similar flavor to **Roquefort** from France and **Stilton** from the midlands of England. They are all made from cow's milk and are seeded with mold during maturation. The texture is rich and creamy and they crumble on handling.

Gouda is Dutch cheese made from cow's milk. The flavor develops with aging and the older cheeses begin to resemble Parmesan cheese in texture.

Gruyère cheese comes from the Gruyere valley in the canton of Fribourg. It is also a cow's milk cheese with a firm but pliable texture and a nutty sweet flavor.

Kasseri is a salty Greek cheese made from sheep's or goat's milk. It is hard and is good for grating. It is a gold color with a natural hard rind and is sold in blocks.

Mascarpone is from the Lombardy region of Italy. It is made of double or triple heavy cream. It has a rich, soft and delicate texture and is used in desserts and with savory ingredients.

Parmesan cheese is a hard dry cheese originally from Italy. It is made from skimmed cow's milk so it contains very little fat. Parmesan, when freshly grated, is superior to the pre-grated and dried versions. Most of the recipes in this book suggest using the best and most authentic parmesan, **Parmigiano-Reggiano** or **Grana Padano**.

Chiles vary in strength, but generally smaller chiles are stronger. **Poblano** chiles are a large dark-green, almost black variety. The darkest is the richest in flavor. The **jalapeño** chile is a green, smooth, medium-sized chile. **Habañero** chiles from the West Indies are extremely hot and are often made into West Indian habañero chili sauces. Hands should be washed immediately after chopping this pepper. **Chipotle** chiles are dried smoked jalapeño chiles. They have a wrinkled, dark brown skin and a smoky, sweet, almost chocolate flavor. Canned chipotles in adobo can be found in the Mexican section of most large supermarkets. **Adobo** sauce is a dark red chili sauce made with vinegar and herbs used as a marinade or to preserve chipotle chiles. **Cayenne** chiles are long, thin and red and widely available in fresh, dried or powdered forms. Other chiles that can be found in some supermarkets include **scotch bonnet**, **Thai and finger hot** chiles. In most cases when a particular variety of chile is unavailable, other similar sized and colored chiles can be substituted.

Cilantro is also known as **chinese parsley** and fresh **coriander**.

Cornichons or **guerkins** are baby pickles that are traditionally eaten with patés and cold meat pies. They are often available in the pickle section or international food section of large supermarkets.

Court Boullion is a seasoned liquid in which fish or shellfish can be cooked. Press four or five cloves into an onion and simmer gently in water together with peppercorns, carrots, parsley, celery and various herbs. White wine, lemon juice or vinegar can be added to the water. Fish is then simmered gently in the aromatic broth.

Crème Fraîche is heavy cream that has matured but not soured. In France, after cream is pasteurized, the natural ferments and lactic acids are added back to the cream, which then thickens and gets its characteristic nutty flavor. In the United States the ferments are not added back in and so heavy cream has neither the texture nor the flavor of French cream. Crème fraîche has the advantage that it does not curdle when boiled and the thicker texture is perfect for some recipes. It can be purchased in the dairy section of some large supermarkets or you may substitute heavy cream or heavy cream with a little sour cream stirred in. As an alternative, see the index for a crème fraîche recipe that approximates the genuine crème fraîche.

Curry leaves are the green aromatic leaves of an Indian bush. The leaves formed the basis of the original curry powder in ancient Indian cooking.

Dried shrimp are small, peeled, sundried shrimp used in Asian cooking. They are used in small amounts and must be soaked before using.

Galangal comes from the creamy white-fleshed rhizome of the greater galangal. It is like ginger, although the flavor is more delicate and the rhizome is easier to crush. The greater galangal when dried and powdered can be called *laos* powder. The lesser galangal is also sold dried and powdered and is known as *kencur*. It is an important ingredient in Thai cooking.

Harissa is a red pepper sauce that originated in Tunisia. It is hot and is made with dried red chiles, garlic, cumin, coriander, caraway, mint and olive oil. It is a traditional accompaniment for couscous as well as other North African dishes. It can be found in tubes or little cans in international food markets.

Herbes de Provence is a mixture of dried herbs originally from the Provence region of France. It normally contains basil, fennel seed, lavender, marjoram, rosemary, sage, summer savory, and thyme.

Lady fingers are dried sponge cake baked in the shape of a fat finger. They are usually found in stores and are used in dessert dishes. This is in contrast with **Ladies fingers**, which is another name for okra.

Lemon grass has a scallion type base. When the outer, scaly layer is peeled off, it reveals a more tender shoot, which is often called the 'lemon root'. It can be purchased in international markets. It is popular in Thailand and throughout Asia and is used in tea, soups and other dishes.

Manioc is also known as **cassava** or **yucca** and is used to make tapioca. This root vegetable is native to South America but is now also grown extensively in Africa. It is available in Latin American and Caribbean markets. The brown skin is peeled to reveal a white flesh. *Farofa* is manioc flour that has been toasted with a little butter over medium heat until it turns golden brown.

Noodles: Rice noodles, rice vermicelli or **rice stick** are thin Chinese noodles that look white before cooking. If they are cooked in liquid they become gelatinous, whereas if they are deep fried they become crispy strands. They retain this texture when cooled and used in salads. **Mung bean noodles, cellophane noodles** or **glass noodles** are made from mung beans. They are primarily used in soups and stews where they turn transparent and gelatinous. Deep fried they resemble rice noodles, which can be substituted. They are soaked before using except when deep frying.

Nuoc Nam is a fish sauce from Vietnam. Fish sauce is a very popular ingredient throughout Southeast Asia. It has a strong, salty flavor and looks brown in color. It is also known as **Nam Pla** (Thailand), **Patis** (Philippines) and **Shottsuru** (Japan).

Phyllo (Filo) pastry is made of tissue thin sheets of dough, layered to make very flaky pastry. It is used all over the Middle East. The name comes from the Greek word for leaf. Phyllo can be made from scratch but it is extremely difficult to do. Frozen ready-made versions can be purchased and are of a good quality. Phyllo has to be defrosted very slowly in the package so that the sheets of pastry do not break. Once the package is opened, remove enough sheets to work with immediately and cover the rest with a damp cloth so it does not dry out.

Prosciutto or Parma ham is an uncooked, unsmoked ham that is cured in salt. Real Italian proscuitto was unavailable in the United States but can now be purchased in the deli sections of many large supermarkets. It should be cut into tissue paper thin slices.

Puff pastry is a light, multi-layered pastry and is time consuming to make. It is a rich dough with a large quantity of butter. Good quality frozen versions are readily available, although package sizes vary. One variety available is a 17 ounce package of sheets. Each sheet will make a 9-inch (23cm) size dish. Other brands have smaller sheets but these can be stuck together with a few drops of water to fit any size. In France it can be bought fresh.

Rice comes in many varieties. **Basmati rice** is long grained aromatic rice grown in the foothills of the Himalayas. It is often used in Indian cooking. Many Texas and Carolina rices are also long grain but without the distinct flavor of Basmati and other aromatic rice. **Arborio rice** is an Italian medium grain rice with a high starch content. It has a shorter, rounded shape and is traditionally used for risotto because the high starch content leads to a creamier dish. Short grained rice, including **glutinous rice**, **sticky rice**, **sweet rice** and **sushi rice** cook soft and sticky. Short grained rice is commonly used in Japanese and Vietnamese cooking.

Saffron is the orange-red stigma of the small purple crocus. It both flavors and colors food and is expensive because the stigmas are picked by hand. Dried whole saffron threads have the best flavor and only a pinch is usually necessary as a little goes a long way. The whole saffron threads or stigmas are used, usually with some liquid and are stirred well into the food so as to color or flavor the entire dish.

Various kinds of sugar are available in different countries under different names. **Granulated sugar** is slightly coarser than **castor sugar**, *sucre en poudre* and **superfine sugar**. They can be interchanged with little consequence. The finest ground sugar is called **icing sugar**, **confectioners' sugar**, **powdered sugar** or *sucre glacé* and is referred to when recipes require it. **Pearl sugar** is nugget size sugar in clear crystal form. It is popular in many areas of Europe but is hard to find in the United States.

Many English terms for food are different in the United States than in other English speaking countries. For example, in England, zucchini are known as **courgettes**, cornstarch is known as **cornflour**, broiling is called **grilling**, eggplant is **aubergine** and mincing is **chopping finely.**

Bunch sizes for **fresh herbs** and some vegetables vary from city to city and country to country. Standardization is not possible, so use your best judgment.

Safe Handling of Raw Eggs

The Salmonella bacteria, which can cause illness and even death, is occasionally found in raw eggs, even uncracked eggs. The risk is low, but is reduced even further if eggs are properly stored and cooked.

For the classic dishes that depend on raw eggs or lightly cooked eggs, some cooks now substitute pasteurized liquid eggs or dried egg whites. The liquid eggs most closely resemble fresh eggs and are only slightly less efficient than fresh eggs for emulsifying or whipping purposes. Dried whites are best for lightly cooked meringues.

Some cooks refuse to compromise and continue using fresh raw eggs without incident. If you are of this school, minimize risk by using the freshest eggs possible and storing them at temperatures below 40°F.

Measurement Conversion Methods

Metric measurements are used all over the world and are now being introduced to the US. The unit of dry weight on which the calculations in these recipes were based was 28g (grams) to the ounce. These measurements were then rounded up or down, giving 450g to the pound. Hence the relationship is not completely linear when comparing conversions. There are 1000g in a kilogram.

Cups as a measure of weight vary from one ingredient to another according to density. Hence, a cup of diced onions does not compare with a cup of fresh parsley. Although some manufacturers now list on their packaging the metric equivalent of a cup, most do not. Volunteers measured and weighed ingredients to get the correct conversion equivalents.

Liquid measures, when in fluid ounces refer to American, not English measures, and the metric equivalent is in liters or milliliters. A cup as a liquid measure is 237ml (milliliters). There are a 1000ml in a liter.

Teaspoons and tablespoons were considered to be standard 5ml and 15ml sizes respectively.

Temperature

Oven temperatures are in degrees Fahrenheit. The equivalent temperatures are listed below in degrees Celsius. Fan assisted or convection ovens need slightly lower temperatures and a reduced cooking time.

Fahrenheit	Celsius
250-275°	121-133°
300-325°	149-163°
350-375°	177-190°
400-425°	204-218°
450-475°	232-246°
500-525°	260-274°

Appetizers & Beverages

GEFULTE CHAMPIGNON
Stuffed Mushrooms with Gouda Cheese

Makes 20 mushrooms
Prep/Cook Time: 40 minutes

20   large fresh mushrooms
2   tablespoons (30g) butter
1   bunch parsley, chopped
1   clove garlic, minced
1   cup (120g) *Gouda cheese
4   tablespoons crème fraîche (see index for recipe or purchase information)
Salt and pepper to taste

- Preheat oven to 400°.

- Clean mushrooms, remove stems and chop the stems finely.

- In a small skillet, heat butter over medium heat. Sauté chopped mushroom stems with parsley and garlic for 5 minutes or until all liquid has evaporated. Let cool.

- Grate Gouda cheese. Reserve 3 tablespoons of cheese for topping and mix remainder with mushroom stems, parsley, and crème fraîche. Add salt and pepper.

- Fill mushroom caps with cheese mixture. Put in a buttered ovenproof baking dish and sprinkle with reserved cheese.

- Bake until warm and bubbly, about 15 to 20 minutes and serve.

*Gouda is Holland's most famous exported cheese. Gouda is aged anywhere from a few weeks to over a year. The younger the Gouda, the milder the flavor.

BORANI-E ESFENAJ

Spinach and Yogurt Dip

Makes 3 cups
Prep/Cook Time: 20 minutes,
plus 4 hours to chill

1   cup (300g) frozen chopped spinach,
    or 10 ounce package fresh spinach
4   tablespoons oil
2   onions, finely chopped
2   cloves garlic, crushed
1½ cups (375ml) yogurt
½   teaspoon salt
¼   teaspoon freshly ground pepper
¼   teaspoon saffron dissolved in 1 tablespoon hot water, optional

• Defrost frozen spinach and drain well. If using fresh spinach, place it in a pan, cover, and steam 5 minutes or until wilted. Drain water and discard.

• Heat oil in a medium saucepan. Sauté onions and garlic until golden. Add spinach and cook for 2 minutes. Remove from heat and let cool.

• In a serving dish, mix yogurt and spinach and season to taste with salt and pepper.

• Garnish with saffron if desired and refrigerate 4 or more hours before serving.

Variation:

Chopped, cooked beets may be used instead of spinach in Borani-e Esfenaj for a colorful variation.

Borani-e Esfenaj can also be served as a salad or side dish with Khoresh-e Bademjan or Lahem b'Ajeen (see index for recipes).

The Persians conquered and inhabited Iran in 550BC and then established a vast Middle Eastern empire that was the largest of its kind until the coming of Rome.

Yogurt with some sort of vegetable is most always a part of an Iranian meal.

MUHAMMASA
Spicy Arabian Walnut Dip

Makes 3 cups
Prep/Cook Time: 15 minutes

½   cup (125ml) olive oil
3   onions, finely chopped
1   cup (145g) walnuts, crushed in a blender
¾   cup (75g) dried bread crumbs
2   tablespoons *Harissa sauce
½   teaspoon ground cumin
Salt to taste
2   cups (500ml) water
1   tablespoon pine nuts, lightly toasted
Chopped parsley

- Heat oil in a large skillet over medium heat. Sauté onions until soft and golden brown. Lower heat.

- Add walnuts, bread crumbs, Harissa, cumin, salt, and water. Stir gently over low heat until flavors are well blended, about 12 minutes.

- Remove from heat, place in a serving bowl and garnish with pine nuts and parsley.

- Serve with slices of thin pita bread cut into triangles or as a dip with fresh carrot sticks, cucumber slices, and peppers.

Muhammasa is also delicious as a dip with kebabs, grilled meat or fish, spread inside pita bread with grilled meat such as Spicy Lamb Kebabs (see index for recipe) and lettuce and tomato or coleslaw.

*Harissa is a fiery hot sauce that originates in Tunisia. It's a traditional accompaniment for couscous, but is also used in other dishes. Harissa is found in cans or jars in the Middle Eastern section of most international food markets.

ROASTED TOMATO AND ROASTED GARLIC SALSA

Makes 3 cups (800g) of salsa
Prep/Cook Time: 1 hour

4   cloves garlic with skin
¼   cup (60ml) plus 1 teaspoon olive oil
2   pounds (900g) Roma tomatoes
½   onion
½   cup (15g) cilantro
2   *chipotles in adobo from can
¼   cup (60ml) red wine vinegar
1   tablespoon salt
1   teaspoon sugar

- Smear garlic with a little olive oil and roast in oven for 25 minutes, until soft.

- Roast tomatoes under a red hot oven broiler turning every 2 to 3 minutes until skin is blackened on all sides. This is messy but creates a wonderful taste. When tomatoes are blackened, drain in a colander and discard juice.

- Peel the garlic, but leave the skin on the tomatoes.

- Mix tomatoes, garlic, onion, olive oil, cilantro and chipotles in a food processor using on/off pulses until just cut into little pieces. Add half the amount of the vinegar, salt and sugar. Taste and add remaining vinegar, salt and sugar or according to taste.

- Serve with tortilla chips.

Consider making a double batch of this luscious Roasted Tomato Salsa. It freezes well if there's any extra.

*The chipotle chile is a dried, smoked jalapeño. It has a wrinkled, dark brown skin and a smoky, sweet, almost chocolate flavor. Canned chipotles in adobo can usually be found in the Mexican section of large supermarkets.

TAPENADE
Olive and Anchovy Spread

6   ounces (170g) pitted black olives
1   tablespoon finely minced garlic
2   teaspoons anchovies or anchovy paste
½   teaspoon pepper
¼   teaspoon thyme
¼   teaspoon oregano
5   tablespoons olive oil
1   teaspoon wine vinegar

• Combine all ingredients in a food processor and purée.

• Spread on baguette rounds or crackers and serve.

Tapenade is excellent spread on warm bread, with black bean soup and a pitcher of sangría. Key Lime Pie or Flan de Queso (see index for recipes) makes a rich grand finale for this light meal.

Tapenade comes from the Provençal French word for caper, tapeno, and was originally made with capers. Tapenade made with olives is sometimes called olivade. Tapenade is also very nice in small amounts on pizza or spaghetti.

TANDOORI MURGHI KEBABS
Tandoori Chicken Kebabs

Serves 6
Prep/Cook Time: 1 hour,
plus 3 hours to marinate

1½ pounds (675g) boneless chicken,
    cut in 1 inch (2.5 cm) cubes
¼ teaspoon cayenne pepper
1½ teaspoons salt
⅓ teaspoon tandoori masala powder
½ teaspoon paprika
3-4 tablespoons lemon juice
3-4 tablespoons plain yogurt
Wooden kebab sticks

- Preheat oven to 300°. Mix all seasonings in a large bowl. Add lemon juice and yogurt and blend. Add chicken and stir to coat with marinade. Cover tightly and refrigerate to marinate for at least 3 hours, stirring from time to time.

- Thread chicken pieces onto kebab skewers and place in baking pan. Do not overlap. Cover with foil and bake for 30 to 40 minutes or until chicken is tender, removing foil the last 5 minutes of cooking. Serve immediately.

Variation:

For an entrée, use whole chicken breasts or whole bone-in chicken pieces, not skewered, and increase cooking time 10 to 15 minutes, or until chicken is cooked through.

Tandoori is traditionally cooked in an extremely hot cylindrical clay oven called a tandoor which results in very tender meat. As a tandoor is not available in most kitchens, the slow cooking method in this recipe is an alternative that produces a similarly tender result. The kebabs can also be grilled over low heat.

KEFTÉTHES
Greek Meatballs

Keftéthes appear at all festive occasions in Greece and every family has their own treasured recipe.

2	tablespoons olive oil
2	tablespoons (30g) butter
1	medium onion, finely chopped
1	cup (50g) soft white bread crumbs
½	cup (125ml) water
3	egg yolks
2	cloves garlic, minced
2	teaspoons salt
½	teaspoon dried oregano, or 1 tablespoon fresh oregano
3	tablespoons fresh parsley, finely chopped
2	pounds (900g) lean ground beef
3	tablespoons red wine vinegar

Freshly ground pepper
Additional oregano for garnish

- Heat olive oil and 1 tablespoon (15g) butter in large skillet. Add onion and sauté until soft. Empty into a mixing bowl. Mix in bread crumbs, water, egg yolks, garlic, salt, oregano, and parsley. Add ground beef and mix thoroughly. Shape into balls about 1 inch (2.5cm) in diameter.

- Sauté meatballs in remaining oil and butter in skillet, turning to brown all sides. Transfer to a serving dish.

- Pour vinegar into the pan in which the meatballs were sautéed and bring to a boil, scraping drippings from the pan in with vinegar. Pour vinegar over meatballs.

- Grind fresh pepper over meatballs and sprinkle lightly with oregano. Serve warm.

Variations:

This recipe doubles well, but with a larger quantity, it is easier to bake the meatballs. Place Keftéthes 1 inch (2.5cm) apart on a lightly greased baking sheet. Bake at 425° for 20 minutes or until cooked through. In a small saucepan boil vinegar until reduced by half, add drippings from the baked meatballs and heat until blended. Place meatballs in a serving dish, pouring the sauce over them.

Also, fresh chopped spinach, mint, or grated carrot may be added and blended in with the meat mixture. The vinegar may be replaced with lemon juice.

TERRINE DE PORC
Country Herb Pâté

²/₃ cup (55g) crumbled stale bread
½ cup (125ml) good red wine
2 eggs
3 teaspoons salt
1 teaspoon pepper
¼ teaspoon cayenne pepper
3 medium onions, finely chopped
4 cloves garlic, minced
Herbes de Provence to taste
2 pounds (900g) each of calf's liver and minced pork,
    ground together by the butcher, 4 pounds (1.8kg) combined
¾ pound (340g) very thinly sliced lean smoked bacon
Juniper berries for garnish
Bay leaves for garnish
½ cup (125ml) cognac

- Preheat oven to 350°.
- In a large bowl, mix first 9 ingredients and leave for a few seconds until moisture is absorbed into the bread.
- Add ground meat and mix very well with hands.
- Microwave a small ball of meat mixture until cooked, then taste for seasoning and adjust accordingly.
- Cover a metal pâté mold or loaf pan with bacon slices. Pour mixture over bacon, press firmly and decorate the top with bay leaves and juniper berries.
- Cover the pan with aluminum foil and place in a large, shallow pan of warm water. Bake for 1½ hours or until center registers 160°. Remove from oven and remove foil.
- Place a heavy saucepan, which is just smaller than pâté mold or pan, or another loaf pan weighted with heavy cans on top of the pâté to press out the juice and fat. When pâté is completely cool, remove weighted pan.
- Drain all the juice from the pâté pan in a separate dish. As it cools, a jelly will will form on the bottom. Skim the fat off the jelly and keep in the refrigerator as a nice accompaniment to the pâté if desired.
- Pour a glass of cognac over the top of pâté. Refrigerate for at least 12 hours.
- Serve pâté sliced on a platter or out of the mold with jelly if desired. Keeps well in the refrigerator for one week.

Variation:

Mushrooms, pink or green peppercorns or chopped green peppers may be added to the meat mixture.

The sweetly tart flavor of Confiture d'Oignon (see index for recipe) makes the perfect condiment for this pâté. Serve this pâté with toast points, crackers or French bread rounds and cornichons.

Pâté en terrine is a meat or fish preparation put into a terrine lined with bacon, cooked in the oven, and always served cold. The correct French abbreviation for this is terrine, but in common usage the French call it pâté, as do English speakers.

Western Swing Pâté

Serves 16
Prep/Cook Time:
2 hours 15 minutes,
plus 5 hours to chill

1   pound (450g) bacon
1   pound (450g) ground turkey
1   pound (450g) ground pork
1   egg
2   cloves garlic, finely chopped
1   medium onion, chopped
½   cup (110g) red bell pepper, chopped
½   cup (110g) yellow bell pepper, chopped
½   cup (50g) unsweetened corn bread crumbs
2   tablespoons tequila
2   tablespoons fresh cilantro, chopped
1   teaspoon salt
½   teaspoon ground coriander

• Preheat oven to 350°. Line bottom of 5x9 inch (13x23cm) loaf pan crosswise with bacon, reserving 4 slices for the top and bringing slices up sides and over edge of pan.

• In large bowl combine remaining ingredients, mixing with hands or a fork. Spoon into pan. Smooth top. Fold bacon ends over top of meat mixture. Place remaining slices of bacon lengthwise over top of meat mixture. Cover with aluminum foil. Bake 1½ to 2 hours.

• Drain juices out carefully, leaving pâté in pan. Let stand covered 1 hour.

• Cover with plastic wrap and refrigerate until cold at least 5 hours but no longer than 3 days. Loosen pâté from bottom of pan and invert on serving platter. Cut into thin slices. May be served either by the slice as an appetizer or on small thin pieces of bread or cracker as an hors d'oeuvre or cold at a picnic.

The "proper name" for this dish would actually be *Western Swing Terrine*. But as explained in the sidebar on page 21, it's common for this type ground meat or liver dish to be referred to as pâté rather than the more correct terrine.

Strictly speaking, the word pâté should only be applied to a dish consisting of a pastry shell filled with meat, fish, vegetables, or fruit, which is baked in the oven and served hot or cold. The best English translation for pâté is "pie."

Western swing pâté has no liver and has an interesting Mexican flavor twist evident by the use of tequila and cilantro.

U S A

BRUSCHETTA WITH ROASTED PEPPERS AND ANCHOVIES

Serves 4
Prep/Cook Time: 30 minutes

2   medium red peppers
4   anchovies, chopped
2   garlic cloves, minced
4   tablespoons olive oil
Salt and pepper to taste
8   slices *ciabatta bread

- Roast peppers on the grill, high oven broiler, or open gas stove flame until well charred, almost black. Lay in a bowl and cover with a towel or plate to loosen skin and place in the refrigerator until cool, about 5 minutes.

- Remove skin, seeds, and thinly slice peppers. Mix with anchovies, garlic, and olive oil. Season with salt and pepper to taste.

- Toast bread 4 to 5 minutes in 350° oven on each side until lightly browned. Cool on a rack for 5 minutes. Recipe may be prepared ahead to this point and assembled just before serving.

- Divide pepper mixture among bread slices and serve.

*Ciabatta literally means "slipper" in Italian, and the name refers to the shape of the bread, a flattened oval. Ciabatta has come to mean, at least in this country, any airy, dimpled loaf dusted with flour, of just about any shape. A small French baguette sliced into thin rounds works well with this recipe also.

BRUSCHETTA WITH TOMATOES, BASIL AND ONION

Serves 4
Prep/Cook Time: 20 minutes

The name Bruschetta comes from the Italian word bruscare *meaning "to roast over coals."*

3   ripe medium tomatoes
Salt and pepper to taste
1   small sweet onion, finely chopped
2   cloves garlic, finely chopped
5   tablespoons olive oil
8   slices ciabatta or French bread
8   leaves fresh basil, chopped

- Preheat oven to 350°. Wash and chop tomatoes and place in a medium bowl. Add salt and pepper to taste and let tomatoes rest for 5 minutes.

- Place tomatoes in a colander and drain and discard juices.

- Return the tomatoes, onion, and garlic to bowl and add olive oil. Mix gently and let rest for 10 minutes.

- Toast bread in the preheated oven for 4 to 5 minutes each side, until lightly browned and let cool on a rack for 5 minutes.

- Recipe may be prepared ahead to this point and assembled just before serving.

- Arrange the tomato mixture on each slice of bread and sprinkle chopped basil over top. Adjust with salt, pepper, and olive oil to taste and serve within 5 to minutes so bread won't become soggy.

Italy

CHA GIÒ
Vietnamese Spring Rolls with Shrimp

Makes 25 spring rolls
Prep/Cook Time:
1 hour 15 minutes

2   ounces (55g) translucent rice vermicelli,
    soaked 20 minutes until soft
    and cut in 1 inch (2.5cm) lengths
2   tablespoons dried tree ears, cloud or wood ears,
    soaked 20 minutes until soft and diced
½   pound (225g) minced pork
12 medium-sized raw shrimp, shelled, deveined, and cut in half lengthwise
4   ounces (115g) water chestnuts, chopped
1   large white onion, chopped
1   large carrot, shredded
2   tablespoons nuoc mam, fish sauce
1   teaspoon pepper
1   egg, lightly beaten
1   tablespoon cornstarch, optional
1   package *banh trang or spring roll skins
Vegetable oil for frying
Lettuce leaves, cilantro and mint, optional garnish
Bottled or freshly prepared Nuoc Cham Sauce (see index for recipe)

- Mix first 10 ingredients in a large mixing bowl and blend well. Adding a tablespoon of cornstarch will give the mixture a smooth texture, but this is optional.

- In a bowl of warm water, gently lower a sheet of banh trang until soft and shake off excess water. There is no need to soak spring roll skins, if using those instead of banh trang. Very carefully, lay a sheet or skin on a clean chopping board. Place a heaping tablespoon of mixture on sheet, roll over once and fold in sides. Roll over once more and tuck in firmly, patting the ends down. Repeat process until all skins or filling are used.

- Place oil 3 inches (7.5cm) deep in a wok or deep skillet. While oil heats, continue making rolls until all filling is used.

- Gently lower one roll at a time in the oil to deep fry until light brown and crisp. Fry in small batches so that the oil does not cool. Place on paper towel to drain. Place on platter and keep in a warm oven until ready to serve.

- Serve with fresh lettuce, cilantro, and mint leaves with Nuoc Cham Sauce for dipping.

Quintessentially Vietnamese, these delicate, crispy rolls are a refinement from the more robust Chinese rolls.

*The gossamer thin *banh trang (rice paper) can be difficult to handle. Conventional spring roll skins may be used as an easy alternative, but these won't achieve the same crispy results. Banh trang come in packages of 25 or more and are found in the same section as noodles in Asian grocery stores.*

GOUGÈRES
Gruyère Cheese Puffs

Makes 30 to 40 gougères
Prep/Cook Time: 45 minutes

1   cup (250ml) water
7   tablespoons (105g) butter
1   cup (140g) flour
4   eggs
1   cup (120g) Gruyère cheese, grated
Pepper to taste

- Preheat oven to 375°.

- In a 1 quart (1 liter) saucepan, combine water, butter, and a pinch of salt. Heat until butter has melted and mixture reaches a boil. Remove from heat and stir in the flour. Return pan to heat and stir continuously until the paste becomes thicker and does not stick to the sides of the pan.

- Remove from heat and add eggs, one at a time, beating well after each addition. Add cheese and pepper to taste. Blend well.

- Drop the batter by tablespoonfuls onto a cookie sheet. Bake 30 minutes or until golden brown. Serve warm.

Gougères (goo-ZHAIRS) traditionally accompany wine tasting in the cellars of Burgundy, France. They can be eaten as an appetizer or as a bread with soup. Ham or bacon may be added to the batter if desired. Gougères freeze well.

Mushroom Pinwheels

Makes 40 pinwheels
Prep/Cook Time: 25 minutes

1   *tablespoon olive oil*
2   *small onions, finely chopped*
1   *pound (450g) mushrooms, finely chopped*
4   *tablespoons parsley, chopped*
Salt and plenty of freshly ground black pepper
1   *17¼ ounce (490g) package puff pastry sheets*

- Preheat oven to 425°.

- Heat oil in a medium skillet over medium heat. Sauté onions in oil for 5 minutes.

- Add mushrooms to skillet with onions and sauté until liquid has evaporated.

- Add parsley and salt and pepper and mix.

- Spread mushroom mixture over the pastry sheets. Roll up tightly and chill for 30 minutes in refrigerator.

- Cut into ¼ to ½ inch (.6 to 1.3cm) rounds. Place on a baking sheet lying flat and cook for 15 minutes. Serve immediately.

Variation:

Portobello or shiitake mushrooms may used instead of white mushrooms. ½ teaspoon ground cloves and 2 cloves of minced garlic may be added with the onions, and ½ teaspoon fresh tarragon or a dash of cayenne pepper can be added with the parsley.

CHRISTMAS EVE SHRIMP

Serves 6 to 8 for hors d'oeuvres
Prep/Cook Time: 30 minutes,
plus 8 hours to marinate

1   pound (450g) cooked fresh shrimp
½   cup (125ml) cider vinegar
20 bay leaves
2   medium onions, sliced
2   cups (500ml) vegetable oil (do not use olive oil)
¼   cup (60ml) Worcestershire sauce
1   teaspoon salt
1   teaspoon paprika
⅛   teaspoon cayenne pepper

- Peel and clean shrimp, rinse in cold water and drain.

- Heat vinegar in a saucepan with 10 bay leaves, but do not allow it to boil.

- Remove bay leaves and reserve. Let vinegar cool.

- In a large bowl or deep casserole, place a layer of shrimp, a layer of sliced onion, then a few bay leaves. Continue until all shrimp have been used.

- Combine cooled vinegar, oil, Worcestershire sauce, salt, paprika, and cayenne and pour over shrimp.

- Refrigerate at least 8 hours and up to 36 hours to marinate. Drain and serve in a large bowl with toothpicks.

Variation:

Substitute ¼ cup (60ml) of dry white wine and a tablespoon of Worcestershire sauce for the ¼ cup (60ml) of Worcestershire sauce, and substitute 1 tablespoon of celery seeds for the teaspoon of paprika.

Recipe doubles or triples well.

The dish is named Christmas Eve Shrimp because the recipe contributor's family has served it at family Christmas Eve celebrations for four generations.

GRAVAD LAX MED SENAPSSÄS
Lox with Mustard Dill Sauce

Serves 8
Prep/Cook Time: 30 minutes,
plus three days to marinate

L o x
- 1½ cups (45g) fresh dill, chopped
- 2 tablespoons salt
- 2 tablespoons freshly ground white pepper
- ¼ cup (50g) sugar
- 2 center cut fresh salmon fillets with skin, 1½ pounds (680g) each
- ½ cup (125ml) vegetable oil

M u s t a r d   D i l l   S a u c e
- 2 tablespoons regular mustard (do not use Dijon or other strong mustard)
- 2 tablespoons white vinegar
- 2 tablespoons sugar
- 1 egg yolk
- ½ cup (125ml) vegetable oil
- Salt and pepper to taste
- ½ cup (15g) fresh dill leaves, finely chopped

- Combine dill, salt, pepper, and sugar.
- Brush skinless sides of fillets with vegetable oil. Completely cover the skinless side of one fillet with the dill mixture.
- Cover with the other fillet as if making a sandwich with skin sides of fillets facing out. Make sure that the dill mixture prevents the skinless sides of the fillets from touching each other.
- Put the salmon into a plastic bag and then secure tightly with another plastic bag over the first, being careful to keep salmon flat. Put in a glass or steel dish, place another slightly smaller dish on top and put a heavy weight on top of this (a quart (950ml) carton of milk works well).
- Chill in the refrigerator for at least 48 hours, preferably for 72 hours, turning the salmon package every 8 to 12 hours. Be sure the juices stay in the plastic bag. The salmon should marinate in its own juices.
- Prepare the sauce: Mix the mustard, vinegar, sugar, and egg yolk in a blender. Add the vegetable oil, first drop by drop and then in a thin stream, while the blender is going. Add salt and pepper to taste. Transfer sauce to a bowl and mix in the chopped dill. Pour into a serving dish.
- Remove the salmon from refrigerator. Scrape off all the dill mixture and discard. Lay each salmon fillet flat and slice paper-thin layers diagonally across the grain, with a look similar to leaves. Discard skin.
- Serve the lox cold on white toast triangles with a dollop of sauce or place on a platter garnished with twisted lemon slices and dill sprigs and with a separate dish of sauce.

In Sweden Gravad Lax is often enjoyed alone with a shot of ice cold akavit and beer. Gravad Lax is a must at an authentic smörgåsbord, which is a Swedish word that translates to "bread and butter table." The word smörgåsbord has evolved to refer to a buffet consisting of a variety of different foods and is used and understood in many languages.

The word lox *is derived from the Scandinavian word for salmon, which is* lax, *and the German word for salmon, which is* lachs.

LAXRULLAR

Smoked Salmon and Dill Rolls

Serves 8
Prep/Cook Time: 40 minutes

Laxrullar may be prepared one day in advance and stored unsliced in the refrigerator. Slice just before serving.

²⁄₃ cup (95g) flour
½ teaspoon salt
1⅛ cups (280ml) milk
²⁄₃ cup (160ml) heavy cream
3 eggs
½ cup (120ml) sour cream
3 hard boiled eggs, minced
½ pound (225g) smoked salmon, minced
1 tablespoon fresh parsley, finely minced
1 tablespoon fresh dill, finely minced
1 tablespoon fresh scallions, finely chopped
Salt and pepper to taste

- Preheat oven to 450°. Spray a 12x18 inch (30x46cm) baking sheet, with raised edges at least ½ inch (1.3cm) high, with cooking spray. Line baking sheet with parchment paper, 2 sheets overlapped if 1 does not cover. Lightly spray papers with nonstick cooking spray.

- Mix flour, salt, milk, and cream until smooth. Add eggs. Pour batter onto the sprayed parchment lined cookie sheet. The batter should fill the entire bottom of the baking sheet and look like a rectangular pancake.

- Bake in middle oven rack for 15 to 18 minutes or until firm and golden brown.

- Spray another parchment sheet with cooking spray. Remove the pancake from oven, and immediately flip over onto the prepared parchment paper. Gently pull the used paper off the pancake and let cool.

- While cooling, mix sour cream, eggs, salmon, herbs, salt, and pepper in a large bowl.

- Spread salmon mixture in an even layer on top of cooled pancake, then roll lengthwise.

- Slice into 1 inch (2.5cm) rounds and serve.

MARINATED SHRIMP IN MUSTARD SAUCE

Serves 15
Prep/Cook Time: 30 minutes,
plus 4 hours to marinate

2½ pounds (1.125kg) medium shrimp,
   peeled and deveined
¼ cup (8g) finely chopped fresh parsley
¼ cup (30g) finely chopped shallots
¼ cup (60ml) tarragon vinegar
¼ cup (60ml) red wine vinegar
¼ cup (60ml) olive oil
4-5 tablespoons Dijon mustard
2 teaspoons crushed red pepper
Green leaf lettuce for garnish, optional
Toothpicks for serving

- Cook shrimp in boiling salted water in a large pot until barely pink. Drain water from cooked shrimp and transfer shrimp to a large bowl

- Mix all remaining ingredients, except lettuce and pour over warm shrimp.

- Cover and refrigerate at least 4 hours.

- Pour into a serving bowl, which is lined with lettuce for garnish if desired and serve with toothpicks on the side.

The use of mustard as a condiment dates back to ancient Asia, Egypt, and to the Romans who mixed ground mustard seed with wine and called the mixture mustum ardens (burning wine). French mustards, which are sold in the form of paste, are made with a mixture of ground white and black mustard seed, often with herbs added. They are mixed with verjuice (juice of unripe grapes) for Dijon mustard or with unfermented wine for Bordeaux mustard.

SHRIMP BAKED WITH TOMATOES, HERBS AND FETA CHEESE

Serves 6
Prep/Cook Time: 40 minutes

This dish also makes a delicious entrée served over fresh pasta. Serve with a green salad and French bread.

*While feta cheese is lower in fat than many cheeses, it is not lower in flavor. This classic Greek cheese is traditionally made from sheep's milk. American and Danish feta cheeses are often made from cow's milk with salt added and are less expensive, but not as flavorful as the sheep's milk feta.

2   cloves garlic, chopped
1   teaspoon salt
2   medium onions, thinly sliced
⅓   cup (85ml), plus 1 tablespoon olive oil
1½ pounds (675g) tomatoes, peeled and chopped
⅛   teaspoon oregano
½   cup (15g) fresh parsley, finely chopped
2   pounds (900g) raw shrimp, cleaned, shelled and deveined.
Salt and pepper to taste
8   ounces (225g) *feta cheese
1   lemon, cut into 6 wedges

- Preheat oven to 450°.
- With a mortar and pestle or in a small bowl with the back of a spoon, crush garlic and salt until a paste forms.
- In a heavy skillet, heat ⅓ cup (85ml) oil over medium heat. Sauté onion until tender. Add tomatoes, garlic, paste, and oregano. Reduce heat and cook over low heat, stirring occasionally for 15 to 20 minutes. Stir in chopped parsley.
- Place a colander over a large bowl. Place onion and tomato mixture into the colander and let liquid drain into the bowl, and reserve.
- Clean skillet with a paper towel. Add remaining tablespoon of olive oil and sauté shrimp for 2 to 3 minutes over medium heat.
- Add reserved liquid from tomato and onion mixture to shrimp and stir.
- Divide the tomato and onion mixture evenly between 6 small serving plates (such as scallop shells) or place in a medium sized ovenproof casserole dish.
- Arrange shrimp on top of tomato and onion mixture. Sprinkle lightly with salt and pepper and crumble feta cheese over the shrimp.
- Bake in the upper rack of the oven for 10 to 15 minutes. Serve very hot with lemon wedges.

U S A

EGGNOG

Serves 8
Prep/Cook Time: 30 minutes,
plus 2 hours to chill

6   eggs, separated
¾   cup (150g) sugar
2   cups (500ml) milk
2   cups (475ml) whipping cream
1   cup (250ml) whiskey or brandy
Freshly grated nutmeg, optional

- In a large bowl, beat egg yolks with an electric mixer until frothy. Continue beating while adding ½ cup (100g) of sugar, a little at a time, until egg yolks become pale in color and mixture is stiff.

- Add milk and 1 cup (235ml) of the whipping cream to egg yolk mixture and beat well. Gently stir in whiskey or brandy. Set aside.

- In separate, non-aluminum bowl, beat egg whites gradually adding ¼ cup (50g) sugar as whites thicken, until soft peaks form. Set aside.

- Whip remaining 1 cup whipping cream at medium speed until soft peaks form.

- Fold whipped cream and then the egg whites into the egg yolk mixture.

- Chill at least 2 hours and serve with freshly grated nutmeg sprinkled on top.

Note:

Refer to the glossary for information regarding the safe handling of raw eggs.

The name for this popular Christmas drink surely originated in England where nog *is a word for strong ale. Eggnog is also related to sack-posset, a milk, egg, and sherry drink known in England for centuries.*

PONCHE DE CRÈME

Cream Punch

Serves 12
Prep Time: 15 minutes

4   *eggs*
Peel of 1 lime, in large pieces
2   *12 ounce (335g) cans evaporated milk*
2   *14 ounce (390g) cans sweetened condensed milk*
12   *ounces (360ml) rum*
1   *ounce (30ml) brandy*
1   *ounce (30ml) angostura bitters*
Freshly grated nutmeg

- With an electric beater, beat eggs with lime peel for about 10 minutes. Mixture will become very thick and pale colored.

- While continuing to beat, slowly add 1 can evaporated milk, then 1 can condensed milk. Repeat with remaining cans.

- Gradually stir in rum, brandy, and bitters so that the mixture doesn't separate. Remove lime peel and pour over crushed ice in glasses, sprinkle with nutmeg, and serve. Or stir in nutmeg, and refrigerate until ready to serve.

Note:

Refer to the glossary for information regarding the safe handling of raw eggs.

Ponche de Crème can be made weeks in advance as it ages well refrigerated. It is also delicious served immediately. The recipe easily doubles or triples.

Trinidad and Tobago have a truly diverse cuisine influenced by many peoples. The country consists of two islands in the West Indies that lie east of Venezuela in the Caribbean. About 40 percent of the country's people have African ancestry, 40 percent are descendants of India, and the remainder are a mixture of European and Chinese. English is the country's official language, but French, Spanish, and Hindi are also spoken.

34

Breads & Brunch

BASIL, CHEESE AND TOMATO SCONES

Makes 15 scones
Prep/Cook Time: 30 minutes

The original scones were triangular, but today they are made in various shapes. Traditionally scones are eaten for breakfast or tea and can be sweet or savory.

The scone is said to have taken its name from the Stone of Destiny (or Scone), the place on which the monarchs of first Scotland and then Great Britain were crowned. King Edward I brought the stone to England from Scotland in 1296. Since 1996, the stone once again lies in Scotland.

2½ cups (355g) flour
1 tablespoon sugar
2½ teaspoons baking powder
½ teaspoon salt
8 tablespoons (120g) chilled unsalted butter
½ firm tomato, seeded and chopped
½ bunch basil, chopped
½ cup (60g) grated cheddar cheese
2 eggs, beaten

- Preheat oven to 400°.

- In a food processor, mix flour, sugar, baking powder, and salt. Add butter using short, on/off pulses until the butter has been incorporated as small pea-sized pieces.

- Turn mixture into a large bowl and gently mix in tomato, basil, cheese, and eggs using a knife or hands, pressing dough down until mixture comes together.

- Press or roll dough on a floured surface to about ½ to ¾ inch (1.3 to 2 cm) thickness. Cut out scones using either a scone cutter or an approximately 3 inch (8cm) round inverted drinking glass.

- Place scones on an ungreased baking sheet and bake for 10 to 12 minutes until light brown, being careful not to bake too long.

Variation:

Experiment substituting your favorite ingredients such as whole-wheat flour and other herbs.

England

Beer Bread

Makes one loaf
Prep/Cook Time: 1 hour 10 minutes

3 cups (425g) flour
¼ cup (50g) sugar
½ teaspoon salt
1 tablespoon baking powder
1 12 ounce (355ml) bottle lager beer, room temperature
¼ cup (45g) melted butter

• Preheat oven to 350°. Grease 9x5 inch (23x13cm) loaf pan.

• Combine dry ingredients in a large bowl. Mix in beer until well blended.

• Pour batter into the loaf pan. Pour melted butter over batter. Bake 45 to 50 minutes or until light golden brown. Leave bread in pan and cool on a wire rack for about 10 minutes. Remove from pan and serve.

Variation:

Add ½ cup (60g) grated cheddar cheese, 2 chopped green onions and a few jalapeño slices to the batter just before baking.

Beer breads are remarkable. They're easy to make, and require very little in the way of prep time. Beer leavened breads often do best with a slow baking time, usually between 45 minutes and an hour as with this recipe. Serve with hearty soups or stews.

Beer Trivia:

Many years ago in England, pub frequenters had a whistle baked into the rim or handle of their ceramic cups. When they needed a refill, they used the whistle to get service. "Wet your whistle" is the phrase inspired by this practice.

FINNISH CHRISTMAS BREAD

Makes 2 large loaves
Prep/Cook Time: 2 hours,
plus 3 hours to rise

1   package active dry yeast
½   cup (125ml) warm water, 105° to 115°
1   teaspoon salt
1   teaspoon cardamom seeds, slightly crushed
1   cup (200g) sugar
2   cups (500ml) milk, scalded and cooled to lukewarm
4   eggs, beaten and at room temperature
10   cups (1.4kg) flour
½   cup (90g) melted butter

Glaze

1 beaten egg, at room temperature, for glazing
Sugar for topping

- In a large bowl, soak yeast in ½ cup (125ml) warm water until it foams, about 5 to 10 minutes. Grease 2 large baking sheets.

- Add salt, cardamom seeds, sugar, and scalded milk to yeast mixture.

- Add 4 beaten eggs and about 5 cups (710g) of flour and mix well.

- Add melted butter and about 5 more cups (710g) of flour, just enough to make the dough stiff enough to handle, and mix well.

- Let dough rest 15 minutes, and then knead for 10 minutes.

- Cover dough with a cloth and let rise for 1½ to 2 hours in a warm place or until doubled in size. Punch down and let rise again for 1 hour.

- Divide dough into 2 parts to make two loaves of bread. For each loaf, divide dough into 3 parts, form 3 long rolls and braid into 1 very large loaf. Allow braided dough to rest for 10 minutes. Place each loaf on a prepared baking sheet.

- Glaze loaves with beaten egg and sprinkle with sugar.

- Let rise again for 1 hour. Preheat oven to 375°.

- Bake first loaf in the center of oven for 25 to 30 minutes or until golden brown. The second loaf can sit and rise while the first loaf bakes.

This recipe makes 2 very large loaves of bread; use one and freeze the other for later, or cut the recipe by half for a single loaf.

This traditional Finnish Christmas bread, often made with raisins, may be used for dessert bread, sandwich bread or dinner bread. A single, large braided loaf makes an impressive centerpiece.

BUCHTELN
Yeast Buns Filled with Jam

Makes 7 buns
Prep/Cook Time: 45 minutes,
plus 2 hours to rise

2   teaspoons active dry yeast
1   cup (250ml) lukewarm milk
¼   cup (50g) sugar
3½ cups (455g) flour
¼   teaspoon salt
4   tablespoons (60g) butter, softened
2   egg yolks
Damson plum or other jam
Milk for brushing tops, optional
Powdered sugar for dusting

- Stir yeast into milk in a large bowl. Add 1 tablespoon sugar. Let stand 2 minutes until foam appears. Add flour, remaining sugar, salt, butter and egg yolks and knead until dough is very elastic.

- Place dough in an oiled large bowl, cover with plastic wrap or a cloth and leave in a warm, draft-free area. Let rise until doubled, about 1 hour.

- Punch dough down in the center with a closed fist.

- Break or cut pieces of dough slightly larger than an egg, flatten the pieces on a floured board and place a tablespoon of jam in the center of each. Form round balls of dough, the size of an egg, enclosing the jam in the center. Cover with a cloth, and place in a warm draft free area. Let rise 45 minutes to 1 hour until doubled in size.

- Preheat oven to 350°. Grease a 9 inch (23cm) round pan

- Brush surfaces of buns with milk if desired and bake until golden brown, about 20 minutes. Serve warm with a dusting of powdered sugar.

The Austrians are quite fond of a meal consisting of a very light first course, such as soup, followed by a substantial sweet "main" course. Buchteln are an example of such a main course. Children are particularly fond of these buns served topped with warm Southern Custard Sauce (see index for recipe).

CRAQUELIN

Brioche with Melted Sugar Nuggets

Makes 2 loaves
Prep/Cooking Time: 20 minutes,
plus 7 hours 30 minutes
to rise and chill

½   cup (125ml) water, lukewarm
4   tablespoons sugar
4½ teaspoons active dry yeast
2   eggs, separated
1   rounded cup (135g) sugar cubes, or 1 level cup (135g) *pearl sugar
4   cups (570g) flour
2   teaspoons salt
1   cup (250ml) milk, lukewarm
6   tablespoons (90g) unsalted butter, melted

• Mix yeast and 1 tablespoon of sugar with the lukewarm water. Let rest until foamy. Cover egg whites and refrigerate.

• If using sugar cubes, place them in the center of a plastic bag. Close bag and pound gently with a meat pounder or a rolling pin until the cubes are in ¼ inch (.6g) nuggets. Sift out finer sugar that formed and discard. About a level ¾ to 1 cup (112 to 150g) of small nuggets should remain.

• In a large bowl, mix all remaining dry ingredients. Make a well in the center. Add the egg yolks, milk, melted butter and yeast mixture in the well. Mix the ingredients with hands and then knead for 10 minutes.

• Add sugar nuggets or pearl sugar and fold and knead the dough over the nuggets until they are well incorporated. Cover with a towel and let rise in a warm place until doubled, 1½ to 2 hours.

• Punch the dough down. Separate into 2 loaves, and place into 2 buttered 8 to 9 inch (20 to 23cm) loaf pans. Cover pans with plastic wrap, and refrigerate 5 hours to overnight.

• Remove dough from refrigerator and let come to room temperature, about 1 hour. Brush loaf tops with egg whites, discarding or freezing extra egg whites.

• Place the loaves in a cold oven. Turn the oven to 325° and bake for 30 minutes. Loosely cover the loaf tops with foil while baking if needed to prevent over browning.

• Remove brioche from oven and let rest in the pan for 10 minutes. Turn out on a wire rack and cool slightly. Serve in slices immediately or later toasted.

Variation:

This recipe works equally well in a bread machine using the dough setting. Follow the bread machine instructions on the order of putting in the ingredients, leaving out the sugar nuggets and egg whites. Remove the dough from the bread machine when finished. Gently fold the sugar nuggets into the dough. Continue recipe as directed.

If you've ever wondered if making bread at home is really worth the effort, try this recipe to know the answer is a definite yes. A very pleasant surprise is that it's really not much effort; time just needs to be allowed for the rising.

*Pearl sugar is nugget size sugar in clear crystal form and is popular in many areas of Europe, but is hard to find in the United States.

DUMB BREAD

Serves 4
Prep/Cook Time: 25 minutes

¼ teaspoon salt
1 cup (140g) flour
2 teaspoons baking powder
¼ cup (50g) sugar
3 tablespoons (45g) butter
⅓ cup (85ml) milk, approximately

• Preheat oven to 425°. Grease a medium-sized cookie sheet.

• Sift together dry ingredients.

• Cut butter into dry ingredients with pastry knife or fork.

• Gradually add enough milk to make a soft dough. Knead on floured board until dough reaches uniform consistency.

• With hands or a rolling pin, flatten dough to about ¾ to 1 inch (2 to 2.5cm) thickness.

• Place dough on prepared cookie sheet and bake 15 minutes. Serve warm in wedges with butter and jam.

This popular West Indian bread is traditionally served at breakfast with butter and jam. According to the recipe contributor's grandmother, the bread is called dumb bread because it contains no yeast and doesn't rise. Hence, it's too dumb to rise. Another theory is that even the most inexperienced cook can make this "dumb" bread.

MANDELBROT

Almond Biscuits

Makes 24 to 30 slices
Prep/Cook Time: 1 hour

Serve mandelbrot any time of day with a cup of coffee or tea or after dinner for dessert. Mandelbrot recipes are handed down from generation to generation in Eastern European Jewish families. Mandelbrot should be dry and crunchy, much like Italian biscotti.

2   eggs
2/3   cup (125g) sugar
2/3   cup (170g) oil
2   teaspoons almond or vanilla extract
2   cups (285g) flour
2   teaspoons baking powder
2/3   cup (65g) chopped almonds
2   egg yolks
1/8   teaspoon ground cinnamon
1/4   cup (25g) sliced almonds

• Combine eggs and sugar in a medium sized mixing bowl and beat on medium speed until well blended. Increase speed to high and beat until mixture is very light and creamy, at least 10 minutes.

• Add the oil and extract and beat until well blended.

• In another bowl, sift together flour and baking powder.

• With mixer on low, add the flour mixture 1/4 cup (35g) at a time until completely incorporated (best performed with a dough hook, but a mixing blade will work). Blend in the almonds.

• Preheat oven to 350°. Line a cookie sheet with waxed paper.

• With well-floured hands, divide the dough into 2 parts. The dough will be very sticky. Shape each part into a cylinder 2 inches (5cm) in diameter and at least 1 to 2 inches (2.5 to 5cm) shorter than the cookie sheet.

• Lay each cylinder on the cookie sheet, and allow to flatten out a bit. Be sure that the resulting loaves are at least 1 inch (2.5cm) from the sides of the cookie sheet and 1 to 2 inches (2.5 to 5cm) apart.

• Beat the egg yolks with the cinnamon and brush on the loaves. Sprinkle the loaves with almond slices and push on the nuts a bit to make sure they stick.

• Bake for 20 to 25 minutes or until beginning to brown. Remove from the oven and place loaves on a cutting surface. Increase oven heat to 450°.

• Slice loaves into 1/2 inch (1.3cm) slices without allowing them to cool. Place slices on a clean cookie sheet and lightly toast in the oven on each side 3 to 5 minutes, or until golden brown.

Variation:

Try other nuts or add 1/3 cup (55g) chocolate chips to the dough before baking.

BLUEBERRY MUFFINS WITH STREUSEL TOPPING

Makes 24 muffins
Prep/Cook Time: 45 minutes

3   cups (425g) flour
1¾ cups (340g) sugar
1   tablespoon baking powder
10 tablespoons (150g) butter
2   eggs
1   cup (250ml) evaporated milk
1   teaspoon vanilla
1¾ cups (260g) fresh blueberries, washed with stems removed,
      or 1¾ cup (260g) frozen blueberries

• Preheat oven to 350°. Spray muffin pan with cooking spray or butter or line with paper muffin cups.

• Mix flour, sugar, and baking powder in a large mixing bowl.

• Cut in 8 tablespoons (120g) of the butter with pastry blender or with two knives handled scissors-fashion. Reserve 1 cup (150g) of this mixture for the crumb topping.

• Add the eggs, milk, and vanilla to the remaining mixture in the bowl. Beat with electric mixer until just combined.

• Gently fold blueberries into batter with a spatula and immediately spoon batter into muffin cups, filling them ⅔ of the way up.

• Melt the remaining 2 tablespoons butter (30g) and drizzle it over the reserved crumb mixture. Blend with a fork and sprinkle equally over the muffin batter.

• Bake in the center of oven for 20 to 30 minutes or until light golden brown.

Cook's Tip:
Prepare muffin batter and spoon into pan, tightly seal and refrigerate overnight to serve the next morning. Put the streusel topping on just before baking. This works with most muffin recipes. Muffin batter can also be frozen in individual muffin papers in the muffin tins. Tightly seal in a plastic bag, and take out and bake as needed. Allow about 5 minutes more cooking time if the batter is frozen.

U S A

CHOCOLATE CHIP BANANA BREAD

Makes 1 loaf
Prep/Cook Time:
1 hour 45 minutes

Banana Trivia:

In the 1940s and 1950s there was an American radio advertisement that advised cooks that "bananas are a product from the very, very tropical equator, so you should never put bananas in the refrigerator". Because the jingle had to rhyme something with "equator", generations of cooks were raised to believe bananas should not be refrigerated. Except that the skins will turn brown, there is no reason not to refrigerate ripe bananas. In fact, that's the only way bananas will keep for any length of time.

½   cup (120g) butter
1⅔ cups (325g) sugar
2   eggs, slightly beaten
¼   teaspoon salt
1½ teaspoons baking powder
½   teaspoon baking soda
4   tablespoons sour cream
1   cup mashed very ripe bananas, about 2 large bananas
2   cups (300g) cake flour, or 2 cups less 2 tablespoons (285g) all purpose flour
1   teaspoon vanilla
2   cups (340g) chocolate chips stirred with 1 teaspoon flour

- Preheat oven to 350°. Grease and flour a 9x5 inch (23x13cm) loaf pan.
- In a large mixing bowl, cream butter and sugar until light and fluffy. Add beaten eggs and salt. Beat well.
- Dissolve baking powder and baking soda in sour cream. Add to first mixture.
- Stir mashed bananas into mixture.
- Add flour gradually, stirring just to combine. Add vanilla and chocolate chips.
- Pour batter into loaf pan. Bake for 75 to 90 minutes. Check at 60 minutes then check every 10 minutes until knife blade comes out clean.

Variation:

Use 1 cup chocolate chips and 1 cup (170g) fresh cranberries instead of 2 cups chocolate chips. This is not as sweet as the original recipe.

U S A

POPPY SEED BREAD WITH ALMOND ORANGE GLAZE

Makes 2 loaves
Prep/Cook Time:
1 hour 20 minutes

Poppy Seed Bread

> 1½ cups (375ml) milk
> 3 eggs
> 1½ cups (280ml) oil
> 2½ cups (450g) sugar
> 3 cups (425g) flour
> 1½ teaspoons salt
> 1½ teaspoons baking powder
> 1½ tablespoons poppy seeds
> 1½ teaspoons almond extract
> 1½ teaspoons butter flavoring
> 1½ teaspoons vanilla

Almond Orange Glaze

> ¼ cup (60ml) orange juice
> ¾ cup (85g) powdered sugar
> ½ teaspoon almond extract
> ½ teaspoon butter flavoring
> ½ teaspoon vanilla

- Preheat oven to 350° and spray two 9x5 inch (23x13cm) loaf pans with cooking spray.

- In a large bowl, mix all bread ingredients until smooth.

- Pour batter evenly into loaf pans and bake for 1 hour.

- About 10 minutes before taking loaves from oven, stir all icing ingredients in small saucepan over medium heat until heated through and thoroughly blended. Set aside until bread is ready to glaze.

- Remove bread from oven and let cool 5 minutes in pans. Pour glaze evenly over loaves and leave in pans for additional 10 minutes.

- Remove from pans and serve in slices.

Very easy and freezes well.

Cook's Tip:

When freezing baked goods, leave unsealed until frozen. This impedes the formation of ice crystals and prevents a freezer taste. Once the baked goods are frozen, seal in airtight containers or cover with plastic wrap and return to the freezer.

U S A

PUMPKIN BREAD

Makes 3 loaves
Prep/Cook Time:
1 hour 15 minutes

*This bread makes a nice addition to a fall meal and is typical at an American Thanksgiving gathering.
It keeps well refrigerated in an airtight container for up to 1 week.*

3⅓ cups (475g) flour
2   teaspoons baking soda
1½   teaspoons salt
1   teaspoon cinnamon
1   teaspoon nutmeg
3   cups (600g) sugar
1   cup (250ml) vegetable oil
4   eggs
⅔   cup (170g) water
1   14½ ounce (411g) can pumpkin

- Preheat oven to 350°. Grease and flour three 9x5 inch (23x13cm) loaf pans with oil and flour.

- In a large bowl, mix all ingredients together until smooth with an electric mixer on medium-low speed. Pour batter evenly into all three pans.

- Bake for approximately 1 hour or until a knife inserted in the loaf comes out clean. Let sit on a rack and cool to room temperature before serving.

Variation:

If you're buying larger cans of pumpkin for other things like pies, use 2 cups (450g) of pumpkin for this recipe.

USA

SOUFFLÉ AU FROMAGE
Cheese Soufflé with Gruyère

Serves 4
Prep/Cook Time: 1 hour

3   tablespoons (45g) butter
3   tablespoons flour
1   cup (250ml) milk
½   teaspoon salt
⅛   teaspoon pepper
⅓   cup (40g) grated Parmesan cheese
2   tablespoons shredded Gruyère cheese
3   egg yolks, beaten
4   egg whites

• Preheat oven to 350°. Butter and dust with flour one 7 inch (18cm) or 4 individual 1 cup (125ml) soufflé dishes.

• In a medium saucepan, melt butter over low heat. Add flour and stir over low heat for 5 minutes. Remove from heat and slowly stir in the milk. Add salt and pepper, and return to heat. Continue to stir and remove from heat as soon as mixture reaches a boil. Add cheeses and egg yolks and stir well.

• Beat egg whites until stiff, and gently fold into the cheese mixture. Pour into soufflé dish(es) and bake 30 to 35 minutes until browned and center is just set. Serve immediately.

Serve with Mediterranean Summer Salad (see index for recipe) or your favorite salad of greens and tomatoes.

Cook's Tip:
A soufflé should not be left to stand, but the basic mixture can be prepared in advance and kept covered and refrigerated until the stiffly beaten egg whites are added. Do not open the oven door while the soufflé is cooking.

BIRCHER MUESLI

Serves 6
Prep/Cook Time: 10 minutes,
plus overnight to chill

3½ cups (350g) oatmeal, regular
  or quick cooking
⅔ cup (170ml) honey
2   cups (470ml) cream
2   cups (470ml) half-and-half cream
4   ounces (120ml) plain yogurt
½ cup (80g) raisins
1   cup (150g) fresh raspberries or blueberries
¼ cup (30g) chopped pecans

- In a large bowl with a lid or seal, combine all ingredients except berries and pecans and mix. Seal and refrigerate overnight.

- Serve cold in individual bowls, sprinkled with fresh berries and chopped pecans.

Variation:

For a lower fat version substitute half-and-half for the cream, and milk for the half-and-half. Also use non-fat yogurt.

Swiss physician, Maximilian Bircher-Benner, created Bircher Muesli nearly 100 years ago. He formulated Muesli to provide his European spa patients with a nutritionally balanced breakfast as part of an overall healthy diet based on raw foods. His health food ideas were initially rejected. Now, a focus on fresh healthy food is a routine part of a physician's advice.

TORTILLA DE PAPAS
Potato Omelet with Sautéed Onions

Serves 4
Prep/Cook Time: 25 minutes

1	medium onion, sliced
3	medium red or yellow potatoes, thinly sliced
1	clove garlic, crushed
¼	cup (60ml) olive oil
4	eggs, well beaten
½	cup (15g) coarsely chopped parsley

Salt and pepper to taste
Parsley for garnish, optional

• In a large skillet with a cover, heat oil over medium heat. Sauté onion, potatoes and garlic until cooked and the potatoes start to turn golden brown, about 15 minutes.

• Drain any excess oil and add the beaten eggs, parsley, salt and pepper.

• Cook covered until cooked through, about 5 minutes. If the top of the omelet isn't set when the remainder is cooked, place a plate on top of the skillet to flip the omelet and cook on the other side or put under the oven broiler for a few minutes.

• Serve warm in slices like a pie. Garnish with additional parsley, if desired.

Variation:

Substitute 2 cups (260g) packaged frozen potatoes for fresh potatoes, and reduce oil to 3 tablespoons. Add eggs directly into the skillet with potatoes and onions and continue with directions.

Tortilla de Papas is a traditional light supper or lunch dish in Argentina.

Tortilla *is the diminutive of the Spanish word* **torta,** *which means a flat cake.*

BALINAS
Lithuanian Crêpes

Serves 6
Prep/Cooking Time: 20 minutes

Balinas are sweeter and eggier than the Russian Blinchiki (see index for recipe). They may be served flat or rolled as a crêpe with filling. Brown sugar, powdered sugar, maple syrup, sour cream, or fresh fruit are all delicious with balinas.

8   tablespoons (120g) butter
8   eggs, room temperature
½   cup (100g) sugar
1   teaspoon salt
1   tablespoon vanilla
1½ cups (210g) flour
3½ cups (875ml) milk
Vegetable oil for cooking crêpes

• Preheat oven to 200°. Place serving plates in oven to warm.

• Melt butter and set aside to cool but not harden.

• In a medium bowl, beat eggs with a fork and mix in sugar, salt and vanilla.

• While continuing to beat egg mixture, slowly add cooled, melted butter.

• Gradually add flour and milk alternating between milk and flour. Batter should be the consistency of heavy cream soup, thicker than water but much thinner than pancake batter.

• Lightly coat a heavy nonstick 12 inch (18cm) skillet with a thin layer of vegetable oil, and heat over medium-high heat until a drop of water placed in skillet sizzles.

• Pour about 2 tablespoons of batter into skillet and rotate so the batter is spread as thinly as possible on the bottom of the skillet.

• When the top no longer appears moist, turn the balina to cook on the other side, about 30 seconds. Remove from skillet and transfer to warm plate in the oven. Repeat process until all batter is used. Serve hot with preferred condiments.

Lithuania

BLINCHIKI
Russian Crêpes

2½ cups (625ml) milk
2   eggs, separated
½   teaspoon salt
2   tablespoons sugar
1½ cups (210g) flour
Vegetable oil for cooking crêpes
Sour cream
Berry jam or fruit syrup

- Preheat oven to 200°. Place serving plates in oven to warm.

- In a large bowl, beat 1¼ cups (310ml) of milk, egg yolks, salt and sugar until well blended.

- Mix in flour until just blended, being careful not to over mix. Slowly stir in remaining milk.

- In a separate bowl, with an electric beater, beat egg whites until stiff, but not dry, and fold into the batter.

- Lightly coat a nonstick skillet with a thin layer of vegetable oil and heat over moderate heat until a drop of water placed in skillet sizzles.

- While tilting the skillet to make the batter spread as evenly as possible, pour in just enough batter to cover the entire bottom, about ¼ cup (60ml).

- Return skillet to heat until blinchik bubbles. Flip and cook about 30 seconds to 1 minute more. Transfer to a warm plate. Repeat process until all batter is used.

- Fill and roll blinchiki with favorite jam and garnish with sour cream or fill with one tablespoon sour cream and top with fruit syrup.

Blinchiki are quite popular in Russia and are often served with tea. Russians may be second only to the British in their love of tea. Blinchki are used as wrappers for fillings, similar to French crêpes, unlike Blini, another popular Russian pancake which are served flat. The filling for blinchiki can be anything imaginable, but the most traditional ones are ground meat, tvorog (curd) with sugar and sour cream, or baked apples. **Blinchiki** *and* **blini** *are plural; singular are* **blinchik** *and* **blin.**

CRÊPES À LA BIÈRE

Beer Crêpes

Serves 4
Prep/Cook Time:
30 minutes, plus 30 minutes
or overnight to rest batter

2   eggs, room temperature
1   tablespoon sugar
¼   teaspoon salt
⅔   cup, plus 2 tablespoons (200ml) beer
1¼   cups (175g) flour, sifted
1¼   cups (310ml) milk, room temperature
½   teaspoon vanilla
Butter or vegetable oil for cooking crêpes

- Beat eggs with a whisk and mix in sugar and salt. Add ⅔ cup (170ml) beer and mix well. Add sifted flour and mix until a smooth paste forms. Slowly add milk and vanilla.

- Let the batter rest at least 30 minutes at room temperature or overnight in the refrigerator. Just before cooking, stir 2 tablespoons beer into batter until just blended to produce a yeasty beer flavor.

- Preheat oven to 200°. Place serving plates in oven to warm.

- Lightly coat a nonstick skillet or crêpe pan with a thin layer of vegetable oil and heat over medium heat until a drop of water placed in skillet sizzles. While tilting the skillet to make the batter spread as evenly as possible, pour in just enough batter to cover the entire bottom, about ¼ cup (60ml).

- When the top side of pancake is completely dry and no batter adheres to the touch, flip the crêpe, by grasping the opposite edges and turning by hand. Or, if an expert, give the skillet a brisk upward movement and flip the crêpe. Cook a few seconds until other side of the pancake is slightly golden and transfer to a warm plate in the oven. Repeat until all batter is used.

- Serve crêpes immediately with light brown sugar, syrup, or any other sweet topping.

Variation:

These crêpes are also excellent dinner crêpes; omit the vanilla and sugar, and fill with a cheese and mushroom sauce or chicken curry.

---

*Cooking with beer is especially popular in Belgium. Belgians have their own **King of Beer, Duke Jean I (c.1251–1295), or Jan Primus in Flemish who was a connoisseur of beer**. In fact, he introduced a law against the adulteration of beer. It is said that Jan Primus or Gambrinus (as he was known in the rest of Europe) could drink 144 mugs of beer during a single feast.*

DINKYTOWN PANCAKES

Serves 6
Prep/Cook Time: 25 minutes

1½ cups (215g) flour
1 teaspoon baking powder
1 teaspoon sugar
½ teaspoon salt
½ teaspoon baking soda
2 cups (500ml) buttermilk, plus additional if necessary to thin batter
1 extra large egg, beaten lightly
3 tablespoons (45g) unsalted butter, melted
Vegetable oil for cooking pancakes
Butter and pure maple syrup

- Preheat oven to 200°. Place serving plates in oven to warm.
- In a large bowl, whisk together flour, baking powder, sugar, salt, and baking soda.
- In another bowl, stir together buttermilk, egg, and butter.
- Add buttermilk mixture to flour mixture and combine.
- Let batter rest at least 15 minutes or refrigerate overnight.
- Stir batter well and add a little more buttermilk if necessary to thin to a thick pouring consistency.
- Lightly coat a skillet or griddle with a thin layer of vegetable oil and heat over medium heat until a drop of water placed in skillet sizzles.
- Pour batter onto skillet to form pancakes about 6 inches (15cm) in diameter. When bubbles begin to appear and bottom is set, flip the pancakes and cook 1 minute more or until cooked through.
- Transfer pancakes to warm plates or serving platter and serve with pure maple syrup and butter.

Variations:

For a light and blintz like pancake, substitute a 40/60 mixture of sour cream and milk for the buttermilk and increase liquid quantity from 2 cups (500ml) to 2¼ cups (560ml). Add 1 egg white and substitute 3 teaspoons brown sugar for the 1 teaspoon of regular sugar. If you want to go lighter still, substitute sifted cake flour for all-purpose flour.

These pancakes have been served for untold years at Al's Diner in Dinkytown, the village of shops and restaurants that borders the University of Minnesota. Al's coffee and Dinkytown pancakes have provided generations of students with warmth and fuel to venture across the Minnesota campus on all those below-zero winter mornings.

PANNEKOEKEN

Dutch Pancakes with Bacon

Makes 6 pancakes
Prep/Cooking Time: 20 minutes

2   eggs, beaten
1¼ cups (310ml) milk
1   cup (140g) flour
¼   teaspoon salt
12 very lean and thin bacon slices
Vegetable oil for cooking pancakes

If very lean bacon is not available, the bacon should be cooked slightly longer to release most of the fat. Pannekoeken should be thin, about the size of a dinner plate, and are good spread with jam and rolled up. In the Netherlands, pannekoeken are usually eaten for lunch or a light dinner.

- Preheat oven to 200°. Place serving plates in oven to warm.

- Whisk eggs and milk together in a medium bowl.

- Sift flour and salt together and blend with milk and egg mixture until smooth with no lumps.

- Heat a heavy nonstick 12 inch (31cm) skillet over medium-high heat until a drop of water placed in skillet sizzles.

- Place 2 slices of bacon in pan, cook for 2 minutes, and drain off excess bacon fat.

- Pour in a heaping ⅓ cup (85ml) of batter, or enough to cover the bottom of the skillet, over bacon, and cook until bubbles form.

- Flip and cook other side until set.

- Serve immediately or keep warm in oven until all batter or bacon is used and serve.

BLINTZ SOUFFLÉ WITH YOGURT AND STRAWBERRIES

Serves 4
Prep/Cooking Time: 1 hour

3   ounces (85g) light cream cheese, softened
¼   cup (60g) butter, melted
6   tablespoons sugar
1   pound (450g) cottage cheese
½   cup (70g) flour
3   eggs
½   teaspoon fresh lemon juice
½   teaspoon baking powder
½   teaspoon cinnamon
1   cup (235ml) vanilla yogurt
1   cup (150g) sliced fresh strawberries or other berries

- Preheat oven to 350°. Grease 9x13 inch (23x33cm) baking pan or dish.

- In a medium bowl combine cream cheese, butter, and sugar and blend well. Mix in cottage cheese. Mix in flour, eggs, lemon juice, and baking powder.

- Pour into baking pan and sprinkle with cinnamon. Bake about 45 minutes or until golden. Serve warm with yogurt and strawberries.

Although this is called a soufflé, it's much easier to prepare and not nearly so temperamental as a true soufflé. It can be kept warm for a time until ready to be served. It doubles easily and can be served with a variety of toppings. Try experimenting with your favorites.

DUTCH BABY
Puffed Pancake

Serves 4
Prep/Cooking Time: 40 minutes

A puffed pancake
or Dutch Baby
originates in
the Amish
communities of
the United States.
The Amish
immigrated to
North America
in the 1700s as a
result of being
persecuted in
Europe for
breaking with
the teachings of
Martin Luther
over the practice
of baptism.
They were
Anabaptists,
believers in
voluntary adult
baptism, which
was punishable
by death in
16th and 17th
century Europe.
Amish
communities
are highly
concentrated
in Ohio,
Indiana and
Pennsylvania.

3   large eggs
¾   cup (185ml) milk
½   teaspoon vanilla
¾   cup (105g) flour
½   teaspoon salt
1   tablespoon (15g) butter
1   tablespoon vegetable oil
Powdered sugar
Lemon juice

• Preheat oven to 450°.

• Combine first 5 ingredients in a medium bowl and mix on high with electric mixer for 3 minutes.

• Heat a heavy 12 inch (18cm) skillet over medium-high heat until a drop of water sizzles when dropped in the skillet.

• Add butter and oil to skillet and heat until butter melts. Pour all of the batter into the skillet.

• Place skillet in middle of oven and bake 15 to 20 minutes, or until pancake is puffed and golden.

• Remove from oven and serve immediately sprinkled with powdered sugar and lemon juice. The pancake will deflate in the middle a bit like a soufflé.

Variations:

This recipe can be easily doubled and prepared in a 9x13 inch (23x33cm) ovenproof glass dish that has been preheated in the oven. The pancake is also excellent served with maple syrup, or with apples, strawberries or peaches, which have been sautéed in butter and drizzled with honey.

U S A

Soups & Salads

EASY BLACK BEAN SOUP

Serves 6
Prep/Cook Time: 20 minutes

3   15 ounce (420g) cans black beans, with liquid
1   15 ounce (420g) can beef stock
1   6 ounce (177ml) can tomato juice
1/4   cup (60ml) red wine
1/2   4 ounce (112g) can chopped green chiles
3/4   cup (200g) bottled salsa
1   teaspoon grated lime zest
1 1/2 teaspoons lime juice
1   clove garlic, crushed
1   tablespoon chopped fresh cilantro

Topping

1   cup (235ml) sour cream
1/2   4 ounce (112g) can chopped green chiles, drained, optional
2   tablespoons finely chopped red onions

- Mix 2 cans of beans with the stock and tomato juice and process in batches in a food processor or with a processor wand in a 4 quart (4 liter) pot until puréed.

- Add all remaining ingredients, except 1 can beans and cilantro, and process until blended.

- Add remaining can of beans and process briefly until last can of beans is coarsely chopped.

- Bring to a simmer over medium-low heat and stir in cilantro. Serve warm in bowls with topping.

- Mix sour cream and chiles for topping. Place a dollop on top of each bowl and sprinkle with red onions to taste.

Variation:

Add 1/2 pound (225g) of cooked pork, ham, or sausage for a full meal.

LENTIL DHAL
Lentil Soup

Serves 4
Prep/Cook Time: 40 minutes

1½ cups (300g) split and hulled lentils
6   cups (1.5 liters) cold water
½   teaspoon cayenne pepper
½   teaspoon turmeric powder
1½ teaspoons salt
4   tablespoons vegetable oil
2   medium onions, finely chopped
1   clove garlic, crushed
½   inch (1.3cm) piece of fresh ginger, peeled and minced
5   tablespoons canned crushed tomatoes,
       or 5 tablespoons diced fresh tomatoes
1   teaspoon garam masala powder
½   bunch cilantro, cleaned and chopped

- Wash lentils until rinsing water is almost clear. Place lentils in a 2 to 3 quart (2 to 3 liter) pot and add 6 cups (1.5 liters) of cold water, cayenne pepper, turmeric, salt, and 1 tablespoon oil. Bring to boil, reduce heat to low, cover and simmer until all the lentils have completely opened up and appear light and flaky, about 30 minutes.

- While the lentils are simmering, heat 3 tablespoons oil in a small skillet over medium-high heat. Sauté onions until deep golden. Add garlic and ginger and sauté for 2 to 3 minutes. Remove from heat and add tomatoes, garam masala, and cilantro. Mix and return to heat for 1 to 2 minutes.

- Add onion mixture to cooked lentils. Mix thoroughly and serve. Don't add onion mixture before lentils are fully cooked, otherwise they will not achieve a tender consistency and will remain hard. The consistency of the dhal should be like smooth thick soup. If too thin, remove saucepan lid and boil off water. If too thick, add a little water and bring back to boil.

Lentil Dhal is a staple food in India, providing a low fat, high protein diet with plenty of spice and flavor. Serve as a soup over steamed or boiled rice and with Aloo Merich Sabzi (see index for recipe) for a complete meal.

Dal or dhal is a Hindi word for both the variety and preparation of legumes. The dahl in this recipe are lentils that have been split and hulled. They are readily available in most international markets. Hulled legumes cook faster and are easier to digest than the American unhulled lentils.

CHILLED APRICOT SOUP

Serves 8
Prep Time: 15 minutes,
plus 2 hours to chill

2	16 ounce (454g) cans apricot halves, including peel and juice
1	cup (235ml) sour cream
½	cup (125ml) white wine
¼	cup (60ml) apricot liqueur
2	tablespoons lemon juice
2	teaspoons vanilla
½	teaspoon ground cinnamon

- Purée apricot halves in a blender until smooth. Add the remaining ingredients, except cinnamon, and blend together.

- Place soup in the freezer for two hours until very chilled, but not frozen. Stir, sprinkle with cinnamon and serve at once.

Also delicious served with a dollop of sour cream, topped with a mint sprig, in the center of each bowl. If apricot liqueur is not available, an orange liqueur such as Grand Marnier, Curaçao or Triple Sec may be used.

CREMA DE AGUACATE

Ecuadoran Cream of Avocado Soup

Serves 6
Prep/Cook Time: 15 minutes

4   cups (1 liter) chicken stock
2   large soft Haas avocados
Salt to taste
1   teaspoon lemon juice
6   tablespoons sour cream
3   tablespoons chopped chives or green onions

- Heat the chicken stock in a 3 quart (3 liter) pan over medium-high heat until warm.

- Just before serving, purée the avocados in a food processor or blender with ¼ cup (60ml) of the warm chicken stock until completely smooth.

- Add avocado mixture and salt to taste to the remaining stock and warm gently. Do not allow soup to boil as it will separate. Add lemon juice.

- Garnish with dollop of sour cream and sprinkle with chives on each serving.

Variation:

Substitute 2 teaspoons of white wine for the lemon juice

The rich avocado fruit has been a major food for the people of Central America for thousands of years. In many tropical parts of the world it is a basic food and has been called "the butter of the poor." The two most widely marketed avocado varieties are the pebbly textured, almost black Haas and the green Fuerte, which has a thin, smooth skin. The Fuerte is more acidic than the Haas and not as well suited for this soup.

AJIACO

Bogota Chicken and Potato Soup with Greens

Serves 8
Prep/Cook Time:
2 hours 15 minutes

1 *3 pound (1.35g) chicken cut in pieces*
1 *pound (450g) beef bones*
10 *cups (2.5 liters) cold water*
1 *bay leaf*
1 *bunch green onions*
1 *bunch cilantro*
½ *teaspoon dried thyme*
½ *teaspoon ground cumin*
2 *carrots*
Salt and pepper to taste
1½ *pounds (675g) baking potatoes, peeled*
1 *pound (450g) yellow potatoes, peeled*
1½ *pounds (675g) small new red potatoes, peeled*
2 *cups (260g) yellow corn kernels*
1 *bunch *guascas or radish greens, cleaned*
8 *teaspoons capers*
8 *tablespoons heavy cream*
1 *medium, ripe avocado*

- Combine chicken pieces with beef bones and water in 4 quart (4 liter) pot. Bring to boil. Skim off surface foam and oil. Add bay leaf, onions, cilantro, thyme, cumin, carrots, salt, and pepper. Reduce heat to low, cover and simmer 30 minutes or until chicken is tender. Drain and place chicken on a platter and let cool.

- Strain the stock and discard solids. Bring stock to boil. Cut baking potatoes into 1 inch (2.5cm) pieces, add to stock, and cook at medium heat 30 minutes or until potatoes are soft. Remove potatoes and a little broth and purée in blender.

- Skin and de-bone chicken and cut into large chunks. Peel and cube into 1 inch (2.5cm) pieces yellow potatoes and add them to the stock. Add whole new potatoes, corn, and gauscas or radish leaves. Continue to cook covered for 20 minutes or until potatoes are tender. Stir in puréed baking potatoes and chicken. Place 1 teaspoon capers and 1 tablespoon cream in each soup bowl. Ladle soup over cream and capers and top with diced avocado.

Ajiaco (Ah hee ah ko) is traditionally eaten in Bogota, Colombia at Christmas time.

*Guascas is the name used in Colombia for "Little Flower Quickweed," a wild herb common in Latin America, southeast Asia and the eastern United States. In Mexico it is called Piojito. Guascas can sometimes be found in Hispanic or international markets in the United States. One bunch of radish greens or an equivalent amount of turnip or spinach greens have a similar taste and can be substituted.

Colombia

FEIJOADA

**Black Bean and Pork Stew
with Sautéed Collard Greens**

Black Bean and Pork Stew

½	pound (225g) black beans,
1	2 pound (900g) rack pork ribs
½	pound (225g) smoked or Italian sausages
½	pound (225g) pork chops
1	pound (450g) bacon slab or thick sliced lean bacon
3	cloves garlic, minced
2	medium onions, finely chopped

Salt to taste

Sautéed Collard Greens

1	pound (450g) collard greens, washed and trimmed
1-2	tablespoons olive oil
2	cloves garlic, minced

Salt to taste

- Soak black beans in water overnight. The next morning, rinse the beans twice.

- Place beans in a large pot with enough water to go about 1½ inches (4cm) above the beans. Cover and cook over low heat until tender, about 1½ hours. Check water and add more if needed.

- Put all meat except the bacon in another deep pot and cover with water. Add garlic, 1½ onions, and salt. Boil rapidly for 5 minutes then simmer gently until meat is tender when tested with a fork, about 40 minutes.

- Chop the bacon and fry gently in a medium skillet over medium-low heat until all fat is cooked out. Remove the bacon pieces and add to beans.

- Drain all but 1 tablespoon of the bacon fat from the skillet and sauté the remaining ½ onion with the bacon fat until golden brown.

- Add one ladle full of beans and juice to the sautéed onions. Cook gently until the beans are very soft, about 15 minutes. Stir this mixture back into the beans.

- Roll up the collard greens, a few leaves at a time, and slice them as thinly as possible. Heat the oil in a large skillet over high heat until nearly smoking. Add the garlic and almost immediately the collards. Cook 1 to 2 minutes until wilted.

- Drain the meat, saving the broth. If desired, remove meat from bones and chop. Add the meat to the bean mixture and enough of the broth to keep the mixture moist. Cook very gently for 20 minutes and serve with the collard greens.

Feijoada is regarded as Brazil's national dish and reflects the international diversity of Brazil's heritage in its ingredients. Beans originally came from Mexico. Farofa is from pre-Portuguese Brazil, and pork was introduced from Europe. The cooking techniques are from Africa.

Feijoada is traditionally served with boiled rice, farofa (manioc flour toasted with a little butter), slices of oranges, fried bacon, and fried potatoes.

SOUTHWESTERN CHILI

Serves 10
Prep/Cook Time:
2 hours 30 minutes

5   pounds (2.25kg) cubed lean beef
3   tablespoons sugar
2   tablespoons salt
½   cup (85ml) olive oil
5   tablespoons flour
6   tablespoons chili powder
5   garlic cloves, minced
1   teaspoon pepper
1½ teaspoons oregano
1½ teaspoons cumin
5   cups cooked rice
Chopped onions
Sour cream
Shredded cheddar cheese

- In a large heavy pot, combine beef, sugar and salt. Add enough water to just cover beef and bring to a boil. Reduce heat and skim off fat while continuing to simmer.

- In a small heavy skillet over medium-high heat, heat oil, flour, chili powder, garlic, pepper, oregano, and cumin, stirring constantly. Add to the meat and simmer for 1½ to 2 hours. Adjust seasoning.

- Serve over cooked rice and top with onion, sour cream and shredded cheddar cheese.

This is a wonderfully rich and spicy chili which freezes well. A great choice for a Super Bowl party.

Cheddar Trivia:

Cheddar cheese receives its name from the village of Cheddar in the Somerset region of England where Cheddar cheese originated. It ranges in color from cream to pumpkin orange. Orange cheddars are colored with a natural dye called anatto.

U S A

Salmon Bisque

Serves 4
Prep/Cook Time: 30 minutes

½ pound (225g) fresh salmon
¼ cup (35g) minced green onions
1 clove garlic
4 tablespoons (60g) butter
¼ cup (35g) flour
2 cups (500ml) milk
3 cups (750ml) half-and-half
2 heaping tablespoons tomato purée
2 tablespoons dry sherry
1 teaspoon salt
Pepper to taste
1 tablespoon chopped fresh dill

- Place salmon in a shallow pot. Add enough water to cover. Bring to a slow boil and immediately reduce water to a simmer. Cook salmon for 10 minutes or until cooked through. Remove from heat and cool. Take salmon from water; remove and discard skin and bones; and flake salmon meat.

- In a large saucepan sauté onions and garlic in butter until soft, about 3 minutes. Add flour, stirring constantly, and cook 2 minutes until thickened.

- Reduce heat and gently whisk in milk and half-and-half.

- Stir in tomato purée, sherry, salt, pepper, and salmon. Cook 10 minutes. Stir in dill and serve.

This salmon bisque makes a full meal when served with salad and French bread. You can also add more flavor by adding onions, cloves, celery, a bay leaf, or peppercorns to the court bouillon liquid while poaching the fish. These will be discarded after cooking.

WEST INDIAN
LOBSTER BISQUE

Serve 8
Prep/Cook Time: 45 minutes

People of the West Indies use locally available spiny lobsters or rock lobsters for this decadent bisque. Maine lobsters are equally flavorful and the soup can also be made with shrimp or crawfish.

4   pounds (1.8kg) lobster tails
6   tablespoons (90g) butter
1   small onion, peeled and diced
1   small carrot, peeled and diced
3   tablespoons dry sherry
1   cup (250ml) dry white wine
3   tablespoons cognac
½   teaspoon each salt and pepper
¼   teaspoon paprika
3   cups (750ml) milk
½   cup (110g) cooked or canned black beans, drained
Hot pepper sauce to taste
Chopped chives

• With a large chopping knife slice lobster tails, still in shells, into 1 inch (2.5cm) thick segments.

• Melt butter over medium-high heat in medium saucepan. Add lobster tails and sauté until the tails turn pink, about 4 minutes.

• Add carrots and onions and sauté in butter until golden brown.

• Add sherry, wine, cognac, salt, pepper, paprika, and milk. Bring to a slow simmer. Simmer 10 minutes and remove lobster only.

• Continue simmering remaining ingredients for 20 minutes.

• Remove lobster meat from shells, cut half the meat into 1 inch (2.5 cm) pieces and reserve. Cut the remaining meat into large pieces and add to the stock.

• Add cooked black beans to stock, warm, and remove from heat.

• Purée the stock in a food processor. The soup can be prepared to this point ahead of time.

• Reheat soup. Remove to soup terrine and stir in reserved diced lobster meat, adjust seasonings and hot pepper sauce to taste. Serve warm garnished with chopped chives.

BEAN CURD SOUP WITH HAM, MUSHROOMS, AND VEGETABLES

Serves 4
Prep/Cook Time: 30 minutes

2   tablespoons vegetable oil
½   cup (40g) thinly sliced fresh mushrooms
½   cup (60g) canned bamboo shoots, cut in thin slivers
2   cups (240g) shredded cooked ham
7   cups (1.65 liters) chicken stock
1   tablespoon rice wine
Salt and pepper
1   pound (450g) package *soft bean curd (tofu), cut in bite sized pieces
2   cups (200g) sliced bok choy

• Heat oil in a large saucepan over high heat. Sauté mushrooms and bamboo shoots for 1 minute, stirring constantly. Add ham and stir briefly. Add chicken stock, rice wine, salt, and pepper. Bring to a boil.

• Drain the bean curd and add to the soup. Simmer on a very low heat for 15 minutes. Add bok choy. Simmer 2 minutes and serve.

A healthy as well as flavorful soup which is eaten in a bowl with plain white rice. It is a very nice choice for a cold winter night. Experiment with different varieties of mushrooms for this bean curd soup.

*Soft tofu is best used in soup while firm tofu is best in a stir-fry.

Soupe au Pistou
Vegetable Soup with Pistou

Serves 6
Prep/Cook Time:
1 hour 30 minutes

*Pistou
(pees-TOO) is a
popular basil
purée from the
Provence region of
France that can be
stirred into soup,
beef stew, or
served on pasta.
When added to
soup or stew,
the egg yolk
is cooked.
Refer to the
glossary for
instructions for
safe handing of
raw eggs if serving
on pasta, or omit
the egg yolks.
The ingredients
are very similar
to Italian pesto,
which also
comes from the
Mediterranean
area.*

Vegetable Soup

- ¼ pound (115g) green beans,
  cut in ¾ inch (2cm) pieces
- 3 small red potatoes, peeled and cut in ½ inch (1.5cm) cubes
- 4 small carrots, peeled and cut in ½ inch (1.5cm) cubes
- 3 small zucchini, cut in ½ inch (1.5cm) cubes
- 4 small tomatoes, peeled, seeded and chopped
- 8 cups (2 liters) water
- ¼ pound (115g) fresh white beans or 12 ounces (340g) canned cannellini beans
- 2 ounces (60g) spaghetti, broken in thirds

Pistou

- 3 cloves garlic
- 1 bunch basil
- 1 egg yolk
- ⅓ cup (85ml) extra virgin olive oil

Salt and pepper to taste
Grated Gruyère or Parmesan cheese for sprinkling

- In a large Dutch oven, place all prepared vegetables (except cannellini beans if using) in 8 cups (2 liters) water. Bring to a boil, reduce heat and simmer until vegetables are just tender, about 45 minutes to 1 hour.

- Place garlic and basil for Pistou in a food processor and process until finely puréed. Add egg yolk and process until well blended. Very slowly pour in olive oil in a thin, steady stream, processing until the mixture is thick and almost the consistency of mayonnaise. Refrigerate until ready to use.

- Add spaghetti and cannellini beans if using. Cook until spaghetti is cooked, about 15 minutes.

- Just before serving, thin pistou with ¼ cup (60ml) soup broth so that the eggs warm up and don't curdle when added to the soup. Stir thinned pistou into the soup, mixing well. Season with salt and pepper and immediately serve soup topped with Gruyère or Parmesan cheese.

Potato Leek Soup
with Bacon

Serves 8
Prep/Cook Time: 2 hours

8   slices bacon, diced
4   leeks, white and pale green parts only, diced
¾   cup (105g) onions, chopped
4   tablespoons flour
8   cups (2 liters) chicken stock
6   large baking potatoes, peeled and diced
4   egg yolks, beaten
2   cups (473ml) sour cream
Salt and pepper to taste
2   tablespoons chopped fresh parsley

• In a 4 quart pot cook bacon over medium heat until brown. Drain all but
  1 tablespoon fat.

• Add leeks and onions and sauté for 3 to 5 minutes.

• Add flour and cook while stirring for 1 minute. Slowly add chicken stock and
  continue stirring until smooth.

• Add potatoes and simmer for 1 hour. Can be prepared ahead to this point.

• Before serving, combine the egg yolks and sour cream. Stir slowly into the
  soup and simmer over very low heat for 10 minutes. Do not let boil. Add salt
  and pepper to taste. Garnish with parsley and serve.

Potato Trivia:

The potato is native to the Americas. In fact, the word potato is derived from an Indian name for the sweet potato which was **patata.** *The potato was introduced in Europe in the 1500s, but was slow to catch on. In many areas of Europe potatoes were believed to cause lust or leprosy and did not become popular until the 1700s, and in some regions considerably later.*

U S A

WEST INDIAN PUMPKIN SOUP

Serves 6
Prep/Cook Time: 1 hour

1 tablespoon olive oil
1 medium onion, chopped
2 sticks celery, chopped
1 carrot, chopped
3 cloves garlic, chopped
½ habanero or other hot chili pepper, chopped
1½ pounds (675g) *calabaza or butternut squash, peeled and cut in cubes
¼ cup (8g) fresh parsley, chopped
2 bay leaves
2 sprigs fresh thyme, or 1 teaspoon dried thyme
1 tablespoon brown sugar
5 cups (1.25 liters) chicken stock
½ cup (125ml) sour cream
Salt and pepper to taste
Chopped chives, scallions, or paprika for garnish, optional

- Heat olive oil over medium heat in a Dutch oven or large soup pot. Sauté onion, celery, and carrot until soft, about 3 to 4 minutes. Add garlic and pepper and cook for another minute.

- Stir in squash, parsley, bay leaves, thyme, sugar and chicken stock. Bring to a boil and then reduce heat to medium-low, simmer 25 to 30 minutes or until squash is soft. Discard bay leaves and thyme sprigs.

- Purée soup in blender or food processor until very smooth.

- Return to soup pot and add water, if necessary, to adjust consistency. Add sour cream and simmer for 2 to 3 minutes. Adjust sugar, salt and pepper to taste. Garnish with chopped chives, scallions, or paprika, if desired, and serve warm.

*West Indian pumpkin is another name for calabaza, a pumpkin-like squash that is popular in Caribbean cuisine. Calabaza, which ranges in size from as small as a cantaloupe to as large as a watermelon, is typically sold in chunks in Latin markets. Its orange flesh is firm and has a sweet flavor, similar to a butternut squash.

Cook's Tip:
Habanero chiles are very hot. Wash hands thoroughly after chopping.

Avocado, Tomato and Goat Cheese Salad with Pine Nuts

Serves 4
Prep/Cook Time: 20 minutes

Dressing

1   heaping teaspoon Dijon mustard
⅓   cup (85ml) olive oil
Juice of ½ medium lemon
Salt and pepper to taste

Salad

1   head romaine lettuce, cleaned and in bite size pieces
2   medium vine ripe tomatoes, cubed
1   ripe avocado, cubed
3½ ounces (100g) *goat cheese, crumbled
⅓   cup (50g) pine nuts, toasted

- Place all dressing ingredients in a small jar with a lid. Seal tightly and shake until well blended.

- Place lettuce, tomatoes, and avocado in a large salad bowl. Pour over desired amount of dressing and toss gently. Sprinkle with crumbled goat cheese and toasted pine nuts and serve.

*Goat cheese is also known as chèvre cheese. A firm chèvre will crumble better for this salad. A soft goat cheese will taste just as good, it's just a little messier breaking it up to go over the salad. You may need to use a fork.

71

CHINESE CABBAGE AND BOK CHOY SALAD

Indonesia is an island paradise consisting of 3000 islands lying along the equator between Asia and Australia, south of the Philippines. It is the world's largest archipelago and has a fascinating mixture of peoples, cultures and a complex cuisine.

*Napa cabbage and bok choy have thin and delicately mild flavored leaves, unlike the strong-flavored waxy leaves on round heads of cabbage. Chinese cabbage should be eaten within three days of purchase for the best flavor.

Dressing

½	cup (100g) sugar
¼	cup (60ml) vinegar
¾	cup (185ml) light olive oil
1	tablespoon soy sauce

Salad

1	*napa cabbage (Chinese cabbage)
1	*bok choy (Chinese white cabbage)
2	3 ounce (90g) packages ramen noodles
¼	cup (60g) butter
½	cup (50g) sliced almonds
3	tablespoons sesame seeds

• Mix all dressing ingredients in a small pan and bring to a boil, stirring constantly. Boil for one minute and remove from heat. Pour into a sealed container and chill in the refrigerator.

• Chop or shred napa cabbage and bok choy. Place in a bowl and set aside.

• Crush the ramen noodles before opening the package. Open the ramen package and discard the seasoning packet.

• In a small skillet, melt butter. Sauté noodles, almonds, and sesame seeds until golden.

• Toss all salad ingredients in large bowl with dressing and serve.

SALADE AU CHÈVRE CHAUD
Salad with Hot Goat Cheese Dressing

Serves 4
Prep/Cook Time: 30 minutes

S a l a d

8	cups (340g) mixed salad greens
2	tomatoes, chopped
2	spring onions or scallions, chopped
3-4	hard-boiled eggs, cut in quarters
1	stick celery, sliced
1-2	cups (150-300g) of one or combination of
	corn kernels, nuts, sprouts, or carrots to liking

H o t   G o a t   C h e e s e   D r e s s i n g

8	slices bacon, chopped in small pieces
¼	pound (115g) mushrooms, finely chopped
1½	tablespoons red wine vinegar
5	tablespoons fresh goat cheese
1	teaspoon prepared mustard
2	tablespoons whipping cream

Pinch cayenne pepper
Salt and pepper to taste

- Place the salad greens on 4 salad plates. Arrange the next 5 ingredients on top.

- In a frying pan over medium heat, cook the bacon. Drain all but 2 tablespoons bacon fat from the pan.

- Add the mushrooms and cook until soft. Add vinegar, mix well. Add goat cheese, let it melt, stirring well. Add mustard, cream, cayenne pepper, salt and pepper.

- Pour hot dressing on salad and serve immediately.

Salad ingredients may also be arranged by type in attractive patterns on the plate, making an appealing presentation. The amount or use of each salad ingredient can be adjusted to personal taste. Corn kernels from a can are often used in salads in both Belgium and France as demonstrated by this recipe and the very popular Salade Niçoise.

MANGO MARGARITA SALAD

Serves 4
Prep/Cook Time: 15 minutes

Margarita Dressing

¼ cup (60ml) lime juice
2 tablespoons white wine vinegar
⅔ cup (170ml) vegetable oil
⅓ cup (65g) sugar
1 teaspoon tequila
½ teaspoon salt

Mango Salad

1 large ripe but firm mango, sliced or cubed
3 cups (125g) torn green leaf and romaine lettuce, about 6 leaves
1 small ripe Haas avocado, pit removed, peeled, and sliced or cubed
4-8 very thin slices of red onion, rings separated

- Combine all dressing ingredients in a small jar. Cover tightly and shake until blended.
- In a medium bowl toss all mango salad ingredients with desired amount of dressing until well coated. Serve cold on individual salad plates.

Variation:

Reduce the sugar to 1 tablespoon for a dressing that accents the tequila and lime flavors and is less sweet. Also the tequila can be eliminated according to your preference for the flavor.

There may be extra salad dressing, depending on whether you like a lot or only a little. Extra dressing keeps up to 2 weeks tightly sealed in the refrigerator.

Cook's Tips:

Ripe mangos needed for this salad should be sweet smelling and slightly soft to the touch but still firm. To cut a peeled mango, stand it stem down on a cutting board. Slice down as close to the pit on one side as possible. Repeat until all the mango flesh is removed and discard the pit.

SALADE DE MANGUES VERTES
Green Mango Salad

Serves 6
Prep/Cook Time: 20 minutes,
plus 1 hour to soak

15	very young small firm green mangos
1	tablespoon kosher salt
2	green onions, chopped
2	tablespoons fresh parsley
½	tablespoon fresh thyme or ½ teaspoon dried
6	cloves garlic, minced
½	red pepper, chopped

Salt and pepper to taste
¼-⅓ cup (60-85ml) olive oil, optional
Lettuce

- Peel mangos. Grate the mango flesh with a food processor or coarse grid of a cheese grater, discarding the stone.

- Put mangos and kosher salt in a medium bowl with enough water to cover the mango. Let soak for 1 to 2 hours.

- Place green onion, parsley, thyme, garlic, and bell pepper in a food processor and grind finely. Remove to a large bowl.

- Drain and rinse grated mangos and dry on a paper or clean kitchen towel. Combine with the herb mixture and stir until well blended. Add salt and pepper to taste and olive oil if desired.

- Chill until ready to serve. Serve on a bed of lettuce.

Serve as a refreshing relish with a spicy meal such as Poulet au Columbo (see index for recipe).

Guadeloupe is an island in the West Indies which is one of a group of islands forming the French département (administrative district or province) also known as Guadeloupe. The beautiful island of Saint Barthélemy, (Saint Barts) is also an island in the département of Guadeloupe. The French influence, blended with the local flavors of the Caribbean, make for a tantalizing culinary experience.

SOM TAM
Papaya Salad

Serves 6
Prep/Cook Time: 30 minutes

The papaya for this very refreshing salad should be unripe, green, and firm enough to grate.

This salad would be good served with Bul-Kogi or Phad Thai (see index for recipes).

*Dried shrimp are available in Asian markets.

**Fish sauce, also known as nam pla, can be found in the Asian section of most large supermarkets.

1   large green papaya, large enough
      to yield 4 cups (600g) fruit
6   cloves garlic, finely chopped
1   dried chile pepper, soaked in water, or fresh Thai chile
¼   cup (20g) ground *dried shrimp, rinsed in fresh water
3   tablespoons **fish sauce
3   tablespoons sugar
3   tablespoons lemon juice
¼   cup (60g) very small cubes of peeled fresh lemon
Cabbage and/or lettuce, shredded

• Peel, seed, and grate papaya.

• Gently crush grated papaya in a mortar and pestle, or in a bowl with the back of a spoon. Remove and set aside in a medium bowl. Can be prepared ahead to this point.

• Crush garlic, chile, and dried shrimp in mortar, mixing thoroughly, and transfer to the bowl of papaya.

• Add fish sauce, sugar, lemon juice, and lemon cubes to the papaya mixture and toss thoroughly. Adjust the seasonings.

• Arrange lettuce or cabbage on a serving platter, mound salad on top and serve.

ANGOUROSALATA ME YIAOURTI

Greek Cucumber and Yogurt Salad

Serves 6
Prep/Cook Time: 15 minutes

3   medium cucumbers
2   cloves garlic, minced
3   green onions, finely chopped
1   tablespoon fresh chopped dill, or ¾ teaspoon dried dill
Salt and freshly ground pepper
1   tablespoon white wine vinegar
1   cup (235ml) yogurt
Finely chopped parsley

- Peel cucumbers and slice thinly or grate on the slicer side of a grater. Place in a medium bowl. Add garlic, onions, dill, salt, and pepper to taste.

- Mix vinegar and yogurt and add to the salad, mixing well. Place in a serving dish. Garnish with parsley and serve.

Serve with Indian curries or Middle Eastern meat dishes such as Etli Kuru Fasulye or Khoresh-e Bademjan (see index for recipes).

Many Mediterranean and Asian countries have versions of cucumber and yogurt salads such as this one and Mast-o Khujar (see index for recipe) with different flavorings.

MAST-O KHUJAR
Cucumber and Yogurt Salad with Nuts and Raisins

Serves 6
Prep/Cook Time: 10 minutes

3	cups (705ml) plain yogurt
3	cucumbers, peeled, seeded, and chopped
1½	teaspoons salt
½	teaspoon pepper
1	tablespoon fresh chopped mint, or 1 teaspoon dried mint
6	tablespoons chopped walnuts
6	tablespoons raisins

• In a medium bowl, beat yogurt with a spoon until smooth. Stir in remaining ingredients. Place in a serving bowl and chill until ready to serve. Garnish with mint sprigs and walnuts.

Excellent accompaniment for Koresh-e Bademjan or Estamboli Polo (see index for recipes) or curry dishes. To make this dish thicker, drain the yogurt through cheesecloth for one hour before adding in the other ingredients. It can then be served as an appetizer with pieces of bread.

SHIRAZI SALAD

Cucumber and Tomato Salad with Feta

Serves 6.
Prep/Cook Time: 20 minutes,
plus 1 hour to chill

A wonderful salad to serve with grilled meats or to take on a picnic.

2   cucumbers, peeled, seeded and
      diced in ½ inch (2.5cm) pieces
4   green onions, chopped
4   tomatoes, diced
2   tablespoons fresh parsley or cilantro, chopped
1½ cups (120g) crumbled feta cheese
3   tablespoons olive oil
1½ tablespoons lemon juice
Salt and pepper to taste
Lettuce

- Mix first five ingredients together in medium bowl.

- In a small container, whisk together olive oil, lemon juice, salt and pepper. Pour dressing over the cucumber and tomato salad and toss. Chill one hour.

- Place a bed of lettuce on a serving platter. Mound cucumber and tomato salad on top of lettuce and serve.

Cilantro Peach Salad

Serves 6 to 8
Prep/Cook Time: 20 minutes

A delectably refreshing accompaniment for barbecue pork sandwiches or barbecue pork ribs as well as other grilled meats. Best in the summer when peaches are in season.

2½   pounds (1.125kg) fresh ripe, but firm peaches
¼   cup fresh cilantro, chopped finely
3   tablespoons sugar
½   teaspoon whole cumin seeds
1   tablespoon lemon juice
⅛-¼ teaspoon cayenne pepper

• Peel and pit peaches and slice in eighths. Place in a medium bowl.

• In a small bowl, mix remaining ingredients and pour over peaches.

• Garnish with cilantro sprigs and serve. If not using immediately, refrigerate until needed.

Avocado Egg Salad

Serves 6
Prep/Cook Time: 30 minutes

4   *eggs, boiled and chopped*
2   *tablespoons finely chopped onion*
2   *tomatoes, peeled, seeded and chopped*
½   *cup (120ml) mayonnaise*
1   *teaspoon lemon juice*
2   *teaspoons prepared mustard*
½   *teaspoon salt*
½   *teaspoon pepper*
4   *ripe but firm avocados, pitted, peeled and chopped*
Lettuce leaves
4   *slices bacon, fried and chopped*
Cherry tomatoes for garnish

- Combine eggs, onions, and tomatoes.

- Mix in mayonnaise, lemon juice, mustard, salt and pepper. Add avocados and mix gently.

- Layer individual serving plates or a large serving platter with a bed of lettuce leaves or shredded lettuce. Spoon avocado egg salad over lettuce.

- Sprinkle with bacon bits, garnish with cherry tomatoes, and serve immediately.

Variation:

May also be served in the avocado shell for an attractive presentation.

Avocados are rich in linoleic acid, which helps break down cholesterol.

Cook's Tip:

To slice an avocado, cut the avocado in half lengthwise; remove the pit and with a large spoon, scoop out the avocado flesh from the shell in 2 pieces. This method is much less messy than peeling and an avocado shell "bowl" is left for filling if desired.

MELITZANES SALATA

Greek Eggplant Salad

Serves 6
Prep/Cook Time:
1 hour 15 minutes,
plus 4 hours to chill

A great make ahead salad that compliments fish or seafood such as Crème of Mussels with Saffron or Psari tis Skaras me Saltsa Politiki (see index for recipe).

1   large eggplant
1   medium-sized onion, grated,
      or 4 green onions, finely chopped
1   large tomato, peeled and chopped
1   clove garlic, minced
2   tablespoons chopped parsley
½   teaspoon dried marjoram
⅓   cup (85ml) olive oil
2   tablespoons red wine vinegar
½   teaspoon salt
Freshly ground pepper to taste
Romaine lettuce leaves
Chopped parsley
Greek olives

- Place the whole eggplant in a shallow pan and bake in a 350° oven for 1 hour or until firm but cooked. Dip into cold water and peel off the skin.

- Dice eggplant into small pieces and place in a bowl. Add onion, tomato, garlic, parsley, marjoram, oil, vinegar, salt and pepper to taste. Mix well and chill 4 or more hours to allow flavors to blend.

- Line a serving platter or 6 salad plates with Romaine lettuce leaves. Serve mounds of salad on lettuce, sprinkle with parsley and olives.

SALADE LIÉGEOISE
Hot Potato and Green Bean Salad

Serves 8
Prep/Cook Time: 40 minutes

8   *small to medium yellow or red potatoes*
2   *pounds (900g) small fresh green beans,*
      cut in 1½ inch (4 cm) pieces
8   *slices lean bacon, cut in small pieces*
2   *shallots or 1 onion, chopped*
2   *cloves garlic, minced*
3   *tablespoons red wine vinegar*
4   *tablespoons whipping cream or sour cream*

• Peel potatoes and cut in half, or quarters if medium sized. Boil until just soft and drain. Keep warm.

• Clean and cook the beans until just crisp tender. Drain and keep warm.

• Meanwhile, in a large heavy pot, which is not coated with a nonstick surface, fry the bacon and onion over medium heat. Drain all but one tablespoon of the bacon fat from the pan.

• Add garlic. Let the bottom of the pot get lightly brown over low heat. Add vinegar and scrape the bottom of the pot with a wooden spoon. Let the vinegar reduce to about to 2 tablespoons. Add cream, followed by potatoes and beans. Add salt and pepper to taste. Gently mix all ingredients over low heat. Remove from heat and serve warm.

Salade Liégeoise originated in the region of Belgium near the city of Liége. It goes well with pork chops or may be served as a meal in itself. It may be prepared earlier in day, refrigerated and reheated before serving.

Bacon in Europe usually comes in a slab or thick slices. It is leaner and less salty than bacon in the United States.

Southern Coleslaw

Serves 10
Prep/Cook Time: 30 minutes,
plus 12 hours to chill

Slaw

1	head green cabbage, shredded
½	head red cabbage, shredded
5	carrots, peeled and shredded
1	bunch green onions, chopped
1	small bunch fresh parsley, chopped

Dressing

1½ cups (350ml)	mayonnaise
⅓ cup (65g)	sugar
4	tablespoons lemon juice
2	tablespoons Dijon mustard
3	tablespoons champagne vinegar
1	teaspoon kosher salt
2	teaspoons pepper

Parsley for garnish

- Mix all slaw ingredients together in large bowl.

- Shake or whisk together dressing ingredients in medium jar or bowl.

- Pour dressing over slaw and let marinate in refrigerator overnight. Garnish with parsley sprigs and serve chilled.

The word cabbage is a derivation of the French word caboch. Cabbage was highly esteemed by the Greeks and the Romans. Because cabbage holds up well to cold temperatures, coleslaw is a good way to have a salad in winter when the lettuce at the supermarket may not be looking very fresh.

WHEAT BERRY SALAD WITH CURRANTS AND SPICY CURRY DRESSING

Serves 8
Prep/Cook Time: 3 hours,
plus 24 hours to soak and chill

Dressing

4	tablespoons mayonnaise
4	tablespoons plain yogurt
2	cloves garlic, minced
1	teaspoon curry powder, or to taste
½	teaspoon salt
⅛	teaspoon pepper
⅛	teaspoon cayenne pepper
1	teaspoon mustard
2	teaspoon red wine vinegar

Salad

3	cups (420g) *wheat berries
½	teaspoon salt
6	small celery sticks, chopped
6	green onions, chopped
¾	cup (100g) currants, soaked for 1 hour in water and drained
3	tablespoons chopped cilantro

Cilantro sprigs for garnish

- Whisk all dressing ingredients until smooth. Refrigerate tightly covered until ready for use.

- Cover wheat berries in large pot with water. Soak over night. Drain water. Cover wheat berries again with water and drain again.

- Cover the wheat berries with fresh water, add salt and cook in a medium pot for 2½ hours or in a pressure cooker for 1 hour, or until tender. Drain water.

- Toss and combine cooked wheat berries with chopped celery, green onions, currants, and salad dressing.

- Refrigerate tightly covered for 12 hours.

- Mix in chopped cilantro and serve. Place on a serving dish and garnish with cilantro sprigs.

*Wheat berries are whole kernels of wheat with bran and germ intact, and are available in health food stores or many large grocery stores.

This recipe comes from a colonial farm and restaurant named Malwatte in Zimbabwe. The farm is run by a group of British women in the small village of Marondera, a few hours northeast of Harare, the capital of Zimbabwe. Malwatte has long been a popular stopping spot for the colonial families living in Harare who are traveling on a weekend country holiday as it is renowned for its great food and fresh goat cheese.

KARTOFFELSALAT
Potato Salad

Serves 10
Prep/Cook Time: 45 minutes,
plus 1 hour to rest

2   pounds (900g) medium boiling potatoes
1   teaspoon salt
1½ cups (375ml) chicken stock
4   tablespoons white wine vinegar
8   tablespoons sunflower oil
⅓   cup (100g) Dijon mustard
Salt and pepper to taste
⅓   cup (50g) chopped green onions
¼   cup (40g) chopped cornichons or dill pickles
2-3 teaspoons finely chopped chives

- In a large pan, cover potatoes with cold water. Add salt, and bring to a boil. Simmer and cook until just tender. Drain and peel while still warm. Slice potatoes ¼ inch (.6cm) thick and place in large mixing bowl.

- In small pan, bring chicken stock to a boil. Pour over the potatoes and let cool.

- In a separate small bowl, blend vinegar, oil, mustard, salt and pepper and pour over the potatoes.

- May be prepared to this point several hours ahead and chilled.

- Gently blend in green onions and chopped pickles.

- Let rest for at least 1 hour before serving. Add chives just before serving and mix again.

A Swiss or German picnic would usually include grilled sausages and meats, a hard roll to eat the sausage in, mustard, and, most certainly, Kartoffelsalat, all served up with plenty of beer.

The chicken stock (or instant chicken soup mix with water) is added both for the flavor and to add airiness.

ZESTI PATATOSALATA
Warm Greek Potato Salad

Serves 8
Prep/Cook Time: 30 minutes

6   medium boiling potatoes, halved but not peeled
1   teaspoon salt
1   bunch green onions, finely chopped
½   cup (125ml) olive oil
3   tablespoons white wine vinegar
Salt and pepper to taste
1   teaspoon dried dill
Finely chopped parsley for garnish

- In a medium pot, cover potatoes with cold water and salt. Bring to a boil, simmer and cook until tender, about 20 minutes. Drain and rinse under cold water until cool enough to handle.

- Peel and slice warm potatoes into a large serving bowl. Add onions.

- Place olive oil, vinegar, salt and pepper to taste, and dill in a small, tightly sealed container and shake until blended.

- Pour over potatoes and mix lightly.

- Sprinkle with parsley for garnish and serve immediately.

The dressing can also be made with lemon juice and oregano instead of vinegar and dill. The salad is delicious served with smoked sausages and broccoli.

TOMATO, BASIL, OLIVE, AND GOAT CHEESE SALAD

Serves 6
Prep/Cook Time: 10 minutes

Makes a beautiful presentation. Best made in the summer when good, vine ripe tomatoes are plentiful.

6   vine ripe large tomatoes
1   tablespoon balsamic vinegar
5   tablespoons olive oil
Salt and pepper to taste
¼   cup (50g) halved, pitted kalamata olives
⅓   cup (25g) crumbled chèvre (mild goat) cheese
1   teaspoon capers
1   bunch fresh basil leaves, whole or chopped

- Cut tomatoes in ⅛ to ¼ inch (.3 to .6cm) thick slices.

- Arrange slices in a circular pattern on a large round platter.

- Drizzle with vinegar then oil.

- Sprinkle lightly with salt and pepper.

- Sprinkle with olives, goat cheese, and capers.

- Scatter basil leaves on top and serve.

U S A

BLACK BEAN AND RICE SALAD

Serves 6
Prep/Cook Time: 15 minutes,
plus 1 hour to chill

1   cup (200g) rice
2   cups (500ml) water
½   teaspoon salt
2   cups (440g) canned or
        cooked black beans, rinsed and drained
1½ cups (45g) fresh cilantro, chopped
¼   cup (60ml) lime juice
¼   cup (60ml) olive oil
½   cup (70g) chopped onion
2   cloves garlic, minced
Salt and pepper to taste
Cilantro for garnish

- In a medium saucepan cook rice with water and salt. When cooked, let cool.

- Combine all ingredients in medium bowl. Season to taste. Refrigerate 1 to 3 hours before serving. Garnish with sprigs of cilantro.

This delicious fresh salad goes very well with Grilled Ginger, Honey and Sesame Chicken (see index for recipe) and a tomato salad on a hot summer day.

BLACK-EYED PEA SALAD WITH CHAMPAGNE VINAIGRETTE

Serves 8
Prep/Cook Time: 1¼ hours,
plus 4 hours to marinate

8   cups (2 liters) water
1   tablespoon plus 1 teaspoon salt
3   tablespoons dried basil, or ½ cup (15g) chopped fresh basil
3   pounds (1.35kg) frozen black-eyed peas
2   medium sweet red peppers, chopped
1   large red onion, thinly sliced
⅓   cup (85ml) sweet Champagne,
        such as Asti Spumante or other sweet sparkling wine
⅓   cup (85ml) rice wine vinegar
⅔   cup (170ml) safflower oil
1   teaspoon freshly ground black pepper
Basil leaves for garnish

- Combine water, 1 tablespoon salt and basil in a large saucepan. Bring to a boil and simmer for 5 minutes.

- Add peas and cook over medium heat for about 45 minutes, until peas are tender but not mushy.

- Drain and allow to cool.

- Toss in the peppers and onion.

- Whisk the champagne, vinegar, oil and remaining teaspoon salt, and pepper. Pour over the peas and marinate in the refrigerator for 4 to 12 hours. Bring back to room temperature before serving. Place in a serving bowl and decorate with basil leaves and finely diced red pepper.

The sparkling wine provides sweetness to the vinaigrette, as compared to using a wine vinegar.

Black-eyed peas are actually beans and are referred to as beans in many countries. The black-eyed pea is native to Africa. Southerners of the United States owe thanks to the many Africans who were involuntarily brought in to work the antebellum farms for introducing this highly nutritious and flavorful legume into their cuisine. It is a tradition to serve black-eyed peas before noon on New Year's Day to bring good luck in many homes in the southern United States.

Warm Thai Beef and Lettuce Salad with Chile Lime Dressing

Serves 4
Prep/Cook Time: 30 minutes,
plus 1 hour to marinate steak

Dressing

- 1/3 cup (85ml) vegetable oil
- 2 tablespoons lime juice
- 2 cloves garlic, minced
- 2 tablespoons soy sauce
- 1 tablespoon minced fresh ginger
- 1 jalapeño chile pepper, chopped

Salad

- 2 tablespoons lime juice
- 2 tablespoons soy sauce
- 4 tablespoons vegetable oil
- 1 pound (450g) sirloin or filet mignon steak, trimmed of fat and cut into 1 inch (2.5cm) thick slices
- 1 small head romaine lettuce
- 1 small head bib lettuce
- 1 small head curly endive
- 1/2 cup (15g) fresh cilantro, chopped

- Combine all dressing ingredients in a small jar. Cover tightly and shake until blended. Keep at room temperature.

- Combine lime juice, soy sauce, and 2 tablespoons of oil. Marinate steak for 1 hour, turning occasionally.

- Drain marinade from steak and reserve.

- Heat oil in a large heavy skillet over high heat. Sear steak until cooked, about 5 minutes per side.

- Remove skillet from heat, transfer steak to cutting board and slice into very thin slices across the grain.

- Add dressing and remaining marinade to steak juices in skillet. Heat and stir 2 to 3 minutes to blend flavors.

- Clean lettuces, tear into bite size pieces.

- Pour dressing over greens. Add steak and toss. Add cilantro and toss again. Serve immediately.

The chile is a late influx into Thai cooking, having arrived from South America with Portuguese traders early in the 16th century. The chile has become a central player in Thai cuisine.

In addition to its indigenous spices and produce, Thai cuisine owes much of its appeal to herbs and seasonings from China, India, Java, as well as Portugal.

Thailand

CHICKEN, MANGO, AND KIWI SALAD WITH HONEY LIME DRESSING

Serve 4
Prep/Cook Time: 15 minutes,
plus time to cook chicken

Salad

4	boneless chicken breast halves, or about 2 cups (450g) of cooked chicken
½	cup (60g) snow peas, cooked until slightly crisp and sliced lengthwise
4-6	cups (170-255g) torn mixed greens
2	cups (300g) fresh mango, sliced or cubed
1½	cups (225g) kiwi, sliced
2	star fruits, sliced for garnish, optional
2	thin slices red onion, separated

Honey Lime Dressing

⅓	cup (85ml) vegetable oil
½	teaspoon salt
¼	teaspoon black pepper, freshly ground
3	tablespoons honey

Grated zest of 1 lime
Juice of 1-2 limes, about 2-4 tablespoons

- Cook chicken breasts using recipe for Baked Chicken for Entrée Salads (see index for recipe) or use precooked chicken breasts purchased from the supermarket.

- Slice cooked chicken breasts thinly across the diagonal.

- Combine all dressing ingredients in a small jar. Cover tightly and shake until blended.

- Mix with 4 tablespoons of salad dressing with chicken slices and set aside.

- Toss snow peas and greens and divide between 4 plates.

- Top with chicken, fruits and onion slices. Drizzle with remaining honey lime dressing and serve.

If preparing this salad in advance, do not combine the chicken with the other ingredients until ready to serve, as kiwi acts as a natural tenderizer and will cause the chicken to soften too much.

Cook's Tips:

Wash and save a few jam or jelly jars for making and storing homemade salad dressings. Also, make double of a favorite salad dressing. It will keep tightly covered in the refrigerator for 1 to 2 weeks. Half the work is done when the salad is next served.

SESAME CHICKEN AND
CRISPY RICE NOODLE SALAD

Serves 4
Prep/Cook Time: 15 minutes,
plus time to cook chicken

Sweet and Sour Dressing

- ¼ cup (60ml) dark sesame oil
- ¼ cup (60ml) vegetable oil
- ¼ cup (60ml) rice wine vinegar
- ⅓ cup (65g) sugar
- 1 teaspoon salt

Salad

- 4 boneless chicken breast halves
- 1 small head green leaf lettuce
- 1 small bunch romaine lettuce
- 3 tablespoons green onions, chopped
- 1 bunch fresh cilantro, cleaned and chopped
- 1 11 ounce (310g) can mandarin oranges, drained,
      or 2 carrots, peeled and grated
- ½ cup (20g) cooked crispy *rice noodles

Sesame seeds

- Cook chicken breasts using recipe for Baked Chicken for Entrée Salads (see index for recipe) or use precooked chicken breasts purchased from the supermarket.

- Slice cooked chicken breasts thinly across the diagonal.

- Combine all dressing ingredients in a small jar with lid. Tighten lid and shake well to blend.

- Drizzle chicken slices with 4 tablespoons of salad dressing.

- May be made to this point and ingredients refrigerated separately several hours ahead.

- Tear lettuces into bite size pieces or shred.

- When ready to serve, toss all salad ingredients, except rice noodles and sesame seeds, with dressing in large salad bowl. Sprinkle lightly with rice noodles and sesame seeds over individual servings.

Variation:

Add ½ to 1 teaspoon powdered ginger to the salad dressing.

*Rice noodles that are pre-cooked and crispy can be found in the oriental section of most large supermarkets. China Boy is a brand that is widely available. Do not substitute chow mein noodles as they get soggy in the dressing.

LOBSTER AND WILD RICE SALAD

Serves 6
Prep/Cook Time: 20 minutes,
plus 1 hour for rice

Until the late 19th century, lobster was so plentiful that it was used for fish bait. Those days are certainly gone. The most popular variety of lobster in the United States, is Maine lobster, which has a close cousin that lives in the Mediterranean and South African waters.

4   cups (580g) cooked wild rice
2   cups (200g) cooked lobster meat, or 2 to 3 lobster tails
         depending on the size of the lobster
½   cup (70g) coarsely cubed red onion
2   medium-sized unblemished ripe but firm avocados
1   tablespoon lemon juice
1   tablespoon Dijon mustard
2½ tablespoons red wine vinegar
½   cup (125ml) vegetable oil
1   clove garlic, crushed
Salt and pepper to taste
2   tablespoons finely chopped fresh parsley
Lettuce leaves
Lemon slices for garnish
Parsley for garnish

- Put rice in mixing bowl and let cool completely. Add lobster and onion, toss together.

- Peel and pit avocados and cut into ½ inch (1.3cm) cubes. Sprinkle with lemon juice to prevent discoloration.

- Combine mustard and vinegar in small bowl and beat lightly with wire whisk.

- Gradually add oil, beating briskly with a whisk. Add garlic, salt, pepper, and parsley.

- Pour dressing over the rice, lobster, and onion, then toss.

- Gently toss in avocado. Arrange lettuce leaves on serving platter. Pile salad in center and garnish with lemon slices and parsley sprigs. Serve at room temperature.

Variation:

Substitute 2 cups (200g) canned or frozen lobster meat or 2 cups (200g) of shrimp for the lobster.

U S A

SMOKED MACKEREL PASTA SALAD

Serves 6
Prep/Cook Time: 45 minutes

½   pound (225g) farfelle or bowtie pasta
6   tablespoons plain yogurt
2   tablespoons mayonnaise
3½   teaspoons lemon juice
2   Granny Smith apples
1   avocado
Black pepper to taste
3   spring onions, finely chopped
1½   teaspoons whole dill seeds
3   fillets smoked mackerel
2   tablespoons chopped fresh dill
Shredded Chinese cabbage and dill for garnish

A delicious salad that no one expects to like until they try it. The avocado can be replaced with chopped mango, melon, or cut seedless grapes depending on what is fresh.

• Cook pasta in a large pot of boiling salted water until al dente.

• Mix yogurt, mayonnaise, and 2½ teaspoons of lemon juice in a large bowl.

• Core and chop apples and peel, pit, and dice avocado.

• Add apples, avocado, spring onions, dill seeds and black pepper. Toss with pasta.

• Remove skin from mackerel, remove bones and break into bite sized pieces. Very gently fold into salad so that mackerel does not break apart too much.

• Sprinkle with chopped dill and remaining lemon juice. Place Chinese cabbage on a serving platter. Mound salad in center. Garnish with dill sprigs.

Field Greens with Pears, Gorgonzola, and Ravioli

Dressing

2	teaspoons dried rosemary, finely crushed
2	teaspoon ground cinnamon
½	teaspoon salt
6	tablespoons balsamic vinegar
⅔	cup (170ml) walnut or olive oil

Salad

1	9 ounce (250g) package Gorgonzola cheese and walnut ravioli, or cheese ravioli
6	cups (340g) mixed field greens (arugula, radicchio, endive, leaf lettuce)
2	large fresh ripe but firm Bosc pears, cored and cut into thin slices
½	cup (70g) coarsely chopped walnuts, toasted
½	cup (40g) crumbled *Gorgonzola cheese

- Combine all dressing ingredients in a small jar. Cover tightly and shake until blended.

- Cook ravioli according to package directions. Rinse with cold water and drain.

- Tear any large greens into bite size pieces.

- Toss greens and ravioli with half of salad dressing in a large bowl. Arrange on 4 salad plates. Arrange pears on top of salads; sprinkle with walnuts and cheese. Drizzle with remaining dressing to taste and serve.

This is an especially nice entrée salad for a luncheon and also makes a nice side salad, omitting the ravioli.

*Gorgonzola cheese takes its name from a little village outside Milan where it was originally made. Gorgonzola has a similar flavor to Roquefort cheese of France and Stilton cheese of England. It is a perfect accompaniment for pears and crumbled over salads, as with this recipe.

Tofu Salad Dressing

Serves 10 to 12
Prep/Cook Time: 10 minutes

1   block silken tofu,
       about 19 ounces (530g) drained
½   cup (125ml) oil
¼   cup (60ml) vinegar
¼   cup (60ml) tamari or soy sauce
1   tablespoon garlic, crushed
1   tablespoon basil, dried or chopped
1   teaspoon onion, finely chopped

• Crumble or mash tofu and combine with remaining ingredients. Mix well.

Serve over a mixed salad of greens, carrots and tomatoes, sprinkled with sunflower seeds.

U S A

WALNUT OIL AND HERB SALAD DRESSING

4   tablespoons red wine vinegar
2   teaspoons whole grain mustard
2   small shallots, finely minced
2   teaspoons finely chopped fresh parsley
1   teaspoon *herbes de Provence
1   garlic clove, minced
½   teaspoon salt
⅛   teaspoon pepper
½   cup (125ml) walnut oil

• In a medium bowl, mix together all ingredients except oil. Using a hand whisk, pour mixture in a slow stream into oil, whisking until all ingredients are emulsified. Serve over mixed greens or use as a marinade for chicken or beef.

*Herbes de Provence is an assortment of dried herbs commonly used in Southern France. The blend can be found packed in tiny clay crocks in the spice section of large supermarkets. It normally contains basil, fennel seed, lavender, marjoram, rosemary, sage, summer savory, and thyme. Italian seasoning herbs may be substituted if herbes de Provence are not available.

Cook's Tip:

Walnut oil has a delightful flavor but can go rancid quickly and should be refrigerated.

Meat & Game

Beef Stir Fry
with Broccoli

Serves 4
Prep/Cook Time: 20 minutes,
plus 1 hour to marinate

Beef Stir Fry with Broccoli makes a quick one-pan meal that can be adapted depending on what is available. Sliced red or green peppers, thinly sliced cabbage, bean sprouts or pea pods can be added, reducing the amount of broccoli accordingly.

¾   pound (340g) lean beef round or flank steak
4   tablespoons soy sauce
1 ½ teaspoons cornstarch
3   teaspoons dry sherry
3   teaspoons sugar
1   tablespoon dark sesame oil
2   tablespoons water
1   teaspoon minced fresh ginger, optional
1   clove garlic, minced, optional
1   bunch broccoli
4   tablespoons oil
1   onion, peeled, halved and sliced
Oyster sauce and/or soy sauce to taste

• Cut steak across grain to make thin, ⅛ inch (.3cm) thick slices. In a large bowl, mix soy sauce, cornstarch, sherry, sugar, sesame oil, water, ginger, and garlic. Add beef and marinate in refrigerator at least 1 hour.

• Cut broccoli into 1½ inch (4cm) florets. Cut florets into ¼ inch (.6cm) thick slices.

• Heat 2½ tablespoons oil in a large skillet or wok until very hot. Add onion and stir fry 3 minutes. Add broccoli and stir fry 2 to 3 minutes until broccoli is bright green. Remove from skillet and set aside.

• Remove meat from marinade and reserve marinade. Add 1½ tablespoons oil to skillet and heat. When hot, add beef and stir fry 2 to 3 minutes until almost cooked through. Add marinade and return broccoli and onion to skillet. Cook 1 to 2 minutes more until sauce bubbles.

• Adjust flavor to taste by adding oyster sauce and/or additional soy sauce to taste. Serve immediately over white rice.

BISTEK
Steak Philippine Style

Serves 6
Prep/Cook Time: 20 minutes,
plus 3 hours to marinate

2   *pounds (900g) beef sirloin steak*
2   *tablespoons lemon juice*
3   *tablespoons soy sauce*
½   *teaspoon freshly ground pepper*
Salt to taste
1   *onion, thinly sliced into rings*
3   *tablespoons oil*
½   *cup (125ml) water*

- Slice steak across grain in ½ inch (1.3cm) thick strips. Place lemon juice, soy sauce, pepper, and salt in a non-reactive or glass bowl. Add beef slices and turn to coat beef. Marinate for 3 hours.

- In a heavy skillet or wok, cook onion rings in oil over medium-high heat until transparent. Transfer onions to a serving dish and leave oil in the skillet.

- Drain marinade from steak and reserve. Heat the skillet with oil from the onions and cook the steak over high heat, stirring often until cooked. Transfer meat to serving dish with onions.

- Add reserved marinade and water to the skillet. Simmer for 10 minutes and pour over steak and onion rings. Serve warm.

The Philippines, a nation of 7100 islands, is named after Phillip II of Spain and was under Spanish Colonial rule from 1565 until 1898 when it was ceded to the United States for a period. The cuisine, while greatly influenced by the Spanish, maintains much of its Chinese and Malaysian origins. Bistek however is a dish with American influence. The title is actually a corruption of "beef steak."

BUL-KOGI
Korean Barbecued Beef

Serves 6
Prep/Cook Time: 15 minutes,
plus 45 minutes to marinate

2   pounds (900g) sirloin, rib or flank steak
1   tablespoon sesame seeds, lightly toasted
3   green onions, finely chopped
3   cloves garlic, finely minced
¼   cup (60ml) soy sauce
2   tablespoons dark sesame oil
¼   cup sugar
2   tablespoons sherry
½   medium-sized hard Asian or other pear, chopped finely in food processor
Pepper to taste

- Slice meat <u>very thinly</u> diagonally across the grain from top to bottom and score each piece lightly with an "X".

- Combine all ingredients in a large bowl. Marinate at least 45 minutes.

- Drain meat and cook over charcoal, under an oven broiler, or in a hot skillet for 30 seconds per side, or until cooked through.

In a Korean home, a portable Bul-Kogi grill would be placed in the center of the table and each diner cooks the meat using chopsticks to their liking. Sometimes it is served by making little packages of meat and rice wrapped up in a medium sized lettuce leaf and is then eaten with the hands.

Cook's Tip:

If the meat has not been previously frozen, the uncooked meat can be frozen in its marinade and kept for a quick meal at a later date.

BUN XAO THIT BO

Beef with Fine Rice Noodles

Serves 4
Prep/Cook Time: 45 minutes

1   clove garlic, crushed
1   medium onion, finely sliced
2   inches (5cm) lemon grass root, thinly sliced
1   teaspoon salt
1   teaspoon black pepper
2   tablespoons *nuoc nam (fish sauce)
¼   teaspoon sugar
1   pound (450g) beef fillet or sirloin steak, very thinly sliced
6   ounces (170g) rice noodles
1   cup (70g) bean sprouts
1   cup (115g) crisp salad greens, shredded
4-6 tablespoons shredded cucumber
1   small bunch mint, stems removed and chopped
2   tablespoons oil
**Nuoc Cham Dipping Sauce (see index for recipe)
4   tablespoons chopped peanuts

- In a medium bowl, combine garlic, onion, lemon grass root, salt, pepper, fish sauce, and sugar. Add beef and marinate for 30 minutes.

- Blanch rice noodles in boiling water for 5 minutes, drain, and set aside.

- Divide bean sprouts, salad greens, cucumber, and mint and put in four individual deep bowls. Top with rice noodles.

- Heat oil in skillet over high heat and fry beef mixture until just cooked. Divide into four portions and add to bowls.

- Dribble over with Nuoc Cham Dipping Sauce and chopped nuts and serve.

Vietnamese cooks use an abundance of fresh coriander, mint and scallions as well as fish sauce, rice or rice noodles and chiles. The food is usually cooked with water and little oil, so it is quite low in fat.

*Nuoc nam is Vietnamese fish sauce and can be purchased in most large supermarkets. **Nuoc cham is a Vietnamese condiment that is based on nuoc nam (fish sauce) combined with various seasonings (see index for recipe).

Gyuniku Tataki-zukuri

Japanese Beef Tartare

Serves 6
Prep/Cook Time: 20 minutes,
plus 2 hours to marinate

1   pound (450g) fresh lean sirloin,
        tenderloin or fillet of beef
Salt and pepper to taste
2   tablespoons oil
3   tablespoons *ponzu soy sauce

- Rub salt and pepper on beef. Heat oil over high heat in a medium skillet. Sear all sides of beef. This should take about 10 minutes. Traditionally the steak is eaten medium rare.

- Put meat in a plastic, zippered bag and add ponzu sauce. Refrigerate at least 2 hours. Take meat out of bag and slice very thin. Serve cold or at room temperature with fresh ponzu sauce.

Serve Japanese Beef Tartare with Sesame Spinach (see index for recipe) and rice.

*Ponzu is a Japanese sauce made with soy sauce, rice wine vinegar, sake, and seaweed. It is available at Japanese grocery stores. An equal mixture of soy sauce, lemon juice and rice wine vinegar may be substituted for ponzu if it is not available.

BOBOTIE
Curried Beef Casserole

Serves 8
Prep/Cook Time:
1 hour 30 minutes

2	medium onions, finely chopped
4	tablespoons (60g) butter
2	tablespoons curry powder
2	teaspoons ground turmeric
1	clove garlic, crushed
½	tablespoon fresh grated ginger
1	green chile, chopped
2	tablespoons brown sugar
3-4	slices white bread
1	cup (250ml) milk
2	pounds (900g) lean ground beef or lamb
4	teaspoons apricot jam
2	teaspoons lemon juice
Salt to taste	
6	bay leaves
3	eggs

- Preheat oven to 350°.

- Melt butter in a medium skillet over medium heat. Sauté onions until transparent. Add curry, turmeric, garlic, ginger, chile, and brown sugar. Cook until mixture becomes dry and set aside.

- In a large bowl, soak bread in ½ cup (125ml) milk. Combine meat, soaked bread, sautéed onions, apricot jam, and lemon juice. Season with salt.

- Spoon meat mixture into greased 1 to 2 inch (2.5-5cm) deep casserole or baking pan. Smooth the surface of the meat mixture and press in the bay leaves.

- Beat remaining milk and eggs, and pour over the meat. Bake about 45 to 60 minutes until golden and cooked through. Serve warm.

Bobotie is the national dish of South Africa. It originated from the Malaysian sector of the population, which came to South Africa to work on sugar plantations. Bobotie is a delicious blend of the spicy Dutch East Indian Empire tastes from Malaysia and Indonesia and local ingredients such as apricots. Serve Bobotie with Yellow Rice and Raisins (see index for recipe), chutney and a green salad or vegetable.

KHORESH-E BADEMJAN
Eggplant and Beef Casserole

Serves 6
Prep/Cook Time: 2 hours,
plus 1 hour to soak eggplant

Khoresh-e Bademjan freezes well and the eggplant may be prepared up to two days ahead and refrigerated until ready for use. Serve with Herbed Rice (see index for recipe) for an elegant dinner.

2   medium eggplants, or 6 Italian eggplants
¾   cup (185ml) oil
2   onions, halved and sliced
1½   pounds (675g) London Broil or other lean beef, cut in 1 inch (2.5cm) cubes
1   tablespoon tomato paste
2   8 ounce (225g) cans tomato sauce
1   teaspoon salt
¼   teaspoon fresh ground black pepper

• Peel eggplants and cut into slices about ¼ inch (.6cm) thick. If using the smaller Italian eggplant, cut in slices lengthwise, not rounds. Soak in water for 1 hour. The soaking takes out the bitterness. The water will turn yellow.

• Remove eggplant from water, rinse, and dry.

• Heat ¼ cup (60ml) oil in a large skillet over medium-high heat. When hot, sauté eggplant until deep golden brown. Do not undercook. Transfer eggplant slices to paper towels as they cook to absorb oil. Add more oil, up to ½ cup (125ml) total as needed.

• Sauté onions in remaining oil until golden. Stir in beef. Cover and cook over medium-low heat for 30 minutes, or until liquid produced by meat is reduced to half. Stir occasionally while cooking.

• Add tomato paste, tomato sauce, and salt. Cover and simmer 30 minutes. Add half of eggplant slices. Cover and simmer for another 30 minutes.

• Preheat oven to 350°. Keeping prettier slices aside, place remaining eggplant slices at the bottom of an ovenproof dish. Pour stew over them and arrange pretty eggplant slices on top. Bake for 20 minutes.

Variation:

For a vegetarian entrée, substitute 2 cups (340g) cooked garbanzo beans for the beef. Also, 2-3 dried limes or 1-2 fresh limes cut into quarters may be added to either version with the tomato sauce.

Pastel de Papas

Argentinian Beef and Potato Pie

Serves 6
Prep/Cook Time: 45 minutes

2	tablespoons olive oil
1	medium carrot, shredded
1	green onion, chopped
½	medium white onion, chopped
½	red bell pepper, chopped
6	pitted black olives, chopped
1	teaspoon minced garlic
2	pounds (900g) ground beef
2	tablespoons tomato sauce
1	15½ ounce (440g) can of corn
1	teaspoon oregano
1	teaspoon basil
1	teaspoon parsley
3	eggs, hard-boiled and sliced
2	cups (500g) cooked mashed white potatoes
1	tablespoon grated Parmesan cheese

Salt and pepper to taste

- Preheat oven to 350°. In a large skillet, heat oil over medium-high heat. Sauté carrot, green onion, white onion, red pepper, olives, and garlic until just tender, about 5 minutes. Remove from skillet.

- Brown beef in the same skillet. Drain fat from beef and add sautéed vegetables, tomato sauce, corn, and remaining herbs. Mix well.

- Gently fold in the boiled egg slices and place mixture in an ovenproof baking dish.

- Combine grated cheese with mashed potatoes. Spread on top of meat mixture.

- Bake covered 15 minutes. Remove cover and bake for 10 minutes until potatoes are lightly browned.

Argentina's official language is Spanish, but like most of the Americas, its population is made of people from many national backgrounds and the cuisine reflects that diversity.

Pastel de Papas is very similar to Shepherd's Pie, a casserole of ground lamb and mashed potatoes that is popular in England, and shows the English influence in Argentina. Some recipes for empanadas in Argentina use a filling similar to the meat from this Pastel with corn, olives and hard-boiled eggs.

PICADILLO

Cuban Beef with Peppers and Raisins Wrapped in Warm Tortillas

Serves 6
Prep/Cook Time: 30 minutes

Picado *means "chopped finely" in Spanish. Picadillo is a name for a whole range of dishes with ground beef mixed with tomatoes, onions, olives, peppers, nuts, raisins, fruits or whatever happens to be on hand. It is served alone or as a type of filling or hash. This Cuban version wrapped in warm tortillas is an easy and different family meal served with yellow rice and a green vegetable or salad.*

2½ pounds (1.125kg) lean ground beef
1 tablespoon oil
2 medium onions, chopped
3 cloves garlic, finely chopped
1½ large green peppers, chopped
1 tablespoon oregano
¾ cup (150g) pitted green or black olives, sliced
1 cup (160g) raisins
1 23 ounce (645g) can tomato sauce
2½ tablespoons ground cumin
Corn tortillas

- In a large skillet, sauté beef over medium-high heat until just browned. Drain fat.

- Add oil, onions, garlic, and green peppers, and sauté for 5 minutes.

- Add all remaining ingredients except tortillas and simmer for 15 minutes or until peppers are softened. Serve with warm corn tortillas.

Tourtière

Quebec Christmas Pie

Serves 8
Prep/Cook Time:
2 hours 15 minutes,
plus 2 hours to chill dough

Meat Filling

1-1½   pounds (450-675g) ground pork
1-1½   pounds (450-675g) ground veal
1   pound (450g) ground beef
3   small onions, finely chopped
2   cloves garlic, chopped
1½   cups (375ml) boiling water
3   small yellow potatoes, peeled and grated
Salt and pepper to taste
¼   teaspoon cinnamon
½   teaspoon ground cloves
1   teaspoon allspice

Shortcrust Pastry

1   egg, beaten
1   tablespoon vinegar
Ice water
5   cups (700g) flour
⅛   teaspoon salt
1   pound (450g) shortening
1   egg yolk
½   cup (125ml) milk

- In a large skillet over medium heat sauté meats, onion, and garlic until meat is no longer pink. Add boiling water, potatoes, and seasonings. Cover and simmer 1 hour, stirring often. Adjust seasonings. Drain fat from meat and let meat cool.

- Preheat oven 375°.

- In a glass measuring cup add vinegar to beaten egg. Add enough ice water to make 1 cup (250ml) of liquid.

- In a large bowl, mix flour and salt. Cut shortening into flour until it crumbles. Make a well and pour in the liquid mixture. Mix gently with a fork. Gather the dough into a ball, and refrigerate 2 hours.

- Divide the chilled dough into 4 equal parts. Roll out one part of dough into a circle. Place ¼ of the meat mixture in middle of dough. Fold dough over the meat filling to make a half circle shape and seal well. Prick the upper crust with a fork to vent steam. Repeat for 3 more pies.

- Mix the egg yolk and milk in a small bowl and brush the mixture on the tops of the meat pies. Bake on a cookie sheet for 45 minutes or until golden.

Canada

Tourtière is a wonderful traditional Quebec Christmas meat pie. This recipe may be halved for a smaller meal.

Short Cut Tip:

Four pre-packaged refrigerated pie crusts may be substituted for the pastry. Line each of two 9 inch (23cm) pie plates with a crust. Divide the meat filling between the two pies and top each filling with another crust. Cut holes for steam. Brush tops with eggs and bake as indicated above.

DOLMADES
Stuffed Bell Peppers

Serves 6
Prep/Cook Time:
1 hour 20 minutes

Vegetables stuffed with meat are very popular throughout the Middle East and each country has its own variation. They are called domathes, *in Greece,* dolmeh *in Persia and* mihshi *in the Arab lands.*

Eggplant, tomatoes and zucchini are other popular Middle Eastern stuffed vegetables and are excellent substituted for the green peppers in this recipe.

Dolmades are even better made a day ahead and reheated.

1	pound (450g) lean ground beef or chicken
1	large onion, finely chopped
1	cup (200g) uncooked rice
1	cup (240g) canned chopped tomatoes, with juice
1	cup (30g) chopped fresh parsley
½	cup (15g) fresh dill or 1 tablespoon dried dill
½	cup (15g) fresh mint or 1 tablespoon dried mint
2	teaspoons salt
¼	teaspoon black pepper
6	large red, green or yellow bell peppers (mixture)
1	cup (250ml) water
1	tablespoon (15g) butter, melted

• Combine by hand meat, onion, rice, tomatoes with juice, parsley, dill, mint, 1 teaspoon salt, and pepper.

• Cut tops from peppers and reserve. Remove seeds, wash, and drain.

• Fill each pepper with meat mixture and place the tops on the peppers.

• Place stuffed peppers in a heavy pot in an upright position close together. Pour water around peppers and add butter and remaining teaspoon salt to the water. Cover pot and simmer 45 minutes to 1 hour or until peppers are tender.

TOMATES Y CEBOLLAS RELLENOS

Tomatoes and Onions Stuffed with Beef

Serves 6
Prep/Cook Time:
1 hour 30 minutes

3   medium tomatoes
3   medium onions
3   medium red potatoes, diced
1   pound (450g) lean ground beef or veal
2   cloves garlic, minced
2   tablespoons chopped parsley
2   tablespoons fresh chopped basil
2   slices bread, soaked in water
1   egg, beaten
½   cup (70g) flour
3   tablespoons olive oil
⅛   teaspoon pepper
1   teaspoon salt
3-4 tablespoons tomato juice or water as needed

- Preheat oven to 375°.

- Cut tomatoes and onions in half. Create a bowl in each half by removing the inner portions of the tomatoes and onions and set these outer portions aside.

- Chop the removed inner parts of the tomato and onions into small pieces and place in an ovenproof casserole. Stir in diced potatoes.

- Mix ground meat, garlic, parsley, basil, and soaked bread.

- Fill tomatoes and onions with meat mixture. Dip in beaten egg and then roll in flour.

- Sauté stuffed tomatoes and onions in 2 tablespoons olive oil until each side is golden brown.

- Place stuffed tomatoes and onions on top of chopped vegetables. Add a few tablespoons of water or tomato juice as needed, and 1 teaspoon olive oil.

- Bake uncovered for 45 minutes to 1 hour, adding water as needed to keep the chopped vegetables moist.

Variations:

Chopped turkey may be substituted for the beef, and celery hearts may be substituted for halved tomatoes and onions.

This is a recipe from the Sephardic Jewish community of Spain. The tomatoes and onions are easy to hollow out using a small spoon. The tomatoes should not be too ripe as they will be more difficult to work with.

BEEF BRISKET WITH CHILI-BEER SAUCE

Serves 4 to 6
Prep/Cook Time: 3 hours

This recipe easily doubles or triples to feed a large crowd. It tastes best when made the day before and reheated. Cooking beef stew and brisket with beer is a traditional Belgian method of cooking. The addition of chili sauce is an innovation from the United States.

6   ounces (180ml) beer
2   pounds (900g) boneless beef brisket
1   teaspoon cumin powder
1   teaspoon celery powder
1   teaspoon garlic powder
1   teaspoon onion powder
Salt and pepper to taste
1   12 ounce (340g) jar chili sauce
1   large onion, peeled and quartered
10 red potatoes, peeled
6   large carrots, peeled and cut in 1 inch (2.5cm) pieces

• Preheat oven to 325°.

• Pour beer in the bottom of a large ovenproof Dutch oven.

• Rinse and dry brisket and place over beer.

• Sprinkle brisket evenly with seasonings. Pour chili sauce on top, spreading to cover meat. Place vegetables around and on top of brisket.

• Cover tightly and cook in preheated oven for 2 hours, basting vegetables with sauce once or twice during cooking.

• Remove vegetables and meat from Dutch oven, and slice meat in ½ inch (1.3cm) thick slices across the grain.

• Return meat to Dutch oven, place vegetables on top and cover. Bake until meat is tender, about 1 hour. Serve with vegetables.

BOEUF MODE

French Pot Roast with White Wine

Serves 6
Prep/Cook Time:
3 hours 15 minutes

Serve with a Chinon or Beaujolais wine.

2	tablespoons olive oil
1	2 pound (900g) beef rump roast
2	whole cloves
1	large onion
1	tablespoon tomato paste
2	cups (500ml) dry white wine
2	cloves garlic, minced
½	teaspoon dried thyme
3	bay leaves, crumbled

Salt and pepper to taste

1½ pounds (675g) carrots, peeled and sliced into ½ inch (1.3cm) rounds

- Heat oil in a heavy ironclad pot or Dutch oven over medium-high heat. When oil is hot, brown beef on all sides.

- Push cloves into onion and add to pot with beef. Stir in tomato paste, wine, garlic, thyme, bay leaves, salt, and pepper. Bring to a boil. Reduce heat to low and simmer covered for 1½ hours. Add carrots. Cover and cook for 1½ hours more, or until the meat is very tender.

- Remove meat to an oval platter, surround with carrots and cover with gravy remaining in pot. Serve with small boiled potatoes, rice, or thick egg noodles.

CARNE ESTOFADA

Spanish Beef Stew

Serves 6
Prep/Cook Time: 2 hours

2   pounds (900g) lean beef, cut into
       small chunks
Salt and pepper to taste
1   clove garlic, thinly sliced
2   medium onions, thinly sliced
3   tablespoons olive oil
1   cup (250ml) red wine
1   14½ ounce (411g) can beef stock
2   vine ripe tomatoes, peeled and chopped
1   tablespoon flour
3   tablespoons warm water
1   10 ounce (280g) package frozen artichoke hearts,
       or one 14 ounce (395g) can artichoke hearts
¼   pound (115g) salt pork
2   medium white potatoes, cubed
2   carrots, sliced

- Sprinkle beef with salt and pepper to taste.

- Sauté garlic and onions in olive oil in a large pot until light brown. Add beef and brown on medium-high heat. Add red wine, beef stock, and tomatoes.

- In a separate small bowl, add warm water to the flour and make a smooth paste. Stir paste into beef and stock until smooth. Simmer covered for 1 hour.

- While the beef is cooking, cut artichoke hearts into strips, and cut the salt pork into very small pieces.

- When the beef has cooked 1 hour, add all vegetables and salt pork. Simmer for an additional 30 minutes or until potatoes and carrots are cooked. Adjust salt and pepper to taste and serve.

GULYÁS

Hungarian Gulash

Serves 8
Prep/Cook Time: 3 hours

2   medium onions, coarsely chopped
¼   cup (60ml) oil or bacon drippings
2½   pounds (1.125kg) chuck or round beef, in ¾ inch (2cm) cubes
2   large cloves garlic, finely chopped
¼   teaspoon caraway seeds
1½   teaspoons salt or to taste
Black pepper to taste
2   tablespoons sweet Hungarian paprika
1   12 ounce (350ml) bottle beer
4   cups (1 liter) water
⅓   cup (80g) tomato paste
1   medium vine ripe tomato, in 1 inch (2.5cm) cubes
2   green bell peppers, cleaned and sliced in rings
3-4 medium yellow potatoes, peeled and in ¾ inch (2cm) cubes
¼   teaspoon bottled hot pepper sauce or to taste
6   tablespoons sour cream, optional
Additional paprika to dust over sour cream, optional

- In a large pot or Dutch oven with a lid, sauté onions in oil or bacon drippings until translucent, but not brown. Add beef, stir and cook with onions for 10 minutes. Add garlic, caraway seeds, salt, and black pepper. Remove from heat and add paprika, beer, and water. Cover and simmer over low heat for 2 hours. May be made to this point and refrigerated up to 1 day ahead.

- Skim excess fat from surface. Add tomato paste, tomato, bell peppers, potatoes and pepper sauce. Adjust salt and pepper, and simmer for 30 minutes. Add water if too thick, or remove cover and simmer until excess liquid evaporates if too thin. Mash a few of the potato cubes to thicken the stew.

- Serve warm in individual bowls topped with a tablespoon of sour cream and a light dusting of paprika on the sour cream, if desired.

This marvelously hot, spicy meat stew originated with the Magyar tribes that roamed Central Europe long before Hungary was a state. The Magyar tribes first lived between the Volga River and the Ural Mountains in what is now Russia. They moved southwest and in the year 800 conquered and settled what is now Hungary. Today, Magyars make up 95% of Hungary's population.

Pork is the most popular meat in Hungary. Authentic gulyás would be made with pork and pork fat.

RINDERROULADEN
Beef Roulades with Bacon and Peaches

Serves 4
Prep/Cook Time: 2 hours

Peaches and sour cream make an enchanting flavor adaptation of the traditional German rouladen, which is prepared with pickles rather than peaches. Beef rolls are referred to in France as roulade and in Italy as braciola.

6   thin slices roulade beef, 3x4 inches (8x10cm),
        by ⅓ inch (1cm) thick or
        6 thin slices pounded round or flank steak
Salt and pepper to taste
2   tablespoons prepared mustard
9   slices lean bacon
1   large onion, finely chopped
2   tomatoes, thinly sliced
1   16 ounce (450g) can peaches, drained and sliced thin
Toothpicks
½   cup, plus two tablespoons (80g) flour
1   cup (250ml) beef stock
¼   cup (60ml) sour cream

• Rinse and dry beef. Sprinkle lightly with salt and pepper.

• Spread beef strips with mustard and place 1½ slices of bacon on each. Spread onions, tomato slices, and peaches equally on the beef strips.

• Roll and secure ends with toothpicks. Dredge in ½ cup (70g) flour, discarding any excess flour.

• Heat oil in large heavy skillet and brown rouladen. Add stock and simmer covered 1 hour and 15 minutes. Check occasionally, and add water if sauce evaporates. Recipe can be made ahead to this point.

• Mix 2 tablespoons flour with enough water to make a smooth paste with no lumps, and slowly stir into rouladen sauce. Simmer, stirring constantly, until mixture thickens. Remove from heat and add sour cream. Serve warm.

GSCHAETZLETS ZÜRCHER ART
Veal with Mushrooms in Wine and Cream Sauce

Serves 6
Prep/Cook Time: 30 minutes

Veal

1   pound (450g) mushrooms, quartered
4   tablespoons (60g) butter
Juice of 1 lemon
2   pounds (900g) veal cutlets, cut into thin strips
1   onion finely chopped

Sauce

1   cup (250ml) white wine
1   cup (235ml) cream
1   teaspoon paprika
Salt and pepper to taste

- In a 2 quart saucepan, place mushrooms, 2 tablespoons (30g) butter, and lemon juice. Cover and cook slowly until soft. Remove mushrooms with a slotted spoon and keep warm, reserving the broth in the pan.

- Melt 2 tablespoons (30g) butter on medium-high heat in a heavy skillet. Add onion and meat and brown until veal is cooked through. Remove meat from skillet and keep warm.

- Add wine to onions in skillet and heat on medium for 1 minute. Add mushroom broth and stir for 1 minute. Add cream, paprika, salt, and pepper. Cook slowly for 1 to 2 minutes, stirring frequently. Remove from heat. Add meat and mushrooms and serve immediately.

Variation:

This dish is also delicious when an equal amount of pork tenderloin is substituted for the veal.

Also, substituting crème fraîche for the cream in this recipe will result in a lighter sauce, which will not curdle easily

Gschaetzlets *are thin strips of meat and in this recipe are cooked in the Zurich style. This dish is very well known all over Switzerland and Germany, and is tradiationally served with buttered noodles.*

Crème Fraîche

1   teaspoon buttermilk
1   cup (235 ml) heavy cream

Heat ingredients until just warm, about 85°. Leave uncovered overnight until thickened. Stir and refrigerate tightly covered for up to 10 days.

INVOLTINI DI VITELLO
Veal Rolls with Fresh Sage, Ham, and Parmesan

Serves 6
Prep/Cook Time: 40 minutes

12   large thinly sliced prime veal scaloppini,
        about 1½ pounds (675g)
12   slices good quality deli-sliced boiled ham
½   cup (45g) Parmesan cheese chips
12   large, fresh sage leaves, rinsed
4   tablespoons extra virgin olive oil
½   cup (125ml) very dry white wine
Fine sea salt or regular salt to taste
Toothpicks as needed

- Pound each veal scaloppini to a uniform thickness with a flat meat pounder. Trim loose portions.

- Lay each scaloppini slice flat on a cutting board one at a time. Place a ham slice on top to cover the whole scaloppini. At one short edge, place a sage leaf and one or two chips of the Parmesan, and roll the scaloppini so that each encloses all the other ingredients in a cylindrical roll (involtino). Secure the opening with one or two toothpicks.

- Heat a large skillet with olive oil over medium-high heat. Sauté the involtini quickly until golden on all sides. Add salt and pepper to taste, and add wine. Turn heat to medium-low, and let wine evaporate, about 10 to 12 minutes. Remove from heat. Let sit 5 minutes. If the wine evaporates so that there is no sauce, add a few tablespoons of hot water.

- Place involtini in a serving dish. Spoon sauce that formed in the cooking pan over the top and serve.

Serve with Sautéed Fennel and Onion or Sautéed Belgian Endive and Spiced Cheese Potatoes (see index for recipes).

VEAL AND HAM PIE

Serves 6 to 8
Prep/Cook Time: 2 hours

Pastry

1³/4 cups (250g) flour
1   teaspoon baking powder
¹/4   cup (60g) soft butter
3   tablespoons oil
Refrigerated cold water
1   egg yolk

Meat Filling

1¹/4 pounds (570g) ground veal
1¹/4 pounds (570g) lean ham, ground finely in a food processor
2   tablespoons finely chopped parsley
2   teaspoons ground ginger
2   teaspoons marjoram
¹/4   cup (60ml) chicken stock
2   teaspoons salt
¹/2   teaspoon pepper
2 hard-boiled eggs, shelled
Gherkin pickles

- Sift flour with baking powder. Blend in butter and oil. Blend in cold water a tablespoon at a time until mixture makes a ball. Split into two balls, one half the size of the other.

- Preheat oven to 400°. Roll larger ball of pastry to fit a 5x9 inch (13x23cm) loaf pan and line pan with pastry.

- Mix all filling ingredients, except hard-boiled eggs and gherkin pickles.

- Put half of the meat filling mixture into the pastry-lined pan. Place whole hard-boiled eggs in a line along the center of meat layer. Place gherkin pickles around eggs, if desired. Cover with remaining meat filling.

- Roll remaining pastry, place on top and seal.

- Mix egg yolks and 1 to 2 tablespoons cold water to form an egg wash. Cut slits into top pastry and brush with egg wash.

- Bake for 30 minutes, then reduce heat to 325° and bake 1 hour more. Cut in slices and serve cold or at room temperature.

The English and Scots are very taken with cold pies of one kind or another. Veal and Ham Pie is a good example and is a typical pub food. Confiture d'Oignon (see index for recipe), chutney or Branston Pickle, which can be purchased in the international food section of many large supermarkets are good condiments for Veal and Ham Pie.

ESTAMBOLI POLO
Sautéed Lamb with Rice and Vegetables

Serves 6
Prep/Cook Time:
1 hour 30 minutes

Estamboli comes from the word for Istanbul and probably originated from a time when the Persian Empire included Istanbul.

Rice
1½ cups (300g) long grain rice
4 cups (1 liter) water
2 teaspoons salt

Green Beans
½ pound (225g) fresh green beans, or 10 ounce package frozen
4 cups (1 liter) water
2 teaspoons salt

Lamb and Vegetables
2 medium onions, halved and sliced
2 tablespoons (30g) butter
¾ pound (340g) lamb tenderloin, cut in 1x¼ inch (2.5x0.6cm) strips
½ teaspoon salt
½ teaspoon turmeric
¼ teaspoon pepper
3 large tomatoes cut in ½ inch (1.3cm) slices
1½ tablespoons lemon juice
¼ cup (60ml) water

- Rinse rice several times in warm water to remove starch. Bring 4 cups (1 liter) water and salt to a boil in a large pot. Add rice and cook at a low boil for 5 to 10 minutes until rice is no longer crunchy, but still firm. Drain rice in a colander and set aside.
- Preheat oven to 350°.
- Wash and trim green beans. Cut into 1½ inch (4cm) lengths. In a medium pan, bring 4 cups (1 liter) water and salt to a boil. Add beans and cook for 10 minutes, until slightly softened. If using frozen beans, thaw and set aside.
- Sauté onions in a skillet with 1 tablespoon (15g) butter. Add meat and seasonings, and sauté until meat is tender, about 12 minutes. Add tomatoes and lemon juice. Simmer covered over low heat for 20 minutes. Add green beans and simmer for 10 minutes.
- Melt remaining butter. Pour in bottom of a large deep ovenproof casserole dish with a cover. Loosely spread a thin layer of rice over the bottom of the casserole.
- In a large bowl or the pot the rice was cooked in, gently mix together remaining rice with meat and vegetable mixture. Transfer to the casserole by piling loosely in the shape of a hill, higher in the center. With the handle of a spoon, poke 5 holes in the mixture, 1 in the center and 4 around the sides. Spread ¼ cup (60ml) of the water on top. Cover and bake for 30 minutes.

Variation:
Beef tenderloin may be substituted for lamb. Another method of cooking Estamboli Polo is to layer a thinly sliced potato or large outer lettuce leaves on the bottom of the casserole, instead of rice.

Iran

ETLI KURU FASULYE
Lamb and White Bean Stew

Serves 6
Prep/Cook Time: 3 hours,
plus 12 hours to soak beans

1 pound (450g) dry Great Northern beans
3 onions, chopped
2 cloves garlic, chopped
6 tablespoons (90g) butter
2 pounds (900g) lamb shanks or shoulder, in 1½ inch (4cm) chunks
3 tomatoes, diced
1 tablespoon tomato paste
4 cups (1 liter) beef stock
2 tablespoons paprika
Salt and pepper to taste
Chopped parsley for garnish, optional

This hearty lamb and white bean stew is a staple of the Turkish diet. Like chili or vegetable soup in the United States, it is often served at the end of a cold winter's day.

- In a large bowl, cover beans with water and soak overnight. Drain.

- In a large pan, add beans and enough water to cover them. Boil beans for 30 minutes. Drain and set aside.

- In a large pot, sauté onions, garlic, and butter. Add meat. Cover and cook 20 to 30 minutes over medium heat, stirring frequently or until mixture releases its moisture, reabsorbs it, and browns.

- Stir in tomatoes, tomato paste, ½ cup (125ml) beef stock, paprika, salt, and pepper to taste. Cover and simmer for 20 minutes.

- Add beans. Add beef stock to barely cover beans and simmer gently, adding hot water in small quantities, as needed, to keep beans covered, until the meat and beans are very tender, about 1½ hours.

- Serve with white rice and garnish with chopped parsley.

Variations:

Replace the paprika with hot peppers for a spicier stew. A combination of beef and lamb can be used rather than all lamb.

HÛNKÂR BEGENDI
Sultan's Delight, Lamb with Eggplant Purée

Serves 8
Prep/Cook Time: 2 hours

This celebrated dish is reputed to have been created in the early 17th century for Sultan Murad IV of Turkey. It features a simple lamb stew served together with an eggplant purée.

2	pounds (900g) lean boneless lamb in ¾ inch (2cm) cubes
6	tablespoons (90g) butter
2	onions, chopped
3	tomatoes, diced, or 1 pound (450g) canned tomatoes, drained and chopped

Salt and pepper to taste

2	cups (500ml) beef stock or water, hot
2	medium eggplants
3	tablespoons flour
3	tablespoons lemon juice
1½	cups (375ml) hot milk
½	cup (60g) kasseri cheese, grated, or Roquefort, Romano or Gruyère

- In a large heavy pot with a lid, sauté lamb in 2 tablespoons (30g) butter for 3 to 4 minutes over high heat. Add onions. Cover and cook over medium heat, stirring frequently, until the meat releases its moisture, reabsorbs it, and browns in its own juice, about 20 minutes.

- Stir in tomatoes. Turn the heat to low. Add salt and pepper to taste and ¾ cup (185ml) of the hot beef stock. Cover and simmer 1 to 1½ hours until meat is tender. As it cooks, check liquid occasionally. Add hot stock, ⅓ cup (85ml) at a time as needed, to keep meat moist and in ample sauce but not watery. Keep warm until ready to serve or reheat when ready to serve.

- Place unpeeled eggplants directly on a gas burner over a high flame or over a grill. Turn frequently to cook on all sides. When the skin is charred and black and eggplants are thoroughly soft, remove from heat. Cool and peel, carefully removing all the pieces of burnt skin. Wipe eggplant clean and place in a bowl.

- Take small pieces of eggplant by hand and squeeze out all the water. Melt remaining 4 tablespoons (60g) butter in a saucepan. Blend in flour, stirring for 2 to 3 minutes over medium heat. Stir eggplant into flour and butter mixture. Finish adding eggplant and beat with a fork over low heat until smooth. Stir in lemon juice. Gradually add hot milk, beating briskly with a wire whisk until smooth and bubbling. Add cheese, correct seasonings and pour into a serving dish.

- Transfer the lamb with onions and tomatoes to a platter and serve with the eggplant purée.

LAMB BIRYANI
Lamb Curry with Cashews

Serves 6
Prep/Cook Time: 2 hours

3   medium onions
4   cloves garlic
1   2 inch (5cm) piece ginger, peeled
7   tablespoons vegetable oil
2   pounds (900g) boneless leg of lamb, fat removed, cubed
2   tablespoons plain yogurt
2   large tomatoes, peeled and chopped
½   teaspoon cayenne pepper
1   teaspoon turmeric
1   teaspoon cumin powder
1   teaspoon coriander
1   teaspoon garam masala
½   cup (75g) roasted cashews
½   cup (15g) chopped cilantro

- Quarter 1 onion and blend with garlic and ginger in a food processor to a paste.

- Heat 4 tablespoons oil in a heavy saucepan over medium heat. Add garlic and onion paste, and cook for 5 minutes.

- Add lamb and yogurt. Cook while stirring 5 minutes.

- Add tomatoes and spices. Bring to a boil, reduce heat and simmer covered for 1 hour, 15 minutes.

- About 15 minutes before lamb is done, quarter and slice remaining 2 onions. Sauté until the onions turn light brown in remaining 3 tablespoons oil and drain.

- Serve topped with sautéed onions, cashews, and cilantro.

Biryani was a favorite of the Mogul emperors who ruled India in the 16th and 17th centuries. It is a meal in itself and may be eaten with just yogurt and relish. However, at more festive times other meat or vegetable curries often accompany it.

Serve Biryani over Fragrant Basmati Rice with Mushrooms (see index for recipe).

India

123

SPICY INDIAN LAMB KEBABS

Serves 8
Prep/Cook Time: 35 minutes,
plus 1 hour to marinate

2   pounds (900g) lean ground lamb
1   onion, minced
1   2 inch (5cm) piece ginger, finely chopped
4   cloves garlic, minced
2   tablespoons chopped cilantro
3   tablespoons plain yogurt
2   tablespoons fresh or bottled Mint Cilantro Chutney (see index for recipe)
3   tablespoons *chick pea flour
1/4 teaspoon cayenne pepper
1   tablespoon cumin powder
1   teaspoon salt
Vegetable oil for basting
1   large onion sliced and sautéed, in 2 tablespoon (30g) butter or oil
Lime wedges
Additional Mint Cilantro Chutney as a condiment

- Mix all ingredients together in a large bowl. Cover and refrigerate for an hour to allow flavors to blend.

- Make into 20 to 24 long oval shapes.

- Preheat broiler or grill. Broil or grill kebabs 20 to 25 minutes until well browned (no pink in center). Baste with a little oil occasionally and turn after 10 minutes of cooking.

- Serve hot with lime wedges and Mint Cilantro Chutney.

The kebab originated in Turkey and eventually spread to the Balkans and the Middle East, India and, later, to the world. The name is a shortened form of the Turkish sis kebab, sis meaning skewer and kebab meaning roast meat. These kebabs also make appealing hors d'oeuvres when formed into smaller portions.

*Chick pea flour can be found in international or Indian food markets. Whole wheat flour may be substituted.

LAHEM B'AJEEN
Lamb in Pastry Rolls

Serves 8
Prep/Cook Time: 1 hour,
plus 5 hours to thaw phyllo

Pastry
- 1   17 ounce (490g) package frozen phyllo pastry
- ¼   cup (45g) melted butter

Meat and Nut Filling
- 1   large onion
- 1   pound (450g) lean ground lamb
- 3   tablespoons (45g) butter
- 2   tablespoons vinegar
- 2   tablespoons lemon juice
- 2   teaspoons salt
- ¼   teaspoon pepper
- ¼   teaspoon allspice
- ½   teaspoon ground cinnamon
- ¼   teaspoon ground cloves or nutmeg
- ½   cup (75g) roasted pine nuts

- Defrost phyllo according to package directions (about 5 hours). Set aside and prepare filling.

- Finely chop onion in food processor. In a large skillet over medium heat, brown lamb. Drain fat and remove lamb from pan. Wipe fat from pan with a paper towel. Add 3 tablespoons (45g) butter to pan and melt over medium heat. Add onion and cook until tender. Return meat to pan with cooked onion and remaining ingredients. Mix well. Remove from heat. Keep refrigerated if not using immediately.

- Spray 9x13 inch (23x33cm) baking dish with cooking spray. Preheat oven to 375°.

- Remove 4 sheets of phyllo dough as one piece, then roll into a loose roll. Slice the roll into 3 equal pieces. (Keep other phyllo dough sheets wrapped until ready to roll so they will not dry out.)

- Remove a single strip of cut phyllo (there are 12 strips after cutting the rolled 4 sheets into 3 sections), lay flat and put 2 teaspoons of filling on one end. Spread the filling almost to the sides and roll the phyllo around the filling as if rolling a short cigar with open ends. Place in baking dish. Repeat until filling is used. (You may have left over phyllo, which can be frozen for other uses.)

- Brush tops of rolls with melted butter and bake 10 to 15 minutes or until lightly golden. Serve warm.

Lebanese cuisine, culture and language come from the Arabs. Lebanon, however is an ancient society of many influences. This homeland of the Phoenicians was known as the "granary of the Roman Empire" and was a trading link between East and West for thousands of years.

Serve Lahem b'Ajeen as an appetizer as well as main course. Like many Arab dishes, it is great made ahead or frozen and reheated.

TALAS KEBABI

Lamb Wrapped in Phyllo with Tomatoes and Garlic

Serves 4
Prep/Cook Time: 50 minutes,
plus 5 hours to thaw phyllo

Talas Kebabi is a traditional and elegant Turkish main dish which is easy to prepare. It can be served with Herbed Rice and Avocado, Tomato and Goat Cheese Salad with Pine Nuts or Shirazi Salad (see index for recipes).

16   sheets thin phyllo pastry
1½   pounds (675g) boneless lamb
        (sirloin part of the leg)
¾   cup (180g) butter
2   medium onions
5   shallots, optional
2   medium tomatoes, chopped
2   cloves garlic, mashed
2   cloves garlic, minced
1   cup (30g) fresh chopped parsley
1½   teaspoons thyme
Salt and pepper
1   egg yolk lightly beaten for glaze

- Thaw phyllo according to package directions, about 5 hours.
- Trim lamb and discard fat. Cut into very thin strips about ⅛ to ¼ inch (.3-.6cm) thick.
- Cut onion into halves, then slice halves very thinly.
- Heat a heavy skillet over high heat. Sir in meat, onions, and shallots with 2 tablespoons (30g) butter. Stir fry 3 to 4 minutes or a little longer until meat releases its moisture, reabsorbs it, and browns lightly in its own juice. Stir in tomatoes and mashed garlic. Cook 1 to 2 minutes. Remove from heat. Add minced garlic, parsley, thyme, salt, and pepper. Mix thoroughly.
- Preheat oven to 400°. Melt remaining butter. Remove 16 defrosted phyllo sheets. Wrap and refreeze the rest.
- Spread 2 phyllo sheets open one on top of the other on a flat surface. Brush with melted butter, keep other sheets well covered with a barely damp cloth to prevent drying. Lay another double layer directly on top of the first; brush with butter. Fold in half to form a rectangle. Brush the new top layer with butter.
- Spread ¼ of the meat filling in the middle of top layer; covering an area about 4x5 inches (10x13cm). As if wrapping a package, fold one corner of the pastry over the filling, brush with butter, and repeat with other corners. Place seam side down on a baking dish and brush top with generous amounts of butter. Repeat the process with the remaining 12 sheets and filling.
- Brush tops of pastries with egg yolk. Bake 20 minutes. If tops are browning too rapidly, cover with a sheet of foil during the last 5 to 10 minutes of baking. Serve hot.

KÖNIGSBERGER KLOPSE
Poached Meatballs in Lemon and Caper Sauce

Serves 4
Prep/Cook Time: 1 hour

Meatballs

2	stale rolls
1	cup (250ml) milk, hot
2	onions
2	whole cloves
1½	teaspoons salt
1	bay leaf
1	pound (450g) ground meat, (beef, veal or half beef and half pork)

5 anchovies, finely chopped
1 tablespoon parsley
Grated peel of 1 lemon
2 eggs
¼ teaspoon nutmeg
Pepper to taste

Sauce

2	tablespoons (30g) butter
2	tablespoons flour
1	cup (250ml) beef stock, warm
2	tablespoons capers, or more to taste
1	tablespoon lemon juice
2	egg yolks

Salt and pepper to taste

- Soak rolls in hot milk for 30 minutes in a large bowl.
- Finely chop 1 onion and set aside. Pierce the other onion with 2 cloves and place in a large pot of water with 1 teaspoon salt. Add bay leaf and bring to a boil while preparing meatballs.
- With hands, squeeze milk out of the soaked rolls, discarding milk. Mix rolls with meat, chopped onion, anchovies, parsley, lemon peel, eggs, nutmeg, remaining ½ teaspoon salt, and pepper to taste. Shape into small meatballs, about 1 inch (2.5cm) in diameter.
- Bring a large pot of water to a boil. Drop meatballs into boiling water, reduce heat, and simmer uncovered, about 20 minutes or until meatballs rise to the surface and are cooked through.
- Melt butter in a small saucepan over medium heat. Gradually stir in flour. Continue stirring, and cook for about 30 seconds. Slowly stir in stock, cook while stirring until the sauce is smooth, about 2 minutes. Add capers, salt, and pepper to taste. Reduce heat to medium-low and stir in lemon juice. Turn off the heat and immediately stir in egg yolks.
- Place meatballs with sauce in a serving dish, adjust salt and pepper, and serve immediately.

Germany

Königsberger Klopse are named for the city of Königsberg, a part of Imperial Germany until it was taken by the Russians in World War II and renamed Kalingrad as it remains today.

Until the Franco-Prussian War of 1897 created Imperial Germany, there was only the separate German speaking kingdoms of Prussia, Saxony, Wurttemberg, and Bavaria. During the Imperial period there was an exciting sharing and blending of the foods of the formerly independent kingdoms and one grand German cuisine was established which remains intact.

Serve Königsberger Klopse over boiled noodles or potatoes.

Filet à la Chantilly

Pork Tenderloin with Brandy Cream Sauce

Serves 4
Prep/Cook Time: 1 hour

1½ pounds (675g) pork tenderloin
½ teaspoon paprika
Salt and pepper to taste
12 slices bacon
1½ cups (350ml) whipping cream
1-2 tablespoons ketchup
1 tablespoon brandy

- Preheat oven 425°.

- Cut tenderloin in 12 equal slices.

- Mix paprika, salt and pepper, and dip both sides of tenderloin pieces into mixture.

- Wrap 1 slice of bacon around each piece of tenderloin.

- Place in greased baking dish and bake for 30 to 40 minutes or until bacon is cooked.

- Whip cream. Fold in ketchup, brandy, and more pepper to taste.

- Top each tenderloin slice with one teaspoon of the mixture and serve immediately with remaining cream sauce offered on the side.

The name Chantilly is given to hot or cold sauces to which whipped cream is added. Although the name is derived from the château of Chantilly, whose cuisine enjoyed a fine reputation in mid-17th century France, these preparations named after it were not created there, but in fact originated in the last century. This recipe came from a family in the French speaking area of Switzerland.

Don't be turned off by the ketchup in this recipe. It adds a nice color to the sauce without masking the flavors of the brandy and cream.

GINGER PORK WITH MELON

Serves 4
Prep/Cook Time: 20 minutes

1   tablespoon oil
1   pound (450g) pork tenderloin,
        in ½ inch (1.3cm) cubes
½   medium yellow onion, thinly sliced
1   clove garlic, minced
1   tablespoon grated fresh ginger
2   tablespoons soy sauce
¼   cup (60ml) dry sherry
2   tablespoons rice wine vinegar
1   tablespoon cornstarch
3   cups (450g) cubed cantaloupe or honeydew melon

• Heat oil in a wok or heavy skillet over medium-high heat. Brown pork cubes, stirring, until lightly browned. Stir in onion, garlic, and ginger. Cook and stir for another 2 to 3 minutes.

• In a small bowl, mix together soy sauce, sherry, vinegar, and cornstarch. Add mixture to skillet and cook 2 to 3 minutes, stirring, until sauce thickens. Stir in the melon and heat through before serving. Serve with rice and stir-fried vegetables.

Melon is believed to have been popular in China as far back as 2300 BC and ginger was one of the spices that the Chinese traded to the Romans for gold and silver.

Hong Kong

SAHNESCHNITZEL

Pork Chops Baked in a Fresh Herb Cream Sauce

Serves 8 to 10
Prep/Cook Time:
1 hour 20 minutes,
plus 24 hours to marinate

Sahneschnitzel has a flavor and texture similar to beef stroganoff, but is made with pork. Serve with boiled or oven roasted potatoes, or buttered egg noodles.

Salt and pepper to taste
16-24 small thin boneless pork chops
1-2   tablespoons butter (15-30g) or oil
6   cups (1.5 liters) onion soup, or 2 packages dry onion soup mix
        prepared to make 6 cups (1.5 liters) soup
2   cups (475ml) whipping cream
1¼   cups (300ml) *crème fraîche
1   teaspoon fresh chopped parsley
1   teaspoon fresh chopped dill
1   teaspoon fresh chopped chives
Additional chopped fresh herbs for garnish

- Salt and pepper pork chops. In a heavy skillet, sear pork chops quickly in butter or oil, a few seconds per side. Place chops in a large deep ovenproof dish.

- Mix soup with whipping cream, crème fraîche, and herbs. Pour mixture over chops. Pork chops should be totally covered, if not, add additional water and whipping cream to cover.

- Tightly cover dish with plastic wrap and refrigerate for 24 hours to marinate.

- Preheat oven to 400°.

- Remove plastic wrap and bake pork chops for 1 hour uncovered.

- Serve warm from oven, garnished with additional chopped herbs.

WITLOF MET HAM EN KAAS

Belgian Endive with Ham and Cheese Sauce

Serves 4
Prep/Cook Time: 40 minutes

8   *endives, about 2 pounds (900g)*
1   *teaspoon sugar*
8   *slices cooked ham*
3   *tablespoons (45g) butter*
¼   *cup (35g) flour*
1½   *cups (375g) milk*
¾   *cup (90g) Gouda, Emmentaler or Gruyère cheese, grated*
1   *teaspoon Worcestershire sauce*
Salt and pepper to taste

- Cut a very thin piece from the bottom of each endive and remove the core with a sharp pointed knife. Bring a pan of salted water to a boil. Add the endives and sugar and simmer for 20 minutes or until tender. Drain well and wrap each endive in a slice of ham. Place in an ovenproof 8x12 inch (20x30cm) casserole.

- Melt butter in a medium saucepan. Blend flour into butter. Slowly add milk, stirring constantly, over medium heat until mixture thickens. Cook on low heat for 5 minutes, stirring constantly.

- Remove from heat. Add cheese, Worcestershire sauce, salt, and pepper to taste. Pour sauce over endives. Can be prepared ahead to this point.

- Preheat broiler. Put casserole under oven broiler until cheese is melted and light golden.

Witlof translates to "white leaf." Endive is grown in complete darkness to prevent it from turning green. This growing method was developed by Monsieur Brézier. When exposed to light, endive becomes bitter. Buy crisp firmly packed heads with pale, yellow-green tips. Store endive refrigerated, wrapped in a paper towel inside a plastic bag for no more than a day.

Codorniz en Pimientos
Quail Baked in Sweet Peppers with Brandy Sauce

Serves 6
Prep/Cook Time: 2 hours

6   quails, cleaned
2   cups (500ml) brandy
Salt to taste
6   strips of salt pork or bacon
6   red bell peppers, each large enough to hold a quail
2   tablespoons olive oil

• Preheat oven to 450°. Sprinkle the interior of each quail with brandy and salt.

• Carefully cut the top off each pepper and clean out the seeds and ribs.

• Wrap each quail with a strip of salt pork or bacon and insert a wrapped quail inside each red pepper. Sprinkle the tops with brandy.

• Put the peppers upright in a casserole with oil, cover and bake for 30 minutes. Lower heat to 300° and cook for 1 hour, spooning brandy and juices over peppers occasionally.

• Sprinkle with salt to taste and serve with the brandy sauce that has formed in the pan while baking, skimming fat as necessary.

There are various methods for cooking quail in red peppers originating from the Catalan region of Spain. The quail in its rich sauce goes well with Greek Eggplant Salad (see index for recipes).

Poultry & Seafood

CHINESE ALMOND CHICKEN

Serves 4
Prep/Cook Time: 15 minutes

4   boneless chicken breast halves
½   tablespoon rice wine or white cooking wine
½   teaspoon sugar
½   teaspoon salt
1   egg white
1½ cups (150g) sliced almonds
Oil for deep-frying chicken

- Cut chicken breasts into ¼ inch (0.6cm) slices.

- Mix wine, sugar, salt, and egg white until well blended. Add chicken slices and coat well with mixture.

- Roll chicken breast slices in almonds.

- In a deep skillet or wok, deep-fry in heated oil until crispy and cooked through, about 1 to 2 minutes. Place on a serving dish and serve with white rice.

This is a simple method of preparing a light fried chicken, Chinese style. Sprinkle with very finely chopped green onions for color when serving. Sesame seeds may be substituted if almonds are not on hand.

Almonds are native to Asia, and dishes combining the sweet crispness of almonds with chicken are very common in southern Chinese cuisine.

GRILLED GINGER, HONEY, AND SESAME CHICKEN

Serves 6
Prep/Cook Time: 30 minutes, plus 2 to 8 hours to marinate

½   cup (125ml) soy sauce
2   cloves garlic, crushed
2   tablespoons minced fresh ginger, or 1½ teaspoons dried
4   tablespoons sesame seeds
½   teaspoon dried thyme
¼   cup (60ml) honey
3   tablespoons brown sugar
⅛   teaspoon allspice
6   boneless chicken breast halves

• Combine first 8 ingredients in a large zip lock plastic bag. Add chicken, seal bag, and turn to coat chicken with marinade. Refrigerate 2 to 8 hours, turning from time to time.

• Remove chicken from marinade and cook over a hot grill until cooked through, about 10 to 15 minutes on each side.

Variation:

The marinade for this recipe works well with pork also. Substitute a 1 to 2 pound (450-900g) pork tenderloin for the chicken breasts. Grill the tenderloin, over a low fire, with the grill lid down, about 40 minutes or until the meat reaches 140°F. Slice and serve.

Cook's Tip:
Wrap peeled garlic clove(s) in a piece of sturdy plastic wrap, leaving room for the garlic to spread. Hit garlic clove(s) with a meat pounder until crushed. Unwrap garlic and use. There will be no smelly fingers or garlic press to clean.

MAKKHANI MURGHI MASALA

Chicken Buttermasala

Serves 4
Prep/Cook Time: 30 minutes,
plus 2 to 3 hours to marinate

The marinated chicken from this recipe may be baked using the same method as with Tandoori Chicken Kebabs (see index for recipe) if you prefer baking to frying.

1	teaspoon ground cumin
½	teaspoon cayenne pepper
½	teaspoon turmeric
1	teaspoon garam masala
½	teaspoon ground coriander

Salt to taste

4	boneless chicken breast halves, cut in 1 inch (2.5cm) cubes
5	teaspoons oil
2	medium onions, chopped
3	cloves garlic, crushed
2	medium tomatoes, sliced thinly
1	teaspoon minced fresh ginger, or ½ teaspoon dried
3	tablespoons sour cream
2	tablespoons (30g) butter

• Combine the first 6 ingredients in a medium bowl.

• Stir cubed chicken with seasoning mixture. Cover and refrigerate 2 to 3 hours for flavors to blend.

• Heat 3 teaspoons oil in a large skillet over medium-high heat. Sauté about ¼ to ⅓ of the marinated chicken in oil until cooked through. Remove cooked chicken to a small bowl and continue with remainder until all chicken is cooked. Set aside.

• Add remaining 2 teaspoons oil to the hot skillet and sauté onions and garlic until translucent. Add tomatoes and ginger, and fry until mixture is soft.

• Add chicken. Stir the mixture over high heat until chicken is heated through.

• Just before serving, stir in sour cream and butter. Serve with rice.

PETTI DI POLLO ALLA CALABRITTO

Chicken Breasts with Porcini Mushroom
and Prosciutto Cream Sauce

Serves 6
Prep/Cook Time:
1 hour 15 minutes,
plus 2 hours standing time

2   ounces (55g) porcini mushrooms
4   tablespoons olive oil
1   teaspoon curry powder
2   tablespoons (30g) butter
6   boneless chicken breast halves
¾   cup (185ml) dry sherry
¼   cup (60ml) heavy cream
1   cup (80g) sliced fresh mushrooms
12   thin slices of fontina cheese
12   thin slices of prosciutto ham
Salt and pepper to taste

- In a small bowl cover mushrooms with warm water. Soak for ½ hour. Drain and reserve mushroom water. Chop mushrooms, and set aside.

- Mix 3 tablespoons olive oil with curry powder in a deep dish. Add chicken breasts and toss to coat. Let sit 10 minutes. Drain oil from chicken into a skillet. Add 1 tablespoon (15g) butter. Heat skillet on medium heat until oil is hot. Brown chicken breasts. Remove from skillet and set aside.

- Add porcini mushrooms to skillet and stir for 3 to 4 minutes over low heat. Add half of the sherry and cook until it evaporates. Add ¼ cup (60ml) mushroom water and stir. Add heavy cream, salt, and pepper, and stir. Bring to a boil and simmer for 5 minutes over medium heat and set aside.

- In another skillet, add 1 tablespoon (15g) butter and 1 tablespoon olive oil and sauté fresh mushrooms on medium heat until the water from the mushrooms evaporates, stirring often. Add remaining sherry and cook until it evaporates. Add salt and pepper.

- Place chicken breasts in a medium-sized ovenproof glass dish and cover chicken with prosciutto and fontina cheese.

- Mix fresh mushrooms with porcini mushroom sauce and pour over chicken breasts. Cover and refrigerate 2 hours.

- Remove cover and bake in a 400° pre-heated oven for 20 to 25 minutes, or until heated through, and serve.

This dish was a favorite of the Calabritto family, a noble Neapolitan family of ancient lineage. It makes an elegant and interesting entrée for a dinner party that can be made ahead and put in the oven just before guests arrive.

ROMANO CRUSTED CHICKEN BREASTS WITH TOMATO CREAM SAUCE OVER PASTA

Serves 4
Prep/Cook Time: 45 minutes

The secret to this dish is timing. The chicken, the sauce, and the pasta need to be ready at the same time. The resulting flavor is fabulous!

C h i c k e n   B r e a s t s

4   boneless chicken breast halves
1½   cups (200g) bread crumbs
3   ounces (90g) Romano cheese, grated
2   tablespoons fresh chopped oregano or 1 teaspoon dried oregano
2   tablespoons fresh chopped basil or 1 teaspoon dried basil
1   tablespoon salt
2   tablespoons white pepper
½   cup (70g) flour
3   whole eggs, beaten
½   cup (125ml) olive oil

S a u c e   a n d   P a s t a

2   tablespoons (30g) butter
1   large shallot, minced
8   ounces (225g) Roma or Italian Plum tomatoes, peeled, seeded and diced
½   cup (125ml) dry white wine
1   ounce (30ml) chicken stock
8   ounces (225g) cappellini pasta or thin pasta
1   cup (235ml) whipping cream
Salt and white pepper
2   tablespoons fresh basil leaves
Grated Romano cheese

- Flatten chicken breasts between 2 sheets of plastic wrap with a meat pounder until ¼ inch (0.6cm) thick. Mix bread crumbs, Romano cheese, oregano, basil, salt, and white pepper. Recipe may be made up to 10 hours ahead to this point, with bread crumb mixture and chicken stored separately and tightly covered in the refrigerator.
- Dredge each chicken breast in flour, then egg, then bread crumb mixture
- Heat olive oil in a large skillet. When olive oil is near the smoking point, place chicken breasts in the skillet and immediately reduce heat to medium. Cook chicken on each side approximately 2 minutes until completely cooked through, being very watchful of the time and temperature, as the bread crumb mixture contains cheese and will burn easily. Keep chicken warm in a 200° oven while preparing sauce and pasta.
- In a large skillet over medium-high heat, melt butter. Sauté shallot with butter for 2 minutes. Add tomatoes and cook until most liquid is reduced. Add wine and chicken stock, turn heat to high and reduce liquid to half.
- While sauce reduces, prepare pasta according to package directions.
- Add cream to reduced sauce and cook 4 minutes. Season sauce to taste with salt and white pepper.
- Toss drained pasta with sauce. Place chicken pieces over pasta and garnish with fresh basil leaves and Romano cheese. Serve immediately.

I t a l y

ARROZ CON POLLO

Cuban Chicken and Rice

Serves 4 to 6
Prep/Cook Time:
1 hour 30 minutes

1	4-5 pound (1.8-2.25kg) chicken cut into pieces, or 4 chicken breasts with or without skin
3	tablespoons olive oil
3	cups (750ml) water
³⁄₄	teaspoon salt
¹⁄₂	teaspoon ground pepper
1	tablespoon tomato sauce
2	bay leaves
1	onion, finely chopped
¹⁄₂	green bell pepper, seeded and finely chopped
¹⁄₂	red bell pepper, seeded and finely chopped
1	tablespoon minced garlic
¹⁄₂	teaspoon ground oregano
¹⁄₂	teaspoon thyme
1	tablespoon dry white wine or sherry
1	tablespoon cider vinegar
¹⁄₂	teaspoon saffron for color
1	12 ounce (355ml) (+/-) bottle of beer
1¹⁄₂-2 pound cured ham steak, cut into small cubes	
1¹⁄₂	cups (300g) short grain Valencia rice
¹⁄₂	cup (120g) green peas
¹⁄₂	red bell pepper, cut in long strips
2	12 ounce (340g) jars white asparagus spears

This is one of the most frequently eaten dishes in all of Latin America. It is a version of paella. Serve with Patacones or Mango Margarita Salad (see index for recipes) and cold beer.

• Brown chicken in olive oil in a large stockpot. When browned, add next 14 ingredients. Cover pot and cook until chicken is tender, about 30 to 40 minutes.

• Remove chicken and set aside. Add enough beer to the liquid in the pot to make a total of 5 cups (1.25 liters). Add rice and ham steak cubes. Cook on medium-low heat, stirring occasionally until rice is tender. Add more beer or water as necessary as rice should be moist.

• Remove chicken from bones and mix into rice.

• Turn out onto a platter. Attractively arrange peas, red pepper strips, and asparagus spears around and on the Arroz con Pollo and serve.

CHICKEN COUSCOUS

2½ tablespoons olive oil
8   pieces of chicken
2   onions, chopped
¾   pound (340g) small carrots, peeled and chopped
½   cup (90g) dry chickpeas, soaked overnight, or
        a 15 ounce (420g) can chickpeas, drained
1   small turnip, peeled and chopped
2½ tablespoons tomato paste
½   teaspoon harissa or more to taste
1½ teaspoons salt
½   teaspoon black pepper
3   cups (750ml) water
1   pound (450g) zucchini, sliced in ½ inch (1.3cm) pieces
½   butternut squash, peeled, seeded, and chopped
4   green bell peppers, chopped
2   tablespoons (30g) butter
1   10 ounce (280g) box quick plain couscous

• Heat 2 tablespoons oil in a large deep saucepan, over medium-high heat. Add chicken and brown about 2 minutes on each side. Add onions, carrots, chickpeas, turnip, tomato paste, harissa, salt, pepper, and water. Simmer covered for 30 minutes. Add zucchini and squash and cook for an additional 15 minutes. Add peppers and cook for 10 minutes. Take the chicken out, remove the meat from the bones, and replace the meat in the saucepan.

• Remove 3 cups (750ml) broth from the saucepan and bring to a boil in a separate medium saucepan. Remove from heat. Add 1 tablespoon (15g) butter, ½ tablespoon olive oil, and couscous. Stir, cover, and let stand for 5 minutes. Add more hot broth if the couscous is too dry. Mix in remaining 1 tablespoon (15g) butter and fluff grains with a fork.

• Put couscous in a large serving dish, top with chicken and vegetables, cover with the rest of the broth and serve very hot.

Variation:

For a spicier couscous, reserve ¼ cup (60ml) of the broth and mix with 2 tablespoons harissa. Serve the sauce in a small serving bowl and pass to spoon over the couscous.

Couscous is a staple of Tunisian cuisine and is traditionally prepared in a couscoussière, a two-part pot. The bottom part is a large round pan in which the stew is cooked and the top is a steamer with holes where the couscous is steamed over the stew.

Tunisia's history and cuisine is extraordinarily rich and ancient. The Phoenicians began the Carthaginian Empire in Tunisia in about 1100 B.C.. The Romans, Vandals, Byzantines, Arabs, and the Ottoman Empire have since ruled it. France controlled Tunisia from 1881 until its independence in 1956 and much of the food has a French influence.

Tunisia

PASTEL AZTECA

Aztec Chicken Layered with Corn Tortillas
Chiles and Queso Fresco

Serves 10 to 12
Prep/Cook Time:
1 hour 30 minutes

8	chicken breast halves
3	fresh *chiles poblanos
1	large onion, coarsely chopped
1	clove garlic, crushed
1	28 ounce (790g) can tomato sauce

Canola or safflower oil for frying tortillas
20-24 corn tortillas
1	15 ounce (420g) jar Mexican heavy cream
1	15 ounce (420g) round Mexican cheese
	(queso fresco or farmers cheese), crumbled

- Use Poached Chicken for Entrée Salads and Other Dishes recipe (see index for recipe) for cooking chicken breasts, or your favorite method. Shred cooked chicken breasts.

- Preheat oven to 350°.

- If using fresh chiles poblanos, broil them close to the heat source until blackened. Place broiled chiles in a plastic bag to sweat for 10 to 15 minutes. Peel, seed; and slice chiles.

- In a food processor, blend onion and garlic in about 3 tablespoons of the tomato sauce until very finely ground. Then blend in remainder of tomato sauce and set aside.

- Heat about 3 tablespoons of oil in skillet until oil bubbles when a tortilla is dipped in it. Quickly fry tortillas, one at a time, for a few seconds until heated but still soft, adding more oil if necessary. Place fried tortillas on paper towels to absorb the oil.

- Place one layer of tortillas in a deep casserole or 9x13 inch (23x33cm) pan and cover amply with tomato sauce.

- Continue layering with tortillas, chicken, Mexican cream, remaining tomato sauce, cheese, and some slices of chiles ending with tomato sauce and cheese.

- Bake for 30 minutes or until sides are bubbly. Slice and serve immediately.

Pastel Azteca doubles well and is an excellent choice for a large dinner party.

*Chiles poblanos are best known as being the chile of choice for chiles rellenos. The darkest colored poblanos have the richest flavor. The very best poblanos are grown in central Mexico.

Fresh poblanos as well as Mexican cream can be found in the produce section of many large supermarkets and Mexican markets. The flavor of fresh chiles poblanos are best, but canned chiles may be substituted. Also, crème fraîche can be substituted for the Mexican cream.

CHICKEN QUESADILLAS

Serves 4 to 6
Prep/Cook Time: 30 minutes

Chicken Quesadillas are a great use for left over rotisserie or roasted chicken

Optional Condiments

1	medium avocado, peeled and sliced
1	teaspoon lemon juice
2	cups (85g) shredded leaf or iceberg lettuce
1	vine ripe tomato, chopped in fine cubes
⅔	cup (155ml) sour cream
1	cup (270g) tomato salsa, bottled or fresh

Quesadillas

8	prepackaged flour tortillas
Butter for frying	
2	cups (450g) shredded cooked chicken
2	cups (240g) grated Monterey Jack cheese
2	green onions, chopped fine, optional

- Toss avocado slices with lemon juice. Arrange lettuce, tomatoes, sour cream, and avocados attractively on a plate. Cover with plastic wrap and refrigerate. Pour salsa in serving dish and refrigerate.

- Preheat oven to 200°. Place a serving platter in oven. Position ingredients by stove.

- Heat skillet over medium-high heat and melt enough butter in skillet to cover bottom. When butter sizzles, lay one tortilla in skillet and immediately sprinkle in order ¼ of the cheese, chicken, and onions on tortilla. When cheese melts and under side of tortilla is light golden, place a tortilla on top of filling. Lift from skillet and add more butter to cover skillet and flip tortilla. Cook until other side of tortilla is golden.

- Remove quesadilla to warm platter hooded with aluminum foil and keep in oven until all quesadillas are cooked. Serve warm in slices with desired condiments.

Fresh Tomato Salsa

½ bunch fresh cilantro, washed and dried
1 small white onion
1 large clove garlic
1 jalapeño chile, seeded
5 ripe tomatoes, quartered
1 tablespoon lime juice

Remove large stems from cilantro. Chop coarsely in a food processor and remove. Chop onion, garlic, and jalapeño in food processor until fine. Add tomatoes and process until coarsely chopped. Remove salsa to serving dish or jar and stir in lime juice and chopped cilantro. Cover tightly and chill. Keeps up to 1 week in refrigerator.

CHICKEN CATALAN

Serves 8
Prep/Cook Time:
1 hour 15 minutes,
plus 12 hours to marinate

2   2½ pound (1.13kg) chickens, quartered,
     or 8 boneless chicken breast halves
8   cloves garlic, peeled and puréed
2   tablespoons dried oregano
Salt and pepper to taste
¼   cup (60ml) red wine vinegar
¼   cup (60ml) olive oil
½   cup (100g) pitted prunes
¼   cup (40g) pitted Spanish olives
¼   cup (40g) capers
1   teaspoon caper juice
3   bay leaves
½   cup (100g) brown sugar
½   cup (125ml) white wine
2   tablespoons chopped parsley

- In a large bowl, combine chicken, garlic, oregano, pepper, salt, vinegar, oil, prunes, olives, capers, caper juice, and bay leaves. Cover, refrigerate, and let marinate overnight.

- Preheat oven to 350°.

- Arrange chicken in a large shallow baking pan and pour the marinade over the chicken. Sprinkle with brown sugar and white wine. Basting frequently, bake until chicken is tender and cooked through, about 45 minutes.

- When ready to serve, transfer the chicken to a warm platter with a slotted spoon. Surround the chicken with the prunes, olives, and capers. Moisten the chicken with spoonfuls of juice, but do not drown. Sprinkle with chopped parsley and serve.

Variation:

2½ pounds (1.13kg) of lean pork may be substituted for the chicken. Bake uncovered in a casserole instead of a large shallow baking pan, and serve as a stew.

This recipe doubles well for a larger group. The combination of olives, capers, garlic and oregano makes this recipe a classic Mediterranean combination. It is extremely easy to make and works well for a large party. Serve over white rice.

143

CORONATION CHICKEN

Serves 8 to 10
Prep/Cook Time: 2 hours,
plus 12 to 24 hours to chill

2   3-4 pound (1.35-1.80kg) whole chickens
1   tablespoon oil
½   medium onion, finely chopped
1   tablespoon curry powder
1   rounded teaspoon tomato paste
1   cup (250ml) red wine
¾   cup (185ml) water
1   bay leaf
1   teaspoon salt or to taste
1½   tablespoons sugar
1   slice lemon
2   tablespoons lemon juice
4   cups (946ml) mayonnaise
2   tablespoons heavy cream
2   tablespoons apricot jam or mango chutney

Here are two variations of a culinary tribute to a beloved monarch.

Coronation Chicken was created for the Coronation of Queen Victoria of Great Britain on June 20, 1837. Queen Victoria's reign lasted until 1901 and was a prosperous and peaceful period of England's history.

• Use Poached Chicken for Entrée Salads and Other Dishes recipe (see index for recipe) for cooking chicken, or your favorite method. Discard skin and bones. Cut chicken into fork sized pieces.

• Sauté onion in oil until translucent, about 3 minutes. Add curry powder and sauté 2 minutes. Add tomato paste, wine, water, bay leaf, salt, sugar, lemon slice, and lemon juice. Simmer 15 minutes uncovered. Remove from heat, strain and cool.

• Mix cooled onion mixture with cream, mayonnaise and apricot jam. Add chicken. Blend well and chill 12 to 24 hours for flavors to blend.

CORONATION CHICKEN WITH GRAPES AND YOGURT

Serves 4 to 6
Prep/Cook Time: 25 minutes,
plus 12 to 24 hours to chill

4   chicken breast halves
1   cup (235ml) plain yogurt
½   cup (120ml) mayonnaise
1   tablespoon apricot jam
1   teaspoon curry powder
1   cup (200g) of halved, white or green, seedless grapes

- Use Poached Chicken for Entrée Salads and Other Dishes recipe (see index for recipe) for cooking chicken breasts, or your favorite method. Cut chicken into cubes.

- Mix all ingredients except grapes and chill tightly covered 12 to 24 hours for flavors to blend.

- Mix in grapes, reserving about ¼ cup (50g) to sprinkle on top of salad for garnish, and serve.

On Queen Victoria's Diamond Jubilee celebrating the fiftieth year of her reign, another famous dish was created in her honor, Cherries Jubilee.

145

ORIENTAL POT ROAST CHICKEN

Serves 6
Prep/Cook Time: 1 hour

Oriental Pot Roast Chicken is especially good served on rice with stir fried vegetables. This dish was donated by a family of Japanese/ Hawaiian descent and is a delicious example of the way a recipe absorbs influences from around the world.

2   teaspoons fresh grated ginger
1   clove garlic, minced
⅓   cup (85ml) soy sauce
1   teaspoon brown sugar
2   teaspoons vegetable oil
1   3-4 pound (1.35-1.80kg) chicken
4   ounces (115g) button mushrooms
¼   cup (60ml) water
2   teaspoons cornstarch
1½ teaspoons water
1   bunch chopped green onions

- Mix ginger, garlic, soy sauce, and sugar together. Rub over chicken inside and out. Reserve any leftover sauce.

- Over medium-high heat in a large Dutch oven, heat oil and brown chicken on all sides. Add mushrooms and sauté for 2 minutes. Add reserved soy sauce mixture and ¼ cup (60ml) water to pot. Cover and simmer until chicken is cooked, about 45 minutes.

- Remove chicken from pot, remove bones and skin, and discard. Cut chicken meat into 2 inch pieces. Place on serving platter.

- Skim fat from top of broth. Mix cornstarch with water to form a paste and add to liquid in pot to make gravy, whisking well. Simmer until heated through.

- Pour gravy over chicken and garnish with green onions.

POULET SAUTÉ MARENGO

Chicken Marengo

1	3-4 pound (1.35-1.80kg) chicken, cut in pieces or 4-6 chicken breast halves

Salt and pepper to taste

¼	cup (35g) flour
3	tablespoons (45g) butter
1	tablespoon olive oil
1	pound (450g) mushrooms, quartered
2	cups (300g) chopped tomatoes
1½	cups (375g) white wine
10	pearl onions, blanched in boiling water for 1 minute and peeled
2	cloves garlic, chopped
1	teaspoon herbes de Provence or dried Italian seasoning
1	bay leaf
10	black olives without pits
¼	cup (60ml) cognac, optional

- Sprinkle chicken with salt and pepper, dredge in flour. Melt 2 tablespoons butter with olive oil in a large Dutch oven or other large heavy pan with a cover. Sauté chicken pieces in batches until all are lightly browned and remove from pan.

- Add remaining butter to Dutch oven and sauté mushrooms for 5 minutes. Stir in tomatoes, wine, onions, garlic, herbs, and bay leaf. Heat through. Return chicken and any accumulated juices to Dutch oven. Add olives and bring to a boil. Reduce heat to medium, cover and simmer for 20 minutes. Uncover pot and add cognac. Simmer until chicken is cooked through, about 10 minutes. Season to taste with salt and pepper and serve warm over rice or noodles.

Chicken Marengo, an excellent dinner party dish, is best made a day in advance which allows time for the flavors to blend, and time for the cook to relax before the guests arrive.

Chicken Marengo is named after the Battle of Marengo, June 14, 1800, where Napoleon Bonaparte defeated the Austrians. Bonaparte, along with his general staff, had gone ahead of his army and was far from his supply wagons. His chef sent men out in the local area to find provisions for the celebration meal and this legendary dish was created.

Spicy African Chicken in Peanut Sauce with Foufou

Serves 6
Prep/Cook Time: 1 hour

1   pound (450g) cassava or yucca, peeled
4   tablespoons peanut oil
6   boneless chicken breast halves, cut into 1½ inch (4cm) cubes
1   6 ounce (170g) can tomato paste
⅛   teaspoon baking soda
1   medium onion, finely chopped
2   cloves garlic, finely chopped
1   teaspoon cayenne pepper, or to taste
3   cups (750ml) chicken stock
½   teaspoon black pepper
2½   rounded teaspoons natural peanut butter
2   10 ounce (280g) packages frozen spinach, defrosted and drained, optional
1½   teaspoons salt

• Chop cassava or yucca into chunks. Bring a large pot of water to a boil. Put in the cassava and cook for 40 to 50 minutes until soft.

• Heat oil in a Dutch oven or large skillet over medium heat. Brown chicken, a few pieces at a time. Return all chicken to skillet.

• Add tomato paste and simmer uncovered for 5 minutes. Add baking soda and stir well to reduce the acidity of the tomato paste. Add onion, garlic, and cayenne pepper. Simmer for 2 minutes.

• Stir in chicken stock and black pepper, and cook covered over medium-high heat for 10 minutes.

• Stir in peanut butter until well blended. Add spinach, and simmer covered for 2 minutes. Add salt.

• Drain the cassava and mash well (traditionally done with a mortar and pestle) to make foufou.

• Serve chicken and sauce in a wide shallow bowl with foufou on the side for dipping.

In Africa, everyone would eat this dish from a communal bowl by taking a walnut sized ball of foufou with one hand and making an indentation in it with the thumb of their other hand, creating a spoon with which to eat the chicken and sauce.

Chicken with groundnuts is popular in many parts of Africa. It is also made with less chicken stock and called Groundnut Stew. Peanuts, known as groundnuts in Africa, are legumes not nuts. They are native to the Americas and were carried to Africa, Asia, and Europe by Portuguese and Spanish explorers in the 1500s.

COLOMBO DE POULET

Guadeloupan Chicken Curry

Serves 6
Prep/Cook Time: 1 hour

1	4-5 pound (1.8-2.25kg) chicken, cut into 8 pieces
½	cup (125g) olive oil
¼	cup (60ml) cider vinegar or lemon juice
3	garlic cloves, minced
2	onions, chopped
3	green onions, chopped
1	tablespoon parsley, chopped
1	teaspoon dried thyme
3	tablespoons *Colombo powder, or curry powder
¼	teaspoon cayenne pepper, or to taste
¼	cup (60ml) water
6	carrots, peeled and diced
3	small white turnips, peeled and diced
3	small green mangoes, peeled and diced
1	zucchini, diced

Salt and pepper to taste

- Brown the chicken in oil in a large skillet on medium heat. Transfer chicken pieces to a Dutch oven and discard grease.

- In the same skillet, add the vinegar or lemon juice and allow to boil for a few seconds, scraping up any browned bits. Pour over chicken.

- Add garlic, onions, green onions, and parsley to chicken. Stir and simmer over medium-low heat for a few minutes.

- Add the thyme, Colombo powder, cayenne pepper, and water and stir well. Add carrots, turnips, mangoes and zucchini, stir and cover. Simmer for 30 minutes, stirring occasionally and adding a little water if needed. Adjust seasonings and serve over rice.

*Poudre de Colombo or Colombo Powder is a curry paste from Guadeloupe. It can be made from 3 cloves garlic, 2 fresh hot red chiles, ⅛ teaspoon turmeric, and 1 teaspoon each of ground coriander and mustard. The ingredients are mashed together and keep for up to 6 weeks in the refrigerator.

Green Mango Salad (see index for recipe) makes a refreshing accompaniment.

Kaeng Kai

Coconut Chicken Curry

Thailand is in
Southeast Asia
and in Southeast
Asia, only the
Vietnamese eat
with chopsticks.
If you've ever
gotten a funny
look when asking
for chopsticks in a
Thai restaurant,
now you
know why.

1-2 tablespoons Thai red curry paste or to taste
2   tablespoons cooking oil
1½ 13.5 ounce (400ml) cans unsweetened coconut milk
5   boneless chicken breast halves, cut in long strips
⅔   cup (170ml) water
1½ tablespoons sugar
4   tablespoons fish sauce
1   19 ounce (530g) can bamboo shoots, drained, in thin strips
⅓   cup (10g) fresh basil leaves, cut in slices

- In a 5 quart (5 liter) or larger saucepan over medium-high heat, fry curry paste in oil until fragrant, about 1 minute.

- Reduce heat, add half the coconut milk a little at a time. Cook and stir until coconut milk begins to have a glossy sheen.

- Add chicken, stir and cook 10 minutes.

- Add the other half of the coconut milk, water, sugar, and fish sauce.

- Heat to a slow boil. Add bamboo shoots and cook for 15 minutes or until chicken is cooked through.

- Add basil on top and remove from heat. Serve with steamed rice.

Variations:

This deliciously spicy curry can be rendered milder by using less curry paste, if desired. For a lower fat version substitute light unsweetened coconut milk.

KHEEMA MURGHI DHANIA

Turkey with Mint, Peas and Indian Spices

Serves 4
Prep/Cook Time: 45 minutes

2   *cloves garlic, coarsely chopped*
1   *inch cube (2.5cm) of ginger,*
       peeled and coarsely chopped
3   *medium onions, coarsely chopped*
½-⅔ *teaspoon turmeric*
½   *teaspoon cayenne pepper*
1   *tablespoon vegetable oil*
1   *pound (450g) ground turkey*
1-1½ *cups (150-225g) frozen peas, rinsed*
Salt to taste
1   *bunch fresh mint, chopped*
1   *teaspoon garam masala*
1½   *tablespoons lemon juice*

- Place garlic, ginger and half of the chopped onions in a blender or food processor and blend to a purée. Transfer mixture to a bowl and add turmeric and cayenne. Mix thoroughly.

- Heat oil in a 2 quart (2 liter) pan over medium-high. Sauté remaining onions until deep golden brown. Stir garlic and onion purée into saucepan with sautéed onions and cook for 4 minutes. Add a little water if mixture begins sticking to the bottom of the pan.

- Mix in turkey, breaking up any large lumps which may form while cooking. Cook turkey until brown. Stir in peas and salt. Cover and cook for 25 minutes, stirring occasionally.

- Add mint, garam masala, and lemon juice. Cover and cook 2 to 3 minutes more, stirring occasionally. Serve hot.

Serve with Vegetable Curry with Potatoes and Peppers, or Lentil Dahl, and Mast-o Khujar (see index for recipes), mango chutney, and rice.

POACHED CHICKEN FOR SALADS AND OTHER DISHES

Makes 2-3 cups (450-700g)
Prep/Cook Time: 25 minutes

Poached Chicken Breasts

4	chicken breasts halves, bone-in or boneless
½	onion
1	stalk celery or ½ teaspoon celery salt
1	teaspoon salt or chicken stock crystals

- Place all ingredients in a skillet or heavy shallow saucepan. Add enough water to just cover chicken.

- Cover pan and bring to a boil. Immediately reduce heat to low, and cook at a very low simmer until tender and no longer pink, about 12 minutes.

- Remove from heat. Let chicken cool in the broth. Remove chicken and discard any bones or skin.

- Use as directed in salad or other dish recipe. If refrigerating for later use, add a little broth to the chicken and store tightly covered.

Poached Whole Chicken

1	3-5 pound (1.8-2.25kg) chicken, neck and giblets removed
½	onion
1	stalk celery, or ½ teaspoon celery salt
1	teaspoon salt or chicken stock crystals

Makes 3 to 4 cups (700-900g)
Prep/Cook Time: 1 hour

- Place all ingredients in large pot. Add enough water to just cover chicken.

- Cover pot and bring to a boil. Immediately reduce heat to low, and cook at a very low simmer until tender and no longer pink, about 45 minutes to 1 hour.

- Remove from heat. Let chicken cool in the broth. Remove chicken and discard bones and skin.

- Use as directed in salad or other dish recipe. If refrigerating for later use, add a little broth to the chicken and store tightly covered.

BAKED OR ROASTED CHICKEN FOR SALADS AND OTHER DISHES

Make 2-3 cups (450-700g)
Prep/Cook Time: 40 minutes

Baked Chicken Breasts

4   boneless or bone-in chicken breast halves,
2   tablespoons (30g) butter, melted
2   tablespoons vegetable oil
Salt to taste

- Preheat oven to 300°.

- Wash chicken breasts and pat dry with paper towels. Place breasts on a broiling rack over a foil-lined broiling pan.

- Combine butter and vegetable oil and brush over chicken breasts. Sprinkle with salt.

- Bake until tender and juices run clear, about 30 minutes for boneless breasts and 45 minutes for bone-in, basting often.

- Remove from oven and wrap in aluminum foil or place in a dish with a tight cover with a bit of the juice while still warm.

- When cool to the touch, remove any skin and bones if applicable, and use as directed in salad recipe or refrigerate immediately for later use.

Roasted Whole Chicken

1   3-5 pound (1.8-2.25kg) chicken,
      neck and giblets removed
2   tablespoons (30g) butter, melted
2   tablespoons vegetable oil
Salt to taste

Makes 3-4 cups (700-900 g)
Prep/Cook Time:
40 minutes

- Preheat oven to 400°.

- Wash chicken and pat dry with paper towels. Place chicken breast side up, on a baking pan lined with foil.

- Combine butter and vegetable oil and brush over chicken. Sprinkle with salt.

- Bake until tender and juices run clear, about 1 hour, basting occasionally.

- Remove from oven and let cool to touch. Remove meat, discard bones and skin, and use in recipe as directed.

The Baked Chicken Breast recipe increases well. It is a very good method to use when large quantities are needed

Shortcut Tip:

Roast two chickens at once. Eat one for dinner and use the meat of the other later in Chicken, Mango and Kiwi Salad with Honey Lime Dressing, Chicken Quesadillas (see index for recipes), or any of the many other recipes in this book calling for pre-cooked chicken. Sprinkle the dinner chicken with a little lemon pepper or seasoning salt before roasting.

MURGHI KOFTAS

Turkey Meatballs with Yogurt Masala Sauce

Serves 4
Prep/Cook Time: 1 hour

Serve with Vegetable Curry with Potato and Peppers (see index for recipe) and rice. Koftas also make nice hors d'oeuvres served using cocktail skewers or toothpicks.

Turkey Meatballs

1	teaspoon salt
½	teaspoon garam masala
¼	teaspoon cayenne powder
½	bunch cilantro, chopped
3	tablespoons plain yogurt
1	pound (450g) ground turkey

Sauce

2	tablespoons vegetable oil
4	medium onions, chopped
2	cloves garlic, finely chopped
1	1 inch (2.5cm) cube ginger, peeled and finely chopped
4-5	tablespoons crushed tomatoes
1	teaspoon salt
¼	teaspoon cayenne powder
½	teaspoon turmeric
½	teaspoon garam masala
½	bunch fresh cilantro, chopped
3-4	tablespoons plain yogurt

- In a bowl mix salt, garam masala and cayenne. Add cilantro and yogurt and mix. Add meat and mix thoroughly.

- Form meatballs of approximately 1¼ inch (3cm) diameter, dipping hands in water occasionally to keep the meat from sticking. Lay out meatballs separately on a tray.

- Heat oil in a medium saucepan over medium-high heat. Sauté onions in oil until light brown. Add garlic and ginger and sauté for 3 to 4 minutes more.

- Add tomatoes, salt, cayenne pepper, turmeric, garam masala, cilantro, and yogurt and cook for another 1 to 2 minutes, stirring well.

- Gently add meatballs to saucepan. Add sufficient boiling water to just cover meatballs. Bring water back to a boil.

- Cover saucepan and gently simmer for 25 minutes or until the meat is cooked and the meatballs are tender. If the sauce appears watery and does not cling to the meatballs, uncover the saucepan and heat on medium-high heat to evaporate some of the water. If the sauce is too dry, add boiling water as required to achieve a smooth sauce.

KESHI YENA
Edam Cheese with Caribbean Chicken Filling

Prep/Cook Time:
2 hours 45 minutes,
plus 3 hours to marinate

³/₄ pound (340g) boneless chicken breast halves
³/₄ pound (340g) boneless chicken thighs
Juice of one lime
2¹/₂ teaspoons salt
Ground pepper to taste
2 teaspoons poultry seasoning
5 medium onions, 3 chopped and 2 sliced
4 tablespoons (60g) butter
12 peppercorns
1 celery stalk with leaves
1 bay leaf, bruised
3 tomatoes, peeled and chopped
1 green bell pepper, chopped
1 tablespoon fresh parsley, chopped
Tabasco sauce
2 tablespoons ketchup
¹/₄ cup (50g) pitted green olives, sliced
1 teaspoon capers
¹/₄ cup (40g) raisins
2 tablespoons chopped *mustard pickles
3 eggs, beaten
Paprika for powdering dish
2 pounds (900g) Edam cheese, sliced

- Rub chicken with lime juice. Season chicken with ½ teaspoon salt, pepper, poultry seasoning, and ⅓ of chopped onion. Refrigerate for 3 hours.
- In a large heavy pot over medium-high heat, brown chicken in 2 tablespoon butter, about 2 minutes per side. Add 2 quarts (2 liters) of water, remaining 2 teaspoons salt, peppercorns, remaining onion, celery stalk, and bay leaf. Bring to a boil, reduce heat and simmer for 20 minutes. Strain and reserve broth, discarding vegetables.
- Heat remaining butter in separate pan over medium heat. Sauté cooked chicken with tomatoes, sliced onions, green pepper and parsley. Season with Tabasco sauce and adjust salt and pepper to taste.
- Add ketchup, olives, capers, raisins, and mustard pickles and stir well. Simmer about 20 to 30 minutes, or until tomatoes are reduced. Remove from heat and let cool.
- Preheat oven to 350°. Butter large casserole dish and powder sides with paprika.
- Add beaten eggs to the chicken mixture. Line casserole dish with half the cheese slices. The slices should overlap each other. Add filling and cover with remaining cheese.
- Bake for 1 hour 15 minutes. Remove from oven and invert onto a heated platter. Keep warm until ready to serve as the cheese becomes hard if permitted to cool, or serve immediately.

Keshi Yena means filled cheese and is a classic blend of Dutch and Caribbean flavors with the Edam cheese (Dutch) and the spicy stewed chicken (Caribbean). It is usually served with rice and fried very ripe plantains. It is also served as an hors d'oeuvre in thin slices on French bread rounds.

*Mustard pickles are preserved with vinegar to which mustard has been added. They are sold in jars and can be found in the pickle section of most large supermarkets.

Huachinango à la Veracruzana

Red Snapper Veracruz Style

Serves 8
Prep/Cook Time: 1 hour

This popular Mexican coastal dish gets its name from the state of Veracruz, a thin strip of land that runs for approximately 600 miles along the southwestern coast of the Gulf of Mexico.

Red Snapper

1	3 pound (1.35kg) red snapper, filleted
1	tablespoon salt
1	tablespoon pepper
½	cup (125ml) lemon juice
1	onion, thinly sliced
1	cup (250ml) white wine
1	teaspoon basil
1	teaspoon oregano
1	teaspoon rosemary

Sauce

1	clove garlic, minced
1	tablespoon olive oil
1	onion, diced
3	large tomatoes, skinned, seeded and chopped
¼	cup (50g) jalapeño pepper slices
½	cup (100g) sliced black olives
¼	cup (50g) capers

• Preheat oven to 325°. Grease a large shallow baking dish to hold fish.

• Rinse fish, rub with salt and pepper and place in prepared baking dish.

• Add remaining fish ingredients and bake for 35 minutes until fish is cooked through.

• Prepare sauce while fish is cooking. In a small skillet, sauté garlic in olive oil. Add remaining sauce ingredients and simmer until thickened. Pour sauce over fish and serve at once.

Variation:

You can also layer the fish and sauce in a casserole and bake them together for 35 minutes. This can be served with warmed corn tortillas.

Psari tis Skaras me Saltsa Politiki

Broiled Fish with Lemon Sauce

Serves 6
Prep/Cook Time: 15 minutes

2   pounds (900g) Greenland turbot, sole fillets, salmon or halibut steaks
3   tablespoons (45g) melted unsalted butter
Salt and pepper
¼ cup (60ml) olive oil
3   tablespoons lemon juice
3   tablespoons finely chopped fresh parsley
1   green onion, chopped
1   teaspoon dried oregano, or 2 tablespoons fresh oregano

- Preheat broiler on high until broiling element is red. Heat broiling pan.

- Brush fish with melted butter and sprinkle with salt and pepper to taste. Place on hot broiling pan that has been quickly brushed with oil.

- Broil 4 to 5 minutes per side, brushing again with butter when turning. Broil, in total, about 8 minutes for turbot or sole, and 10 minutes for salmon or halibut, or cook until fish flakes when tested with a fork.

- Meanwhile, in a small bowl combine oil, lemon juice, parsley, onion, and oregano, and beat with a fork until just blended.

- Place fish on a warm serving platter. Pour lemon and herb sauce over the fish and serve.

Cook's Tip:
For broiling fish, the broiler pan should be hot before you introduce the fish. Put the pan in the oven and heat it thoroughly then quickly brush it with oil and place the fish, skin side down, on it. The fish will cook perfectly and will be easy to remove from the pan.

Greece

CATFISH CREOLE

Serves 6 to 8
Prep/Cook Time: 1 hour

3   cups (360g) chopped green onions
1   teaspoon crushed garlic
1   cup (220g) finely chopped bell pepper
3   tablespoons vegetable oil
1   cup (30g) finely chopped fresh parsley
1   cup (150g) diced or crushed tomatoes
1   bay leaf
1/2   teaspoon fresh thyme
1/2-1   teaspoon cayenne pepper
1   teaspoon salt
1-1 1/3 cups (250-335ml) dry white wine
2 1/2   pounds (1.12kg) catfish fillets, cut in 2 inch (5cm) wide slices
4-6   cups (590-885g) cooked white rice

- Sauté onion, garlic, and bell pepper in vegetable oil until onion is translucent. Add parsley, tomatoes, bay leaf, thyme, cayenne pepper, and salt. Cook and stir 5 minutes over medium heat.

- Add wine. Cover and cook 25 minutes over medium heat.

- Place catfish in vegetables. Cover and cook, stirring occasionally, on low heat for 15 minutes or until catfish is cooked through. Serve immediately over rice.

In North or South America, a Creole is a person whose ancestors were early French or Spanish settlers of the New World. The word Creole comes from the Spanish word criollo, meaning "native to the place."

Traditional Creole cuisine utilizes butter and cream heavily, whereas Cajun cuisine depends on pork fat. Another difference between the two cuisines is that Creole uses more tomatoes and Cajun more spices. Both cuisines rely on chopped green peppers, onions and celery.

U S A

Fillet of Fish on a
Bed of Fresh Spinach

Serves 4
Prep/Cook Time: 40 minutes

¼   cup (60g) unsalted butter,
        plus 2 teaspoons (10g)
3   10 ounce (280g) packages fresh spinach, cleaned, stems removed
Salt and pepper to taste
4   tilapia, sole, flounder or other mild fish fillets
3   cups (750ml) dry white wine, or enough to cover fish
⅔   cup (155ml) heavy cream

- Preheat oven to 375°.

- In a large skillet, melt ¼ cup (60g) butter on medium heat and sauté spinach in butter. Cover and cook until completely wilted. Drain most of the liquid from the spinach, and sprinkle with salt and pepper to taste.

- Place spinach in a 9x12 inch (22x30cm) baking dish and arrange fish on top. Add enough wine to cover. Season fish with salt and pepper and dot with 2 teaspoons (10g) butter in small slices on each fillet.

- Cover with aluminum foil and bake until fish is cooked through, about 20 minutes.

- Remove from oven, gently stir in cream, without breaking fish, and adjust seasoning to taste.

Excellent served with boiled new potatoes and a green salad with Walnut Oil Herb Salad Dressing (see index for recipe).

Sabzi Polo va Mahi

Royal Iranian Style Fish with Herbed Rice

Serves 8
Prep/Cook Time:
1 hour 15 minutes

3   cups (600g) basmati rice
4   tablespoons salt
1½ cups (180g) chopped scallions
1   cup (30g) chopped dill
1   cup (30g) chopped cilantro
1   cup (30g) chopped parsley
12 tablespoons (180g) unsalted butter
2½ pounds (1.13kg) salmon, orange roughy or sea bass fillets without skin
1½ teaspoons salt
1½ teaspoons turmeric
½   pepper
Fresh parsley for garnish, optional

This dish is not as complicated as it appears and is well worth the effort. It makes a grand impression. The Herbed Rice also can be served at any meal even without the fish.

Sabzi Polo (herbed rice) is one of the traditional dishes eaten to celebrate the Persian New Year, No Rooz, which occurs on the first day of spring and then it is always eaten with fish. In Iran, the fish of choice is usually sea bass.

- Bring 5 quarts (5 liters) of water to a boil in a large pot with salt. Rinse rice in warm water from the tap. Drain rice, and drop into the boiling salted water. Cook for 5 to 10 minutes until rice is al dente. Drain rice in a colander, rinse, and set aside.

- In a large skillet, sauté scallions, dill, cilantro, and parsley in 5 tablespoons (75g) of the butter. Combine the drained rice with the herbs.

- Coat the bottom of a 4 quart (4 liter) pan with 1 tablespoon (15g) melted butter. Sprinkle rice into the pot, a handful at a time, allowing the rice to mound in the center and staying away from the sides of the pot. This allows steam to escape from the bottom of the pan and butter to melt through the rice. Using the handle of a long wooden spoon, make several holes in the rice that reach the bottom of the pan.

- Drizzle 4 tablespoons (60g) of melted butter over the rice. Cover pan with a dishtowel and lay lid on top of towel, folding opposite ends of the towel together over the top of the lid.

- Cook for 20 minutes over medium heat. Reduce heat to low and steam for 30 minutes.

- While rice is cooking, sprinkle fish with turmeric, salt, and pepper. Sauté fish in a skillet with remaining 2 tablespoons (30g) butter, or brush with melted butter and broil until fish is cooked through, about 10 minutes.

- Remove the cooked rice to a large platter and place fish on top, garnished with parsley. Serve *tahdig*, the golden brown crust that will form at the bottom of the rice pot, in a separate dish. To remove *tahdig*, place pot in a basin containing cold water for several minutes, and then turn the pot over onto a round platter to allow *tahdig* to come out.

Salmon Fillets with Sautéed Onions over Creamed Grits

Serves 4
Prep/Cook Time: 30 minutes

Grits

3	cups (750ml) chicken stock
½	teaspoon salt
1	cup (150g) quick (not instant) grits
1	cup (235g) cream

Salmon

2	medium onions, sliced
2	large cloves garlic, minced
¼	cup (60g) unsalted butter
1½	pounds (675g) salmon fillets, all skin removed
¼	teaspoon salt
1	teaspoon lemon pepper
1	tablespoon lemon juice

• Bring chicken stock and salt to a boil in medium pot. Stir in grits and cook over medium heat 2 minutes. Stir in cream and cook 1 minute. Turn off heat, cover, and let rest until salmon is finished, about 20 minutes.

• Sauté onions and garlic in butter over medium heat until transparent.

• Place fish in whole pieces on top of onions and garlic. Sprinkle with salt, lemon pepper, and lemon juice. Cover and steam 10 to 12 minutes over low heat. Uncover and cook another 3 to 5 minutes if necessary to reduce liquid. Serve over warm creamed grits.

Grits are ground hominy, which was one of the first food gifts the American Indians gave to the colonists. Hominy are dried white or yellow corn kernels from which the hull and germ have been removed. This process is performed chemically by soaking the corn in slaked lime or lye.

Cooks in southern areas of the United States have traditionally served grits with seafood and wild fowl as well as with breakfast dishes.

Szechuan Salmon

Serves 4
Prep/Cook Time: 25 minutes

Szechuan Sauce

1	tablespoon cornstarch
3	tablespoons water
3	tablespoons soy sauce
2	tablespoons sugar
2	tablespoons rice wine vinegar
1	1 inch (2.5cm) cube fresh ginger, peeled and minced
1	clove garlic, minced
1	teaspoon red pepper flakes (or to taste)
¾	cup (185ml) chicken stock

Salmon

4	salmon fillets or steaks, 6 to 7 ounces (170-200g) each, skin removed if using fillets
¼	cup (20g) sesame seeds
¼	cup (60ml) vegetable oil
½	cup (125ml) dry white wine, or enough to cover salmon

Sliced green onions for garnish, optional

Szechuan cuisine is known for peppery hot seasoning and sauces as opposed to Cantonese cuisine that has mild flavors.

The sauce for this recipe may be doubled or tripled, and can be kept tightly covered in the refrigerator for weeks. The method of cooking the salmon keeps the fish moist and flavorful.

- Mix cornstarch with water until smooth, adding water as needed to make a thin paste. Set aside.

- Mix all other sauce ingredients in medium saucepan and bring to boil over medium-high heat. As soon as mixture comes to a boil, whisk in cornstarch paste. Add additional cornstarch mixed with water to mixture if a thicker sauce is desired. Remove from heat.

- Preheat oven broiler on 500° until burners are red. Leave door slightly open so burners will stay on. Set a shallow broiling pan in oven to heat.

- Brush salmon with oil and press sesame seeds in both sides of salmon.

- Lightly brush the hot broiling pan with oil and placed salmon in the pan.

- Broil salmon at highest temperature for 1 minute on each side or until sesame seeds are golden not burned.

- Pour wine over salmon. Reduce heat to 400° on the bake setting. Close door and bake for 10 minutes or until fish is firm to touch. Baking times will vary according to thickness of fish.

- Transfer salmon to warm serving platter and pour Szechuan sauce over it. Garnish with green onions if desired, and serve.

JANSSON'S FRESTELSE
Jansson's Temptation

Serves 6
Prep/Cook Time:
1 hour 30 minutes

10	medium boiling potatoes
2	medium yellow onions
1	pint (473ml) heavy cream
1	can of anchovies, including liquid
2	tablespoons bread crumbs
2	tablespoons (30g) unsalted butter

- Preheat oven to 450°.

- Peel potatoes and cut them like French fries.

- Peel and chop onions.

- Grease a casserole dish with butter.

- Place a layer of potatoes, then a layer of onions, then a layer of anchovies with some liquid, and lastly another layer of potatoes.

- Pour cream over the top layer.

- Top it with bread crumbs and butter.

- Bake for approximately one hour or until the potatoes are soft.

The name for this dish is believed to have come from a Swedish man of the same name. The story goes that Jansson, who was born the son of a Swedish fisherman and then became a very popular opera singer, was a notorious flirt. He was also known for his cooking skills and he prepared this now famous dish to lure young ladies to his rooms after an opera performance. Serve with a glass of schnapps and a cold beer.

Sweden

PAIN DE POISSON
Fresh Fish Loaf

Serves 8
Prep/Cook Time:
1 hour 45 minutes

Pain de Poisson is very nice served at a summer luncheon with a tomato salad. It can be made ahead and refrigerated until used.

Court-bouillon is a French cooking term for a broth made by cooking various vegetables and herbs gently in water. A court bouillon is traditionally used for poaching seafood. This keeps the fish moist and flavorful.

Court-bouillon

½	small onion
2	cloves
4	cups (1 liter) water
1	bay leaf
½	carrot, chopped
1	stalk celery, chopped
2	peppercorns
1	slice lemon

Fish and Sauce

1	pound (450g) skinless salmon filets (or salmon and white fish mixed)
⅔	cup (155ml) crème fraîche (see index for recipe or purchase information)
6	eggs, beaten
1	cup tomato sauce

Salt and pepper to taste
½ cup (120ml) mayonnaise
Juice of 1 lemon

- Stick cloves in onion, and place with all remaining court-bouillon ingredients in a saucepan just large enough to fit fish. Bring to a boil. Reduce heat and simmer 20 minutes.

- Add fish to court-bouillon, bring back just to a boil, reduce heat immediately and very gently simmer 10 minutes. Remove from heat and let fish cool in court-bouillon. Recipe can be made to this point 1 day ahead and refrigerated.

- Drain and flake fish.

- Preheat oven to 325°. Butter a 9x5 inch (23x13cm) loaf pan or an ovenproof decorative mold pan.

- In a large bowl, mix crème fraîche, eggs, and tomato sauce. Add fish and a generous amount of salt and pepper to taste, as this dish benefits from a generous amount of both.

- Pour fish mixture into buttered pan. Bake for 1 hour and 10 minutes.

- After baking, cool to room temperature. Remove from pan and serve at room temperature or chilled with mayonnaise mixed with lemon juice.

France

CRAWFISH PIE

Serves 6
Prep/Cook Time:
1 hour 15 minutes

1	9 inch (23cm) pie crust
1	cup (250ml) vegetable oil
¼	cup (35g) flour
1	cup (140g) chopped onions
½	cup (110g) chopped green pepper
½	cup (110g) chopped celery
1	tablespoon minced garlic
½	teaspoon salt
¼	tablespoon ground white pepper
¼	teaspoon cayenne pepper
½	cup (60g) sliced green onion tops
1	tablespoon chopped parsley
3	cups (750ml) *crawfish, fish or chicken stock
3	cups (300g) crawfish meat
1	tablespoon paprika
1	cup (250ml) white wine
1	cup (100g) dry bread crumbs
1	tablespoon Parmesan cheese

- Preheat oven to 450°. Slightly prick pie crust with a fork and bake in heated oven for about 8 minutes. Remove and let cool. Do not turn off oven.

- Heat oil in a large iron skillet on medium high heat until oil begins to smoke. Gradually add flour, stirring constantly until dark brown, about 4 to 5 minutes.

- Lower heat to medium-low and sauté onions, green peppers, and celery until tender. Add garlic, salt, white pepper, cayenne pepper, green onions, and parsley.

- Stir in the stock, bring to a boil, and cook for 15 minutes. Add crawfish and paprika. Bring back to a boil and simmer for 15 minutes. Add wine, bread crumbs, and Parmesan cheese, and let simmer until thickened.

- Pour into baked pie crust and bake until hot, about 15 to 20 minutes.

Variation:

Prepare hors d'oeuvre portions by replacing the pie crust with pre-packaged small pastry shells that can be found in the frozen foods section of most supermarkets. Reduce baking time to 10 to 15 minutes.

Crayfish are called crawfish in the southern United States. They are essentially freshwater shrimp, found and enjoyed all over the world. They look like miniature lobsters. The only meat in a crawfish is in its tail, but the juices from the body make a good stock.

*Crawfish stock can be made by cooking the crawfish bodies in 3 cups (750ml) of water with an onion for 30 minutes.

MEJILLONES CON CREMA Y ASAFRAN
Cream of Mussels with Saffron

Serves 4
Prep/Cook Time: 1 hour

4   pounds (1.8kg) mussels
1   tablespoon flour
3   onions, finely chopped
2   tablespoons olive oil
1   cup (250ml) dry white wine
1   bay leaf
1   cup (235ml) cream
¼   teaspoon saffron

- Fill a sink with cold water and mix flour with the water. Carefully pour mussels into water. They should open slightly and make bubbles of air, trying to feed on the flour and thus rinsing their insides. After 10 minutes, remove mussels from the water and rinse again in clear water. Continue rinsing until there is no sandy residue coming from the mussels, about 2 rinses should suffice. With a sharp knife or fingers, remove the beard of the mussels (the fringe protruding from the shell) by pulling energetically on it. Once the mussels are clean, cook within the hour.

- Sauté onions over low heat in a 3 quart (3 liter) pan with olive oil until soft.

- Place cleaned mussels in a large separate pan and add water to ½ inch (1.3cm) over mussels. Bring to a boil, reduce heat, cover and cook at a low boil until mussels open, about 5 to 6 minutes, shaking half way through cooking time to move uncooked mussels to the bottom.

- Remove mussels, discarding any that have not opened. Reserve 4 cups (1 liter) of the broth and discard the rest.

- Remove the meat of the mussels from the shells and set aside.

- Strain reserved broth, then add with wine and bay leaf to the pan with sautéed onions. Cook uncovered at a boil for 20 minutes.

- Remove bay leaf and purée the onion and broth mixture in a food processor. Return to the pan. Add the cream and saffron. Cook and stir over low heat until warm and blended. Add the mussels and cook only until the mussels are heated, about 1 to 2 minutes. Serve immediately.

Europeans are much more enamored with mussels than Americans. Huge quantities of mussels along the coasts of the United States go unharvested. Try this delicious Spanish dish and learn first hand why the Europeans are so fond of mussels.

If you noticed that no salt is listed in this recipe, it was intentional. Mussels are naturally salty and season the broth themselves.

Moules à la Marinière

Steamed Mussels with White Wine Sauce

Serves 4
Prep/Cook Time:
1 hour 15 minutes

3	tablespoons (45g) unsalted butter
3	medium onions, sliced
4	celery sticks with some leaves, chopped
2	cloves garlic, minced
6	sprigs parsley
½	teaspoon dried thyme

Ground black pepper to taste

2	cups (500ml) Sauvignon Blanc wine
6	pounds (2.7kg) mussels in the shell
1	tablespoon flour
¼	cup (7g) finely chopped parsley

- Melt butter in a heavy pot large enough to provide space for all the mussels later. Add onions, celery, garlic, parsley sprigs, thyme and pepper. Cook for 4 to 5 minutes at medium-low heat until vegetables are softened, but not browned. Add white wine and remove from heat and set aside. The broth may be prepared 4 to 24 hours ahead and refrigerated until ready for use.

- To clean the mussels, fill a sink with cold water and mix flour into the water. Carefully put mussels in the water. They should open slightly and make bubbles of air, trying to feed on the flour, which rinses their insides. After 10 minutes, remove mussels from the water and rinse again in clear water. Continue rinsing until there is no sandy residue, about 2 rinses should suffice.

- With a knife or fingers, remove the beard of the mussels (the fringe protruding from the shell) by pulling energetically. Once the mussels are clean, cook within the hour.

- Heat broth over medium-high heat until simmering. (If the pot does not accommodate all the mussels, divide the mussels and broth and cook in two pans.) Carefully pour in the mussels and cover with a tight lid. After about 4 minutes, shake the pan to move the uncooked mussels to the bottom. Continue cooking until most of the mussels have opened, about 5 to 6 minutes. Discard the few mussels that haven't opened. Serve in large soup bowls with the broth.

A very popular Belgian and French dish which is often served with home cooked French fries.

To eat mussels, use a fork to take the first mussel out of its shell, then use the empty shell like pliers to remove the remaining mussels from their shells. Discard the empty shells in a large bowl in the center of the table. Don't ignore the delicious broth after you've eaten the mussels. It is marvelous eaten soaked in bread or as soup using half a mussel shell as a spoon.

CAJUN SHRIMP

Serves 6
Prep/Cook Time: 30 minutes

3   pounds (1.35kg) large raw shrimp, unpeeled
2-3 cloves garlic, crushed
½   cup (125ml) olive oil
¾   cup (185ml) white wine
12   tablespoons (180g) unsalted butter
½   cup (15g) chopped parsley
¼   cup (60ml) Worcestershire sauce
2   teaspoons Louisiana hot pepper sauce
1   teaspoon cayenne pepper
Salt to taste
Juice of 1 large lemon (about 2 tablespoons)
Parsley sprigs for garnish

- Preheat oven to 400°.

- Place shrimp in a large ovenproof dish with cover.

- Mix all ingredients, except lemon juice, and pour over shrimp.

- Bake for 15 minutes, stirring occasionally.

- Pour lemon juice over shrimp and serve garnished with fresh sprigs of parsley.

Serve with rice, a salad, and French bread.

Cajuns are descendants of French Canadians who the British drove from the captured French colony of Acadia, now Nova Scotia, Canada and adjacent areas in the 18th century. The Acadians subsequently settled in the fertile bayou lands of southern Louisiana. It is believed the word Cajun *originated with the native Americans living in Louisiana, who turned the unfamiliar pronunciation of Acadian into* Cajun.

168   *U S A*

KAENG GUNG SAPPOROT

Coconut Shrimp Curry with Pineapple

Serves 4
Prep/Cook Time: 20 minutes

- 3   tablespoons peanut oil
- 1/4 cup (35g) finely chopped onion
- 3   tablespoons finely chopped dried shrimp
- 3   tablespoons finely chopped *lemon grass
- 3   tablespoons finely chopped galangal (Thai ginger with a hot peppery flavor)
- 1/2 teaspoon shrimp paste, optional
- 2   teaspoons chili paste, or 1 teaspoon chili oil
- 2   cups (500ml) unsweetened coconut milk
- 1   tablespoon fish sauce
- 1   teaspoon brown sugar or palm sugar
- 1   pound (450g) raw shrimp, shells removed, 24-30 count
- 2   cups (500g) pineapple chunks
- 4   cups (590g) cooked rice

- Heat large skillet or wok until a drop of water dropped on skillet sizzles. Add peanut oil, onion, dried shrimp, lemon grass, galangal, shrimp paste, and chili paste. Stir fry for 2 minutes until oil is aromatic.

- Add coconut milk, fish sauce, and sugar and bring to a boil. Reduce heat to medium and continue cooking until mixture reduces by half, about 10 to 12 minutes.

- Add shrimp and pineapple, and simmer 3 to 4 minutes. Do not overcook. Serve over steamed or boiled rice.

Many of the spices in this recipe can only be found in specialty food markets in some cities. The recipe is particularly good with them, but if a few that are unavailable are left out, the dish will still be very nice with the basic ingredients. Ginger can be substituted for the galangal.

*Lemon grass is one of the most important flavorings in Thai cooking. Citral, an oil that is also found in lemon peel, gives lemon grass its sour-lemon flavor and fragrance. Lemon grass is available fresh or dried in Asian, and particularly, Thai markets.

OKONOMIYAKI

Japanese Style Seafood Cakes

Serves 8
Prep/Cook Time: 20 minutes

2½   cups (350g) *okonomiyaki flour
1¼   cups (310ml) water
2   eggs
¼   head of cabbage, shredded or finely chopped
4   tablespoons vegetable oil
¾   pound (340g) combination of shrimp, squid, octopus, pork or beef as preferred
3   tablespoons oil

- Mix flour, water, and eggs in a medium bowl. Add cabbage and mix.
- Chop squid or octopus. Thinly slice pork or beef. Combine the seafood and meat.
- Heat oil in medium nonstick skillet over medium-high heat. Lightly cook ¼ of the seafood and meat mixture.
- Pour ¼ of the batter with cabbage over the seafood and meat in the skillet. Cook like a pancake, 5 minutes on one side then turn over and cook for 3 to 5 minutes.
- Repeat with remaining batter and seafood and meat to make a total of four large seafood cakes.
- Serve hot with ketchup, mayonnaise, okonomiyaki sauce, pickled ginger or dried bonito flakes.

Variation:

Okonomiyaki is also commonly prepared and is very good with chicken, leeks, tuna or aonori (blue seaweed which tastes like dill).

Okonomiyaki, which translates to "cook what you like," are a cross between pancakes and pizza. At the many Okonomiyaki restaurants in Japan, the diners make their own pancakes on a griddle in front of the table, choosing from a selection of diced seafood, meat and vegetables.

*Okonomiyaki flour, a mixture of wheat and yam flour, can be purchased at Japanese grocery stores plain or with added flavorings. All purpose flour will work fine if it's not available.

Pasta, Rice & Vegetables

FETTUCCINE WITH CHIPOTLE SAUCE

Serves 4
Prep/Cook Time: 1 hour

*Chipotle chiles are ripened, dried and smoked jalapeño chiles. They are usually found canned in vinegar or an adobo sauce.

6   tomatoes
2   *chipotle chiles
Salt and pepper
1   teaspoon oregano
2   bay leaves
3   tablespoons olive oil
4   tablespoons vegetable oil
1⅓ cups (310ml) heavy cream
½   pound (225g) fettuccine
Parmesan cheese

- Broil tomatoes over an open flame or under oven broiler near the heater element until skin is blackened. Peel the skin from tomatoes.

- Blend tomatoes, chiles, salt, pepper, oregano, and bay leaves in a blender.

- Heat both oils and fry tomato mixture until water has evaporated.

- Add heavy cream.

- Meanwhile, cook fettuccine al dente in a large pot of boiling water. Drain.

- Serve chipotle sauce on top of fettuccine with Parmesan cheese.

GNOCCHI DI PATATE

Potato Gnocchi

1½ pounds (675g) boiling potatoes,
1   cup (140g) (+-) flour
⅔   cup (55g) freshly grated Parmesan cheese, optional

- Boil unpeeled potatoes in a large pot until tender, about 35 minutes. Drain potatoes and return to pan. Shake over moderate heat for a few seconds to dry.

- Cool to handle and peel potatoes. Force through a ricer or food mill set over a large bowl. Knead in ⅔ cup (100g) flour, then add remaining flour gradually, kneading until smooth and soft, but still a bit sticky. Add a little more flour if dough is too sticky to shape.

- On a well-floured surface with floured hands roll dough into ropes about ¾ inch (2cm) thick. Slice ropes at ¾ inch (2cm) intervals.

- Flour hands and work surface well again and flour a fork that has first been dipped in oil. Hold fork horizontally, parallel to the work surface, with convex side of fork facing you. Press a chunk of dough with a finger to the convex side of the fork, making little boats, with fork imprints on one side and a deep impression from the finger on the other. Let drop onto work surface and repeat until all gnocchi are shaped, re-flouring hands and fork after every 2 to 3 gnocchi.

- Bring a large pot of salted water to a boil. Drop about 20 gnocchi in to boil, cook until they float, about 1 to 2 minutes, and remove from water. Place in an individual serving plate and keep warm. Repeat with remaining gnocchi. Toss with desired sauce, add freshly grated Parmesan cheese if desired and serve.

Gnocco *in Italian means a small lump, and as a food refers to a little dumpling.* **Gnocchi** *are most commonly made of potatoes, spinach or Semolina flour and should be very light and airy. They are used as a pasta and are best if served with pesto sauces such as Pesto Povero (see index for recipe), cream sauces or a thick tomato sauce.*

PASTA BALSAMIC

Serves 3
Prep/Cook Time: 25 minutes

½   pound (225g) fettuccine
¼   cup olive oil
2   ounces (55g) mushrooms, sliced
2   cloves garlic, minced
½   ounce (15g) black olives, without pits, diced
2   ounces (55g) sliced Cappacola or smoked ham, diced
3   green onions, chopped
1   ounce (28g) sun dried tomatoes, chopped
2   small Roma tomatoes, diced
6   large basil leaves, cut julienne style
3-5 tablespoons balsamic vinegar
2   tablespoons Romano cheese

- In a large pot of boiling salted water, cook the fettuccine al dente and drain. Transfer the fettuccine back to the cooking pot.

- Heat oil in a medium skillet over medium-high heat. Sauté mushrooms, garlic, and olives for 1 minute. Stir in ham, green onions, and sun dried and Roma tomatoes and cook for 30 seconds.

- Add to fettuccine with basil and balsamic vinegar. Place in a large serving bowl, sprinkle with Romano cheese and serve.

Balsamic vinegar is a specialty of Modena, a province of northern Italy. It is made from the reduced sweet juice of white grapes and aged in a series of barrels made from various woods.

PASTA WITH ZUCCHINI AND WALNUTS IN A CREAM SAUCE

Serves 6
Prep/Cook Time: 30 minutes

Cream Sauce

 2 cups (475ml) heavy cream
 ½ cup (45g) freshly grated Parmesan cheese
 ⅛ teaspoon grated nutmeg
 Salt and pepper to taste

Pasta, Zucchini, and Walnuts

 1 pound (450g) zucchini, cut into 2 inch (5cm) matchsticks
 2½ tablespoons (40g) butter
 1 cup (115g) walnuts
 Salt to taste
 1 pound (450g) linguine (best if fresh)

- Boil cream until thick, reducing to about 1½ cups (350ml). Stir in Parmesan cheese and add nutmeg, salt and pepper to taste. Remove from heat and keep warm until tossed with pasta.

- Sauté zucchini with butter in a skillet over high heat for 1 to 2 minutes stirring constantly. Remove, drain and place in a warm bowl.

- Lightly toast the walnuts in the skillet over high heat, stirring constantly. Add walnuts to the zucchini and salt lightly to taste.

- Cook the pasta in boiling salted water until just cooked. Drain well.

- Toss pasta with cream sauce. Stir in the zucchini mixture and serve at once in warm pasta bowls or warm plates.

Variation:

1½ cups (350ml) of crème fraîche, which does not need to be reduced, may be substituted for the 2 cups (475ml) of cream. Green beans, basil, and garlic can also be substituted for the zucchini and nutmeg.

SOTANGHON

*Philippine Style Noodles with Chicken,
Mushrooms and Sautéed Vegetables*

Serves: 8
Prep/Cook Time: 40 minutes

The trick to
cooking the
noodles is to
wait until the
broth has reached
a full boil before
adding them.
They will cook
very quickly
and soak up
all the liquid.
The primary
flavor should be
of the fish sauce
and pepper.

6	boneless chicken breast halves
2	bay leaves
1	teaspoon peppercorns
1	large onion, quartered
3	cups (750ml) water
2	garlic cloves
½	cup (70g) onion, finely chopped
3	tablespoons vegetable oil
½	cup (30g) dried Chinese mushrooms soaked in warm water
1	cup (175g) julienne cut carrots
1	cup (150g) julienne cut leeks
1	cup (175g) julienne cut celery
½	pound (225g) cellophane (bean thread) noodles, soaked in warm water 30 minutes
¼	cup (60ml) patis or fish sauce

Salt and freshly ground black pepper to taste

• Put chicken, bay leaves, peppercorns, quartered onion, and water in a large saucepan. Bring to a boil over high heat, reduce heat to low and gently simmer 5 to 10 minutes until chicken is cooked. Let cool. Strain broth through a sieve and reserve. Remove chicken and cut meat into thin strips.

• Drain the noodles and cut them into 6 inch (15cm) lengths. Drain the mushrooms and cut into slices.

• In a wok or large skillet, sauté garlic and onion in oil until transparent. Stir in carrots, leeks, and celery and sauté for 2 minutes. Add mushrooms, chicken, and reserved broth. Bring to a boil and add noodles. Stir, add the fish sauce, salt to taste, and lots of freshly ground black pepper and serve.

GRILLED CHICKEN, VEGETABLES, AND GORGONZOLA FETTUCCINI

Serves 4
Prep/Cook Time: 1 hour

3   boneless chicken breast halves, grilled or broiled
6   tablespoons olive oil
1   garlic clove, chopped
1   large carrot, peeled and cut julienne style
1   leek, cut julienne style
¾   cup (185ml) white wine
1   cup (250ml) chicken stock
1   cup (235ml) cream
9   ounces (250g) *Gorgonzola cheese
½   pound (225g) fettuccini
1   large yellow squash, cut julienne style
1   large zucchini, cut julienne style
Salt and pepper to taste
3   Roma tomatoes, diced
½   bunch basil, coarsely sliced across leaves

- Cut grilled or broiled chicken breasts julienne style.

- In a large saucepan heat olive oil over medium-high heat. Add garlic, carrot, and leek and cook 30 seconds.

- Add wine and cook until reduced by half. Add chicken stock and cream and reduce until sauce consistency is reached.

- Remove from heat and stir in Gorgonzola. Set aside.

- Cook pasta in salted water until al dente. Drain.

- Reheat sauce just until bubbling and add yellow squash and zucchini. Cook for 1 minute. Add chicken. Remove from heat, toss sauce with pasta and season with salt and pepper.

- Garnish with tomato and torn basil leaves.

*Gorgonzola is best served very fresh and at room temperature. Fresh Gorgonzola has a creamy consistency and should be very white. Avoid cutting the cheese until you are ready to use it. Once cut, it will begin to dry out and yellow, therefore only the amount needed should be purchased.

Shortcut Tip:

Use a 10 ounce (280g) package of precooked sliced chicken breasts available in the poultry department of most supermarkets.

Spaghetti alla Carbonara

Serves 4
Prep/Cook Time: 30 minutes

12   slices of smoked or regular lean bacon
4   cloves of garlic
3   eggs
5   heaping tablespoons of grated Parmigiano-Reggiano (Parmesan),
      or Grana Padano cheese
4   tablespoons heavy cream
Salt to taste
Freshly ground black pepper
½   pound (225g) spaghetti
Additional Parmigiano-Reggiano cheese for sprinkling

- Slice the smoked bacon in thin strips and place in a medium nonstick skillet.

- Cook the bacon until a little fat is released and add the garlic. Continue cooking until the bacon is slightly crisp. Discard garlic and drain off any excess bacon fat.

- Beat eggs in a bowl. Stir in the Parmigiano cheese and heavy cream. Add salt and lots of pepper to taste.

- In a large pot of boiling salted water, cook the spaghetti al dente and drain. Transfer the spaghetti back to the cooking pot.

- Add the bacon pieces to the spaghetti and toss. Add the egg mixture. Mix well and cook for 2 minutes. Serve hot with Parmigiano-Reggiano cheese sprinkled on top of each portion.

Carbonara hails from Rome, which is known for foods with an earthy flavor. It is claimed that American soldiers stationed in Rome at the end of the Second World War requested bacon and eggs frequently and inspired locals to combine these beloved ingredients with their own pasta.

PHAD THAI
Fried Noodles Thai Style with Pork and Vegetables

Serves 4
Prep/Cook Time: 45 minutes

1   11 ounce (310g) package flat,
     narrow rice noodles
8   tablespoons vegetable oil
1   tablespoon chopped garlic
1   tablespoon chopped shallots
¼   cup (60ml) water
1   3-4 ounce (85-115g) boneless pork loin chop, trimmed of fat
     and cut into small slivers
1   cake firm soy bean curd, cut into small slices
1   teaspoon ground chiles
4   tablespoons sugar
3   tablespoons fish sauce
4   tablespoons rice wine vinegar
3   eggs (optional)
1   pound (450g) bean sprouts
⅓   cup (45g) Chinese leek leaves, or chopped green onions
Shredded lettuce
½   cup (75g) roasted peanuts, finely chopped
1   lemon, cut in 4 slices

- Soak noodles in hot water for 1 hour. Drain.
- Heat 3 tablespoons oil in a frying pan over high heat and sauté garlic and shallots until golden. Add noodles with ¼ cup (60ml) of water and cook, turning constantly with spatula to prevent sticking.
- Move noodles to the side of pan, or remove and set aside.
- Put 3 tablespoons oil into pan and heat. Add pork, bean curd, and dried chiles and stir. Return the noodles to pan and mix thoroughly. Add sugar, fish sauce, and vinegar and mix.
- Move noodles to the side of pan, or remove and set aside.
- Put 2 tablespoons oil into the pan and heat. Break eggs into the pan and scramble with spatula, making a thin layer of eggs over bottom of the pan.
- When the eggs are set, return the noodles and mix with the eggs.
- Add half the bean sprouts and half of the Chinese leek leaves and turn with a spatula to mix.
- Spread shredded lettuce on 4 serving plates. Spoon Phad Thai on top of the lettuce and sprinkle with peanuts, remaining bean sprouts and Chinese leeks, and a slice of lemon.

Variation:
Coconut milk may be used instead of ¼ cup (60ml) water.

Thailand was formerly known as Siam. The country was renamed in 1939 after the last of Siam's absolute monarchs had abdicated. The word **Thai** means free, thus Thailand means "land of the free."

Chicken and shrimp, alone or in combination, are also commonly found in Phad Thai and may be used instead of pork.

LINGUINI WITH SHRIMP, TOMATO, AND BASIL SAUCE

The flavor and fragrance of fresh basil begin to decrease as soon as it is heated. Therefore, for a stronger and richer basil flavor, stir in all the basil, except that to be used for garnish, only after the shrimp are cooked.

4	tablespoons olive oil
1	medium onion, finely chopped
4	cloves garlic, minced
8	fresh ripe medium tomatoes, chopped
6	sprigs parsley, chopped
20	basil leaves, chopped
1	teaspoon dried oregano
½	teaspoon salt
1	very small dried red chili pepper, finely crushed

Juice from 1 lemon wedge
| 1 | pound (450g) medium shrimp, peeled |
| 1 | pound (450g) linguini or thin spaghetti |

Chopped fresh basil for garnish
Olive oil for drizzling

- In a large skillet, heat 4 tablespoons olive oil over medium-high heat. Sauté onion until golden brown. Add garlic and cook until garlic is softened, 2-3 minutes. Add tomatoes. Cook on medium heat about 10 minutes, stirring frequently until a thick sauce forms.

- Add parsley, basil, oregano, salt, chili pepper, and lemon juice. Add shrimp, stir and cook until shrimp turn pink, about 4 minutes.

- Cook linguini al dente in a large pot of boiling water. Drain.

- Serve linguini in 4 bowls, divide sauce over the top, sprinkle with chopped basil, and drizzle with a little olive oil to taste (most people like a couple of tablespoons).

MIEN XAO CUA

Stir Fried Cellophane Noodles with Crabmeat

Serves 4
Prep/Cook Time: 10 minutes,
plus 30 minutes to soak noodles

5   ounces (140g) cellophane
       (bean thread) noodles
4   tablespoons canola or vegetable oil
5   shallots, thinly sliced
5   cloves garlic, chopped
8   ounces (225g) lump crabmeat, or
       2, 6½ ounce (185g) cans lump crabmeat
½   cup (125ml) chicken stock
1   tablespoon fish sauce
2   scallions, sliced
1   tablespoon chopped cilantro
Freshly ground black pepper
Lime slices, optional

• Soak cellophane noodles in warm water for 30 minutes. Drain noodles and cut in half.

• Heat oil in large skillet over high heat. Add the shallots and garlic and sauté until the edges begin to brown. Add the crabmeat and stir-fry for 30 seconds. Add noodles and stir-fry for 1 minute. Add the chicken stock and fish sauce and stir well. The noodles will start to become a little more translucent. Add the scallions and remove from heat.

• Sprinkle with cilantro and pepper and serve with lime slices.

This quick and easy dish is popular among the Vietnamese. It is usually served with a vegetable as part of a meal, or alone as an appetizer.

PENNE MARE E TERRA

Sea and Earth Pasta

The Italian name
for this dish,
which originates
in the regions
around Naples,
translates as "Sea
and Earth Pasta."
It is typically
prepared with
vegetables that
are cultivated
near Naples,
hence the earth
in the title and
the tuna and
anchovies
are the sea.

⅔	cup (100g) chopped onion
2	cups (500ml) beef stock
1	teaspoon tomato paste
3	slices lean bacon, cooked and chopped
¼	cup (60ml) olive oil
½	cup (125ml) dry white wine
½	cup (75g) frozen peas, defrosted
½	cup (125ml) water
1	5-6 ounce (140-170g) can of tuna in oil, drained
2	anchovies, chopped
1	tablespoon capers, chopped

Salt and pepper to taste

1	pound (450g) penne pasta
1	tablespoon (15g) butter, optional

• In a large skillet, cook onion in the beef stock. Add the tomato paste, bacon, and olive oil and cook over medium heat until all water evaporates and continue cooking until onions are golden.

• Add white wine and cook until wine evaporates.

• Add peas and water. Cook until peas are just tender, about 3 to 4 minutes.

• Add tuna, anchovies, capers, salt, and pepper. Warm until heated just through and keep warm while pasta cooks.

• Cook pasta al dente in large pot of boiling salted water. Drain, toss with butter, if desired, and top with tuna sauce.

ÄLPLERMAGRONEN

Rich Macaroni with
Gruyère and Potatoes

Serves 4
Prep/Cook Time: 30 minutes

11   ounces (310g) macaroni
2½ tablespoons (38g) butter
2   large onions, cut into rings and then in half
1   clove garlic, crushed
1   cup (235ml) cream
3   medium yellow potatoes, boiled in their skins
3   tablespoons whipped cream, optional
½   cup (60g) Gruyère cheese, grated
Salt and pepper to taste

- Boil the macaroni in salted water until al dente. Drain.

- In a large skillet, heat the butter. Sauté the onions until golden brown.

- Add the garlic and cream to the onions and simmer for two minutes. Add the cooked macaroni and mix well.

- Peel the potatoes and slice into ¼ inch (.6cm) slices. Add the potatoes, whipped cream, Gruyère cheese, salt, and pepper to the macaroni. Reheat and serve.

Variation:

Another method of preparing Älplermagronen is to first cook the onions until they start to brown and become slightly crispy. Remove from the pan and continue making the Älplermagronen. When serving, sprinkle with the browned onions and a little chopped parsley.

Älplermagronen is the Alpine farmers' macaroni and cheese and is a delicious example of why the Swiss are so well known for their cheese specialties.

PESTO POVERO

Poor Man's Pesto

Serves up to 12
Prep/Cook Time: 10 minutes

6	cloves garlic, or to taste
⅔	cup (100g) pine nuts
½	cup (60g) walnut halves
2½	tablespoons blanched almonds
1	cup (85g) freshly grated Parmesan cheese
4	tablespoons olive oil

- Place all ingredients in a food processor and blend until very smooth. This will make a very thick paste that can be stored in an airtight container for up to two weeks in the refrigerator or much longer in the freezer.

- When serving, remove a desired amount of the paste and add water to achieve the thickness desired for the particular pasta being used.

Variations:

More or less garlic can be used according to taste. Other nuts may be substituted for the ones called for.

Serve Pesto Povero with Gnocchi di Patate (see index for recipe) or other pastas. This pesto has a nice bite. Try using a little of the pesto, and then increase the amount according to taste. The number of servings depends on your preference.

Cook's Tip:

An easy way to keep extra amounts of pesto is to freeze it in an ice cube tray. This also works well with extra broth, tomato paste, or egg whites. Seal in air tight bags until ready to use.

Italy

SALSA BOLOGNESE
Bolognese Sauce

Serves 4
Prep/Cook Time: 45 minutes,
plus 1 hour to soak mushrooms

1/3 cup (25g) dried porcini mushrooms, chopped
1 cup (250ml) warm water
2 sprigs fresh rosemary
2 sprigs of fresh sage
1 celery stalk
1 medium carrot
1 small onion
2 tablespoons extra virgin olive oil
1/2 pound (225g) lean ground beef
1/2 pound (225g) lean ground pork
1 cup (250ml) red wine
1-2 tablespoons tomato paste
1 16 ounce (450g) can Italian tomatoes, chopped
Salt and pepper to taste

- Soak mushrooms in warm water for 1 hour. Tie fresh herbs together with twine.

- Coarsely chop celery, carrot, and onion in a food processor.

- Heat oil in a medium to large heavy pot over medium-high heat and sauté vegetables for 5 minutes.

- Add meat to vegetables and brown.

- Add red wine and cook until wine is evaporated.

- Reduce heat to medium and stir in tomato paste. Add tomatoes, mushrooms with water, herbs, salt, and pepper to taste.

- Reduce heat to low and cook sauce for 30 minutes. Remove herbs and serve.

For the best sauce, ask the grocery butcher to grind the meat fresh. Use a piece of London Broil, sirloin, or lean chuck and pork loin chops with the fat removed. Also, the sauce is best using tomato paste (in a tube) and tomatoes imported from Italy as there are no unwanted added ingredients. Most large grocery stores will have a couple of brands to choose from in the tomato section.

Bolognese sauce may be prepared in larger quantities and frozen.

TIROLER SPECKKNÖDEL

Tyrolean Bacon Dumplings

Serves 4
Prep/Cook Time:
1 hour 30 minutes

½ pound (225g) lean bacon
      (thick cut preferred), cut in small pieces
½ onion, chopped
3 tablespoons parsley
4 eggs
1½ cups (375ml) milk
¾ cups (105g) (+/-) flour
7 dry bread rolls, cut in small cubes

- In a small skillet, sauté bacon and onions until cooked. Drain fat and add parsley.

- In a large bowl, mix eggs with milk and flour.

- Add bacon mixture and rolls and mix well. Adjust with additional flour if necessary to make dough manageable. Let sit for ½ hour.

- Use two tablespoons to form dumplings into round balls about 2½ inches (6.5cm) across.

- Fill a large wide pot with about 4 inches (10cm) water. Bring to a gentle boil, and drop in dumplings carefully. Rapid boiling water will tear dumplings apart. Gently simmer uncovered for 20 minutes, adding water if necessary for dumplings to float.

Speckknödel is a specialty of Tyrol or Tirol. Tyrol, once an independent entity under the Counts of the Tyrol, is a beautiful mountainous region in western Austria and northern Italy. Traditionally Speckknödel is made with Bauernspeck, peasant's bacon. The Bergbauern, mountain peasants, living on the beautiful isolated slopes of the Tyrolean Alps, have made an art of curing bacon for the long winter months.

Serve these Tyrolean dumplings as a side dish with goose or duck and red cabbage, or as a main course with a cabbage salad.

Austria

RISOTTO ALLA PARMIGIANA
Risotto with Parmesan

Serves 6
Prep/Cook Time: 30 minutes

¼ cup (60g) unsalted butter
¼ cup (60ml) extra virgin olive oil
1 small red onion, chopped
2 cups (400g) Arborio Italian rice
2 quarts (1.9 liters) hot beef or vegetable stock
1 cup (85g) freshly grated *Parmigiano-Reggiano

- Melt butter and oil in a heavy large pan over medium heat. Sauté onion until light golden. Continuing to cook, add the rice and stir vigorously with a wooden spoon for about 2 minutes.

- Add two ladles or ½ cup (120ml) of stock and stir. When the rice begins to dry out, add more stock. Adjust heat to medium-low, and continue adding stock and stirring constantly as the rice absorbs it. Continue process until the risotto is tender to the center but the grains are still separate from the other grains, about 18 minutes. Do not let the rice stick to the bottom of the pan. Should the stock run out, add a little water. The risotto should be tender but, like pasta, al dente.

- Turn the heat off, and add all of the Parmesan cheese while stirring vigorously. Remove from heat. Let stand for 2 minutes before serving.

In Italy, risotto is served as a primo piatto, the course between an appetizer and the main dish. Risotto is uniquely Northern Italian and many regions pride themselves on their varieties of rice used.

*Using a top quality Parmigiano-Reggiano cheese is the secret of this rich pasta. The best Parmigiano-Reggiano has the name stenciled on the rind of the cheese and is produced in the Italian areas of Bologna, Mantua, Modena, or Parma, from which the name Parmesan originated. Grana Padano is another excellent choice and is slightly less expensive.

Fragrant Basmati Rice with Mushrooms

Serve Fragrant Rice with Makkhani Murghi Masala (see index for recipe).

*Basmati rice, which means "queen of fragrance" in Sanskrit, has an enticing nutlike flavor and aroma.

2   tablespoons (30g) butter
1   tablespoon vegetable oil
3-4 spring onions, cleaned and chopped
8   ounces (225g) fresh mushrooms, cleaned and sliced
2   cups (400g) *Basmati rice
8   whole cloves
2   cinnamon sticks
3¾   cups (935ml) chicken or vegetable stock

- In a 2 quart saucepan, heat butter and oil over medium-high heat. Sauté onions until translucent. Add mushrooms and cook until soft. When all liquid has evaporated from the onions and mushrooms, remove with a slotted spoon and set aside.

- Pour rice into the saucepan and cook over medium heat while stirring until golden, about 5 minutes. Sprinkle in cloves and cinnamon.

- Slowly stir in stock and return onions and mushrooms to pan. When mixture begins to bubble, reduce heat to low, cover, and simmer until rice is tender, about 15 minutes.

Variation:

Instead of mushrooms and cloves, try using 1 cup each of diced carrots and frozen peas, and 4 cardamom pods with the cinnamon.

Yellow Rice with Raisins, Cinnamon, and Saffron

Serves: 8
Prep/Cook Time: 1 hour

2½ cups (500g) rice
1   cinnamon stick
¼   teaspoon saffron
2   tablespoons (30g) butter
¼   teaspoon turmeric
2   tablespoons sugar
2   tablespoons seedless raisins

- Place rice in 5 cups (1.25 liters) of water. Bring to a boil.

- Add cinnamon stick, saffron, butter, turmeric, and sugar to water.

- Reduce heat to simmer, cover, and cook about 30 minutes. When rice is nearly cooked, add raisins and steam until rice is tender.

This is the traditional accompaniment for Bobotie (see index for recipe). It is also excellent with beef, lamb, or poultry dishes.

Crêpes aux Courgettes
Zucchini Fritters

Serves 6
Prep/Cook Time: 20 minutes

2 medium zucchini
3 tablespoons flour
1 egg
2 tablespoons sour cream
2 cloves garlic, minced
Salt and pepper to taste
Mixture of equal parts vegetable oil and butter for cooking

- Preheat oven to 200°. Place serving platter in oven to warm.

- Wash, dry and finely grate zucchini.

- Press grated zucchini between paper towels to absorb as much water as possible.

- Whisk flour, egg, and sour cream until blended. Mix in zucchini and garlic. Add salt and pepper to taste.

- Heat 1 teaspoon oil and 1 teaspoon butter (5g) in a medium skillet over medium-high heat. Drop by tablespoon onto skillet forming small pancakes. Cook each side 3 to 4 minutes. Remove to a warm platter and keep warm. Repeat process until all fritters are cooked. Serve warm.

Variation:

Crêpes aux Courgettes can be made in the Greek style by adding a little feta cheese, chopped dill and chopped mint.

SABZI BHAJI
Indian Stir-Fried Mixed Vegetables

Serves 6
Prep/Cook Time: 20 minutes

3   large carrots
½   pound (225g) green beans
¼   cauliflower
½   small cabbage
3   tablespoons ghee or vegetable oil
½   teaspoon black mustard seeds
8   curry leaves, optional
2   cloves garlic, minced
2   teaspoons finely chopped ginger
1   teaspoon turmeric
1   teaspoon cayenne pepper or 1 fresh red chile, seeded and sliced
1½ teaspoons salt

• Peel carrots and cut into matchstick strips. String green beans and slice
  diagonally. Cut cauliflower into small slices leaving some stem with the
  florets. Shred cabbage coarsely.

• Heat ghee or oil in a large frying pan and fry mustard seeds and curry leaves
  for 2 minutes, stirring. Add garlic, ginger, turmeric, and chile, and stir for 1 to
  2 minutes, then add carrots, beans, and cauliflower. Stir over medium heat
  until vegetables are half cooked, then add cabbage and continue to toss and
  cook for 5 minutes or until all vegetables are tender but still crisp. Sprinkle
  with salt, mix well, cover and cook for 2 minutes.

Sabzi Bhaji goes well with Turkey with Mint, Peas and Indian Spices (see index for recipe) and rice.

Cook's Tip:
Black mustard seeds add flavor to the oil as they cook, but do tend to pop and fly around like popcorn. Leave the top on for the first two minutes while shaking the pan.

TUSCAN ROASTED VEGETABLES

Serves 4
Prep/Cook Time: 45 minutes

Roasted vegetables are also excellent served cold over mixed field greens as an entrée or side salad drizzled with additional oil and vinegar to taste.

2   *small red potatoes, quartered*
4   *medium carrots, peeled and cut diagonally into ½ inch (1.3cm) slices*
1   *medium red onion, sliced into ½ inch (1.3cm) rounds*
2   *small yellow squash, cut diagonally in ¾ inch (1.9cm) slices*
3   *tablespoons olive oil*
½   *teaspoon Italian herb mixture*
1   *tablespoon balsamic vinegar*
Salt and pepper to taste

- Preheat oven to 450°. Spray an 13x9 inch (33cmx23cm) ovenproof pan with cooking spray.

- Place all vegetables in pan. Toss with oil and then sprinkle with herbs.

- Roast in oven for 30 minutes or until tender, turning half way through cooking time.

- Remove from oven, sprinkle with vinegar and season with salt and pepper to taste. Toss to blend flavors and serve.

Variation:

Red or green bell peppers can be added with other vegetables. Adjust oil and herbs according to quantity of peppers added and to your taste. Sweet potatoes, celery, turnips, zucchini, and parsnips are also excellent roasted.

Italy

KooKoo-ye Bademjan

Persian Eggplant Quiche

Serves 6
Prep/Cook Time:
1 hour 15 minutes

2   large eggplants
Olive oil for cooking eggplant and onion
2   onions, finely chopped
2   cloves garlic, chopped
6   eggs
1   teaspoon salt
1/4 teaspoon ground pepper
1/4 teaspoon saffron dissolved in 1 tablespoon water

- Preheat oven to 350°. Oil a 9x13 inch (23x33cm) ovenproof dish.

- Peel eggplants, slice lengthwise, ½ inch (1.3cm) thick, and soak in salted water for 1 hour until the water turns yellow and removes the bitter taste of the eggplant. Rinse and dry eggplant.

- In a large skillet heat a few tablespoons of oil over medium-high heat. Sauté eggplant slices until golden brown adding oil as needed. Remove from skillet and let cool.

- Mash eggplant with a fork or briefly in a blender.

- In the same skillet, heat 3 tablespoons oil. Sauté the onions and garlic until translucent.

- Place oiled dish into preheated oven.

- Break eggs into a large bowl. Beat thoroughly. Add salt, pepper and saffron. Add mashed eggplant and mix well. Pour mixture into the hot dish from the oven. Return to oven immediately, and bake uncovered for 45 minutes.

- Serve the kookoo in the baking dish or unmold it by loosening the sides with a knife and inverting onto a serving platter. It may be cut into small pieces and served as a vegetable side dish or appetizer.

Kookoo is an Iranian term for a vegetable or meat dish with beaten eggs, baked in the oven. There are various versions, using other vegetables such as zucchini and potatoes and cooking methods. Kookoo can also be cooked on top of the stove in the manner of Tortilla de Papas (see index for recipe.)

ALOO MERICH SABZI
Vegetable Curry with Potato and Peppers

Serves 4
Prep/Cook Time: 40 minutes

Curry Sauce

3	tablespoons vegetable oil
3	medium onions, finely chopped
2	cloves garlic, crushed
1	1 inch (2.5cm) cube ginger, peeled and finely diced
3	tablespoons canned crushed tomatoes
1½	teaspoons salt
1	teaspoon turmeric powder
½	teaspoon cayenne pepper
1	teaspoon *garam masala powder

Vegetables

3	medium red or yellow potatoes, cut into 1 inch (2.5cm) cubes
2	medium green bell peppers, seeded and cut into 1 inch (2.5cm) squares
2	medium red bell peppers, seeded and cut into 1 inch (2.5cm) squares

• Heat oil in a large, heavy, deep skillet over medium-high heat. Fry onions until deep golden. Add garlic and ginger. Cook for 3 minutes, stirring constantly. Add tomatoes, salt, turmeric, cayenne pepper, and garam masala. Cook for 2 minutes.

• Add peppers to sauce. Cover skillet and cook on low heat until potatoes are almost cooked, about 15 to 20 minutes. Stir frequently to prevent potatoes from sticking to pan. If they begin to stick, add 1 to 2 teaspoons of water as required.

• Add peppers to potatoes, stir thoroughly and cook covered on low heat for about 15 minutes or until peppers are cooked but still a bit crisp, and potatoes are soft. Serve hot.

Vegetable Curry with Potato and Peppers is a delicious vegetarian entrée. Serve with basmati rice and a cucumber yogurt salad such as Angourosalata me Yiaourti (see index for recipe). The technique of preparing a curry sauce first and adding vegetables to cook after can be used with almost any combination of vegetables.

*Garam masala is available in Indian markets and the international food section of some large supermarkets, or a recipe can be found in the index of this book.

India

WARM VEGETABLE TERRINE WITH MUSHROOM SAUCE

Serves 12
Prep/Cook Time:
2 hours 45 minutes,
plus 15 minutes standing time

Vegetable Terrine

½ cup (120g) butter
½ cup (70g) flour
1½ cups (375ml) milk
½ cup (60g) grated cheddar cheese
Salt and pepper to taste
8 eggs, lightly beaten
10 ounces (280g) broccoli, chopped coarsely
14 ounces (390g) cauliflower, chopped coarsely
4 carrots, diced

Mushroom Sauce

3 tablespoons (45g) butter
8 ounces (225g) mushrooms, sliced thinly
1¼ cups (300ml) heavy cream

- Preheat oven to 350°.

- Melt butter in a saucepan over medium-low heat and blend in flour until smooth. Stirring constantly, gradually add milk. Stir sauce over medium heat for 2 minutes until thickened and flour has cooked.

- Remove from heat and stir in cheese. Add salt and pepper to taste and cool for 10 minutes. Stir in eggs and set aside.

- Boil, steam or microwave vegetables until tender. Line a 5x8 inch (13x20cm) terrine with plastic wrap. Purée broccoli with ⅓ of the cheese sauce in a blender or food processor. Spread into pan and repeat process with ⅓ of cheese sauce and carrots and ⅓ of cheese sauce and cauliflower. Cover pan with greased foil and place it in a large roasting pan. Pour boiling water in the roasting pan until it comes halfway up sides of the loaf pan. Bake about 2¼ hours or until firm. Remove from oven and let stand for 15 minutes.

- Prepare mushroom sauce while loaf cools. Melt butter in a skillet. Add mushrooms and sauté for 5 minutes or until soft. Add cream and simmer until slightly thickened.

- Invert pan onto serving platter. Slice terrine and serve with warm mushroom sauce.

A beautiful tri-colored dish that is appealing to the eyes as well as the palate.

A terrine is a fairly deep dish with straight sides. Terrines come in a wide range of sizes. The food that is cooked or served in a terrine is also known as a terrrine.

PASTICHIO
Italian Layered Vegetable Tart

Serves 8
Prep/Cook Time:
1 hour 45 minutes

Pastichio *literally translates to "mess" and is used as a name, in Italy, for a dish which includes a variety of ingredients thrown together to make a luscious creation as the Italians can do with just about any food.*

Italian cuisine is probably the oldest in Europe. It is derived from Greek gourmet traditions, these being derived in their turn from oriental cuisine. A recipe for a Pastichio with meat can be found in many Greek cookbooks.

C r ê p e s
- 2   *eggs*
- ½   *cup (125ml) milk*
- ¼   *cup (35g) flour*
- ½   *teaspoon plus 2 tablespoons olive oil*
- *Salt*
- *Olive oil for cooking crêpes*

Z u c c h i n i
- 1½   *pounds (675g) zucchini, halved then cut in ¼ inch (6mm) slices*
- 1   *medium white onion, quartered and finely sliced*
- ¼   *cup (60ml) olive oil*
- ½   *teaspoon chicken bouillon granules, or ½ bouillon cube, chopped in small pieces*
- ¼   *cup (60ml) hot water*

B é c h a m e l   S a u c e
- 4   *tablespoons (60g) butter*
- 2   *cups (500ml) milk*
- ⅓   *cup, plus 1 tablespoon (65g) flour*
- ¼   *teaspoon nutmeg*
- *Salt to taste*

P a r m e s a n   T o p p i n g
- 1   *teaspoon olive oil*
- 1   *cup (85g) grated Parmesan cheese*

- Crêpes: Mix eggs and milk in a medium bowl. Sift flour into the liquid mixture and stir. Add ½ teaspoon oil. Strain out any lumps.

- Put 2 tablespoons oil in a large nonstick skillet and heat over medium-high heat. When hot, pour the oil into the crêpe batter, stir and take out any bits of cooked crêpe. Wipe skillet with a paper towel and put back on heat. Pour in ¼ cup (60ml) of batter, rotating skillet while pouring to spread. When crêpe is set, about 10 seconds, peel up the side with a knife and turn over by hand. Cook the other side 5 to 10 seconds. Crêpes can be made ahead and kept in the refrigerator in an airtight container between individual sheets of waxed paper for 3 to 4 days or frozen.

- Zucchini: Place zucchini and onion in a large skillet. Pour olive oil on top. Sprinkle bouillon on top. Cook for 1 to 2 minutes over high heat. Add hot water, reduce heat to medium, and continue cooking, stirring occasionally until zucchini is soft and cooked through but not tearing apart.

(continued on next page)

Pastichio *(continued)*

- Béchamel Sauce: In a saucepan, melt butter on medium-high heat. When melted, reduce heat to low and add flour while stirring to make a roux. Cook for 1 to 2 minutes. Add milk a little at a time while stirring. Return heat to medium-high. When milk begins to boil, reduce heat to medium. Stirring constantly, add nutmeg and cook 10 minutes.

- Preheat oven to 400°.

- Assemble Pastichio: Spread oil on the bottom of a 9 inch (22cm) round cake pan. Put 1 crêpe on the bottom, then cover with some zucchini and push down to make a flat layer. Add ½ cup (125ml) of béchamel sauce, some Parmesan cheese and repeat, ending with cheese. Bake for 35 minutes. Let sit for 15 minutes before removing from pan. Serve warm in slices like a pizza.

Variation:

Mushrooms are a delicious substitute for the zucchini. Use 12 ounces (335g) of mixed mushrooms (include some portobello), ½ cup (125ml) olive oil and 2 to 3 cloves of minced garlic. Sauté mushrooms and garlic in oil over medium-high heat for 5 minutes. Reduce heat to medium and cook 15 minutes, stirring occasionally.

Shortcut Tip:
Use an 8 ounce (225g) package of lasagna noodles, cooked al dente, instead of the crêpes.

Pastichio is also a lovely vegetarian entrée and makes a full meal for 4 served with a green salad.

Ybor City Vegetable Paella

Serves 8
Prep/Cook Time: 2 hours

This recipe is from the Ybor City area near Tampa, Florida where there is a thriving Cuban community. Traditional paella would have fewer vegetables, and cooked chicken, sausage, and shellfish would be cooked with the rice in the oven.

1	medium eggplant
⅓	cup (85ml) olive oil, plus 1 tablespoon if needed
1	medium onion, chopped
¾	pound (340g) zucchini, chopped in ½ inch (1.3cm) slices
½	pound (225g) mushrooms, quartered
2	medium tomatoes, chopped
5	cups (1.25 liters) chicken stock
2	cups (400g) rice
½	teaspoon crushed saffron

Salt and pepper to taste

1	14 ounce (396g) can artichoke hearts, drained
1	16 ounce (450g) can garbanzo beans, drained
1	3 ounce (85g) jar pitted green olives, drained
1	10 ounce (280g) package frozen peas (not thawed)

- Preheat oven to 350°.

- Cut eggplant in half lengthwise, then cut crosswise into ½ inch (1.3cm) thick slices.

- Heat oil in large ovenproof pan over medium-high heat.

- Sauté onion until tender. Add zucchini and mushrooms. Cook, stirring occasionally, until vegetables are golden brown.

- Add eggplant and 1 tablespoon olive oil if needed. Cook, stirring frequently, until eggplant is tender but still firm. Recipe can be made in advance to this point.

- Stir in tomatoes, stock, rice, saffron, salt and pepper. Heat to boiling over high heat.

- Place pan in oven. Bake uncovered until rice is tender and liquid is absorbed, about 50 minutes. Remove from oven, stir in artichoke hearts, garbanzo beans, olives, and frozen peas. Return to oven and heat through, about 15 minutes.

BLACK-EYED PEA BOURGUIGNONNE

Serves 4
Prep/Cook Time:
1 hour 15 minutes,
plus overnight to soak beans

6   ounces (175g) dried black-eyed peas, soaked overnight and drained
2   tablespoons vegetable oil
1   cup (165g) pearl onions, blanched with skins removed
1   clove garlic, finely chopped
1   cup (175g) sliced carrots, ½ inch (1.3cm) thick
1½ cups (375ml) red wine
¾ cup (185ml) vegetable stock
2   tablespoons tomato paste
2   bay leaves
2   tablespoons parsley, minced
1   cup (225g) button mushrooms
Salt and pepper to taste

- In a large pot, boil peas for 10 minutes. Drain and set aside.

- Wash and dry pot. Add oil to the pot and heat over medium-high heat. Sauté onions quickly until brown. Add garlic and carrots, and sauté for 3 minutes.

- Stir in black-eyed peas, wine, stock, tomato paste and herbs. Bring to a boil. Reduce heat, cover, and simmer gently for 30 minutes.

- Add mushrooms, and cook 20 minutes.

- If a thicker sauce is desired, mash a few of the peas. Season to taste with salt and pepper and serve.

This dish may be made ahead and is a delicious vegetarian version of the classic Beef Bourguignonne. Serve with boiled potatoes or rice and a full bodied young red wine such as Beaujolais, Côtes du Rhône, or Burgundy.

Gallo Pinto

Costa Rican Rice and Beans

Serves 4
Prep/Cook Time: 40 minutes

Gallo Pinto is a staple dish of Costa Rica. It is eaten for breakfast with tortillas and scrambled eggs, or for dinner.

*Salsa Lizano, a Costa Rican sauce, can be found in specialty food markets or substitute Pickapeppa sauce from Jamaica, which is normally stocked in larger grocery stores.

1	cup (200g) long-grained white rice
2	cups (500ml) water
1	large onion, chopped
1	yellow or red bell pepper, seeded and chopped
2	cloves garlic, chopped
2½	tablespoons vegetable oil
1	15½ ounce (435g) can of black beans, drained
4	tablespoons *Salsa Lizano
3	tablespoons fresh chopped cilantro

- In a medium saucepan cook rice with 2 cups (500ml) water.

- Heat oil over medium-high heat in a large skillet. Sauté onion, bell pepper, and garlic until just tender.

- Add black beans, rice, and Salsa Lizano, and stir frequently until heated through.

- Mix in the cilantro and serve.

RED BEANS AND RICE

Serves 6 to 8
Prep/Cook Time: 3 hours,
plus 12 hours to soak beans

1   pound (450g) dry round red beans
2-3 pounds (.9-1.35kg) ham hocks
3   medium onions, chopped
2   ribs celery, chopped
2   green peppers, seeded and chopped
3   cloves garlic, minced
2   bay leaves
Water to cover beans and 3 cups (750ml) water for rice
Salt and pepper to taste
4   tablespoons (60g) butter, optional
1½ cups (300g) white rice

• Clean beans and place in a large bowl. Add water to cover and soak in refrigerator overnight.

• Drain beans and discard water. Place beans in a large kettle or stockpot with ham hocks, onions, celery, green pepper, garlic, and bay leaves.

• Pour over enough cold water just to cover. Cover with lid. Bring to a boil. Reduce heat and simmer 2 to 3 hours, adding more water, if needed, to keep the beans from sticking.

• Cook rice in 3 cups (750ml) water.

• Remove bay leaves and discard. Remove 2 cups (340g) beans from the pot, mash and return to the pot. Stir well.

• Season well with salt and pepper. Add butter if desired. Heat until butter has melted. Serve hot with rice.

This is a Georgia and South Carolina version of a Louisiana specialty with the addition of flavorful ham hocks.

Cook's Tip:

Cooked dried beans are excellent food, are very nutritious as well as being high in fiber. If you have a problem digesting cooked dried beans, soak the beans in cold water overnight; drain in the morning and discard the water. Add fresh water to cook the beans, and when they are tender, discard that also. The enzyme in the beans which can cause stomach problems dissolves in the water and goes down the drain.

PARMIGIANA DI MELANZANE

Eggplant Parmesan

Serves 8
Prep/Cook Time: 2 hours

This recipe comes
from a beautiful
pensione on the
Island of Ischia
in Italy.
Two delightful
sisters who are
famous for their
cooking among
Neapolitan food
connoisseurs host
the pensione.
They graciously
shared the recipe
complete with
their secret
ingredient, the
cocoa powder.
The dish is not
complicated, but
does require time
to prepare and
is well worth
the effort.

3   pounds (1.35kg) eggplant
3   tablespoons olive oil
3   cloves garlic, crushed
1   bunch fresh basil, chopped
3   pounds (1.35kg) fresh ripe tomatoes, diced,
      or 3 pounds (1.35kg) drained canned plum tomatoes
4   egg whites
Vegetable oil for frying eggplant
1½ pounds (675g) fresh mozzarella cheese, thinly sliced
8   ounces (225g) Parmesan cheese, freshly grated
2   teaspoons of Dutch process cocoa powder
Salt and pepper to taste

• Preheat oven to 400°.

• Peel and cut eggplant in slices horizontally, approximately ¼ inch (.6cm) thick. Soak eggplant for 1 hour in cold water with a handful of salt.

• Heat olive oil in a medium-sized stainless steel or other non-aluminum pan. Add garlic and sauté until golden brown. Remove garlic. Add half of basil to olive oil in pan and quickly add the tomatoes. Simmer for 15 minutes. If fresh tomatoes are used, pass through a food mill when cooked. Season with salt and pepper to taste.

• Drain eggplant and pat dry.

• Beat egg whites until soft peaks form. Dip eggplant in egg whites and deep fry in hot vegetable oil until golden brown. Drain on paper towels to remove excess oil.

• Spread a few spoonfuls of tomato mixture on the bottom of a 15x9 inch (38x22cm) ovenproof dish. Add a single layer of eggplant, covering the bottom of the dish. Add a layer of mozzarella, sprinkle a few of the remaining basil leaves and some Parmesan cheese. Continue layering to the top of the dish ending with a layer of tomato sauce. Sprinkle with cocoa powder and Parmesan cheese. Can be prepared ahead to this point and refrigerated, tightly covered, up to 24 hours ahead.

• Bake 20 minutes. Remove from oven and let sit 15 minutes before serving.

LEEK TART

Serves 8
Prep/Cook Time: 1 hour

C r u s t

1	cup (140g) flour
½	cup (120g) unsalted butter, cut into small pieces
3	ounces (85g) very sharp cheddar, or Gruyère cheese, grated

Salt to taste
White pepper to taste

1	egg
1	teaspoon heavy cream

F i l l i n g

7	tablespoons (105g) unsalted butter
1	pound (450g) leeks, including the white part with 1 inch (2.5cm) only of the green, thinly sliced
¼	cup (60ml) water
½	cup (120ml) heavy cream

Salt
Freshly ground pepper

- Preheat oven to 350°.
- Sift flour into a large bowl and cut in butter with fingertips or knife or pastry blender until it looks like cornmeal. Add the cheese. Add salt and pepper to taste.
- Form dough into a ball, wrap in plastic wrap and refrigerate for at least half an hour.
- While the dough is chilling, prepare the filling. Heat half the butter over low heat in a large frying pan with tight lid. Add leeks and cover, cook slowly for 10 minutes. Add ¼ cup (60ml) water to pan, cover and cook another 5 minutes.
- Add remaining butter a little at a time. Do not let leeks brown. Push leeks to side of pan after they have absorbed all butter and moisture and there is no liquid left in pan. Add cream and heat slowly. Season with salt and pepper.
- Press chilled dough evenly into a 10 inch (25cm) tart pan or individual tart pans, pinching together any tears or splits in pastry. Weight crusts and bake about 10 minutes. Remove the weights. Prick the bottom and sides of crusts.
- Lightly beat egg with cream and paint crust with egg mixture. Bake for 10 minutes longer or until crust is lightly browned.
- Fill tart crust with leek filling and serve hot.

Variation:

For a lower fat Leek Tart, cook the leeks in 2 tablespoons (30g) butter and ¼ cup (60ml) of chicken stock, instead of 7 tablespoons (105g) butter.

U S A

Leek Trivia:

Leeks are native to Mediterranean countries, and have been prized for thousands of years. Nero believed leeks would improve his singing voice and is said to have eaten huge quantities. In the sixth century, the Welsh made leeks their national symbol and wore them on their helmets believing it would bring them good fortune and help them win wars.

ZWIEBELKUCHEN
Onion Tart with Bacon

Serves 8
Prep/Cook Time:
1 hour 45 minutes

Crust

2½	teaspoons dry yeast
½	cup (125ml) lukewarm milk
3¾	cups (500g) flour
¾	cup (180g) butter, softened
1½	teaspoons salt
2	eggs

Onion Filling

½	pound (225ml) thick cut lean bacon, cut in small pieces
4	large onions, thinly sliced
2	cups (500ml) Riesling wine
1	cup (235ml) cream
5	eggs, beaten
1¼	teaspoons salt
¼	teaspoon pepper
½	teaspoon cumin
½	teaspoon paprika
1½	cups (180g) grated Gouda or Edam cheese

- Mix yeast in milk. Add remaining crust ingredients and knead well. Put ball of dough in a bowl and place that bowl in another bowl full of cold water. When dough has risen, about 1 hour, roll out to fit on a large baking sheet about 12x18 inches (31x46cm) with an edge around it. Make a small lip around the dough edges to go up the edge of the sheet to hold in the liquid.
- Cook bacon in a large skillet pan until it starts to render the fat. Add onions, and cook until onions are translucent. Drain off bacon fat. Add wine, and continue cooking on medium heat until wine is almost evaporated, about 15 minutes.
- Preheat oven to 350°.
- In a medium bowl mix eggs and cream. Add salt, pepper, cumin, and paprika. Add bacon and onion mixture. Spread evenly over crust. Sprinkle cheese over the entire tart.
- Bake for 30 minutes or until filling is light golden brown. Turn oven off, and let sit for another 10 minutes.
- Cut into squares about 3x4 inches (8x10cm) and serve.

Variation:

The amount of wine can be reduced to ½ cup (125ml) as long as the onions are cooked slowly until soft.

Germany

TORTA DE LEGUMES
Vegetable Torte with Ham and Cheese

Serves 8
Prep/Cook Time: 45 minutes

4	large eggs
1	cup (250ml) cooking oil
3	cups (425g) flour
1	teaspoon baking powder
2	cups (300g) in total combination of diced cooked potatoes, carrots and peas
4	spring onions (scallions), chopped
½	cup (15g) chopped fresh parsley
½	cup (75g) chopped tomatoes
4	ounces (115g) grated cheddar, Swiss or jalapeño jack cheese
3	ounces (85g) cooked ham, cubed

Salt and pepper to taste

• Preheat oven to 350° and grease a 9x13 inch (23x33 cm) baking dish.

• Beat eggs in a large bowl. Add oil, flour, and baking powder. Add all remaining ingredients and fold together well. Pour batter into prepared dish and bake in center of oven until golden and just set, about 45 minutes.

• Cut into triangles and serve hot or at room temperature.

Variation:

This makes an excellent vegetarian entrée with the ham omitted.

This recipe is a wonderfully different way to serve vegetables and is simple to prepare. It is a great accompaniment with roasted or grilled meats and is also a good choice for a picnic with sliced meats or with barbecue. This recipe is Brazilian but is similar to Tortilla de Papas (see index for recipe) from Argentina.

SAUTÉED FENNEL AND ONIONS WITH FRESH THYME

Serves 4
Prep/Cook Time: 20 minutes

1   *large fennel bulb, or 2 small fennel bulbs*
1½ *tablespoons (22g) butter*
2   *tablespoons vegetable oil*
2   *medium red onions, thickly sliced*
2½ *tablespoons sherry vinegar, or red wine vinegar or balsamic vinegar*
3   *sprigs fresh thyme, chopped, or 1½ teaspoon dried thyme*
Salt and pepper to taste

• Trim stalks from fennel bulb, half it lengthwise, and cut into thin slices. In a large skillet, melt butter with oil over medium heat. Add fennel and sauté gently for 5 minutes.

• Raise heat to high, add onions and sauté, stirring frequently for 4 to 5 minutes, until cooked but still slightly crisp.

• Stir in vinegar, and, if using dried thyme, add thyme. Stir until vinegar evaporates. If using fresh thyme, add at this point and serve fennel or keep in a warm oven (200°) for up to 30 minutes, until ready to serve.

ENDIVES BRAISÉS

Sautéed Belgian Endive

Serves 4 to 6
Prep/Cook Time: 35 minutes

6   *Belgian endives, as white as available*
2   *tablespoons (30g) butter*
1   *clove garlic, minced*
Salt and pepper
¼   *cup (60ml) white wine*

- Wipe endives with cloth or paper towel to clean; do not dip in water.

- Cut a cone shape of about ½ inch (1.3cm) deep from stem end to remove most of the bitter part.

- Melt butter in a large skillet with lid. Place endives in butter and cook over low heat. After 10 minutes add garlic, and salt and pepper to taste. Cover and cook until soft and translucent, about 20 minutes, turning endives every 5 minutes while cooking. Add white wine and cook for 3 minutes more. Serve immediately or reheat and serve later.

The buttery endive is an excellent accompaniment for Involtini di Vitello or Filet à la Chantilly (see index for recipes) as well as grilled red meat and lamb.

For an attractive presentation, place endive in a decorative ovenproof dish, brush top with a little melted butter and set under a hot oven broiler until light golden. Sprinkle with chopped parsley and serve.

Fassolákia Yahní

Greek Style Green Beans
with Tomatoes and Fresh Dill

Serves 4
Prep/Cook Time: 40 minutes

Green beans cooked in this style are particularly good served with meat dishes such as Talas Kebabi or Lahem b'Ajeen (see index for recipes).

2   tablespoons olive oil
1   pound (450g) fresh green beans
1   clove garlic, chopped
1   large ripe tomato, chopped
1   large bunch fresh dill, chopped
Salt and pepper to taste

- Rinse, snap the ends off and remove strings from green beans.

- Heat oil in a 2 quart (2 liter) saucepan over medium-high heat. Briefly cook the garlic and chopped tomato for 1 to 2 minutes.

- Place chopped dill and green beans on top of chopped tomato. Do not stir at this point.

- Cover immediately and cook over low heat. Stir occasionally after 10 minutes of cooking. A tablespoon of water may be added if tomato juices evaporate to keep the vegetables from burning.

- Cook until the beans are tender, about 20 to 30 minutes. Season with salt and pepper to taste and serve.

Variation:

Two to three potatoes, peeled and quartered can be added with the green beans. Add ¼ cup water or more with the potatoes to maintain moisture while cooking.

PATACONES
Fried Plantains

Serves 6
Prep/Cook Time: 30 minutes

4   large green plantains, peeled
1   tablespoon salt
Vegetable oil for frying
Salt

- Slice plantains into ½ inch (1.3cm) thick rounds. Place plantains in a large bowl with enough cold water to cover them by 1 inch (2.5cm). Add 1 tablespoon salt to water and allow to soak for 20 minutes. Remove plantains to dry on a paper towel.

- In a large deep skillet, heat 2 inches (5cm) of oil over medium heat. Fry dry plantains in hot oil in batches until golden on each side, about 2 minutes per side. Then lift out and drain.

- With fist, a meat pounder, or bottom of a cup, pound the fried pieces between wax paper to about ⅛ inch (.3cm) thickness.

- Return plantain pieces to the hot oil and refry until crisp and golden, about 1½ minutes per side. Remove and place on paper towel.

- Sprinkle with salt to taste. Serve hot or cold.

Plantains can be purchased green or ripe and blackening. Buy firm green plantains for Patacones. A clove of minced garlic or paprika can also be used to flavor the chips.

Plantains are an ancient fruit native to tropical Asia. They are a popular snack, sliced and fried, in many parts of the world. They are known as Patacones in Colombia, Kluey chap in Southeast Asia, Matoke chips in Kenya, and Plantain chips and tostones in the Caribbean.

Colombia

CREAMY GARLIC MASHED POTATOES WITH ROMANO CHEESE

These would go very well with Keftéthes meatballs or Psari tis Skaras me Saltsa Politiki (see index for recipes) or with any grilled meat, poultry, or fish.

Serves 10
Prep/Cook Time: 40 minutes

2½ pounds (1.125kg) red potatoes, peeled or unpeeled
5 cloves garlic
2 bay leaves
7 tablespoons (105g) butter, melted
1 cup (250ml) milk
5 large basil leaves, chopped
2 teaspoons fennel seeds
1 cup (85g) Romano cheese, grated
2 teaspoons fresh ground pepper
Salt to taste
Basil leaves for garnish

- Cut potatoes in halves or quarters.

- In a large pot of water, combine potatoes, garlic, and bay leaves. Bring to a boil and continue boiling for 20 minutes or until potatoes are tender. Drain water and discard bay leaves. Transfer potatoes and garlic to a mixing bowl.

- Beat potatoes and garlic at medium speed with electric mixer until smooth. Slowly add butter and milk, mixing continuously. Add basil, fennel seeds, cheese and pepper. Add salt to taste. Place in serving dish, garnish with extra basil leaves and serve.

GALETTE
Savory Potato Tart

Serves 4
Prep/Cook Time:
1 hour 15 minutes

Puff pastry for two 10 inch (25cm) pie shells
2   medium yellow potatoes,
        peeled and very thinly sliced
Salt and freshly ground pepper to taste
1   bunch of parsley, finely chopped
7   pearl onions, blanched skinned and finely chopped
2   cloves garlic, finely chopped
1½   tablespoons (25g) butter, in 6 slices
⅔   cup (155ml) sour cream or to taste

- Preheat oven to 350°. Roll out half puff pastry and cover bottom of 9 or 10 inch (23 to 25cm) pie pan. Make sure the edge of the pastry hangs 1 inch (2.5cm) over the sides and cut off the extra length to form a circle.

- Layer half of raw potato slices on top of pastry. Sprinkle with salt, pepper, half of parsley, onion, and garlic. Add 3 butter slices on top. Repeat procedure.

- Roll out rest of pastry. Top pie with second sheet of puff pastry. Close edges tightly, and poke a few holes in the top pastry with a fork to vent steam.

- Bake for 35 to 45 minutes until light golden brown. Remove from the oven and let stand about 5 minutes.

- Cut along the edges of the top pastry with a sharp knife, lift pastry and spread sour cream over the potatoes. Put the top pastry back on and serve.

Variation:

For a flavor change, Boursin cheese, a white, smooth, buttery herb cheese, is excellent substituted for the sour cream.

The French galette probably dates to the Neolithic era, when thick cereal pastes were cooked by spreading them on hot stones. The hearth cakes, or galettes, evolved in the Middle Ages, with several regional varieties. Galettes are usually sweet, but are also often made in the French countryside with potatoes.

Galete may be prepared ahead and reheated, actually the flavor is better the next day.

LATKES
Potato Pancakes

Makes 26 latkes
Prep/Cook Time: 50 minutes

6 large yellow potatoes, peeled
    and coarsely grated
1 yellow medium onion, finely chopped
2 eggs beaten
2 tablespoons flour, or 1¾ tablespoons matzo meal
Salt and pepper to taste
Vegetable oil or olive oil for frying
Sour cream, optional
Applesauce, optional

While Latkes are served in Jewish homes throughout the year, they are an integral part of the celebration of Chanukah. Perhaps this tradition stems from the fact that the patties are fried in oil, representing the miracle of Chanukah, when a one-day supply of lamp (olive) oil lasted for the eight day rededication ceremony of the Temple of Jerusalem in 165 BC, after the temple had been desecrated by the king of Syria.

- Place ovenproof serving platter into oven and preheat oven to 200°.

- Place grated potatoes in colander and rinse under cold water to wash off the starch. Drain.

- Combine potatoes and all remaining ingredients except oil and mix well.

- Coat a 12 inch (31cm) heavy nonstick skillet with a ¼ inch (6mm) layer of vegetable oil, and heat over medium heat until a drop of water placed in skillet sizzles.

- Drop potato mixture by spoonfuls into skillet to form 3 inch (8cm) latkes. Fry on both sides until golden brown, turning only once so latkes do not become soggy. Remove latkes and place on paper towels on the heated serving platter to drain excess oil. Return platter to the oven to keep warm until all latkes are cooked. Serve alone or with sour cream and applesauce.

Variation:

Substitute a mixture of 3 carrots, 2 potatoes and 2 zucchini, all grated, for the potatoes.

Spicy Garlic Roasted Cheese Potatoes

Serves 6
Prep/Cook Time: 45 minutes

6   *medium yellow potatoes or 20 small red potatoes*
4   *cloves garlic, coarsely chopped*
1   *teaspoon salt*
⅓   *cup (85ml) vegetable oil*
½   *teaspoon cayenne pepper or more to taste*
¼   *cup (20g) fresh grated Parmesan cheese*

- Preheat oven to 375°.

- Scrub potatoes and slice lengthwise into 4 to 6 wedges (small potatoes can be left whole or halved).

- Crush garlic with salt, and then combine with oil, cayenne pepper, and Parmesan cheese.

- Toss potato wedges in oil mixture until evenly coated.

- Arrange on rimmed baking sheet.

- Bake for 30 to 40 minutes, or until tender and golden, turning occasionally.

Variation:

For herbed roasted cheese potatoes, substitute 2 teaspoons rosemary for the cayenne pepper.

Spicy Potato Rösti

Serves 6
Prep/Cook Time: 45 minutes

3   large boiling potatoes
Salt and pepper to taste
2   tablespoons butter
1   medium onion, finely chopped
1   green chile, finely chopped
½   cup (225g) cottage cheese
1½ cups (165g) grated cheddar cheese

- Boil potatoes in their skins until cooked enough to take the crispness out, about 10 minutes.

- Preheat oven to 375°.

- Grate potatoes and season with salt and pepper.

- Melt butter in a medium skillet over medium-high heat. Sauté onions until light golden, about 5 minutes. Add chile, cottage cheese and grated cheese and cook for 30 seconds. Add potatoes and mix well.

- Spread the mixture in a shallow ovenproof baking dish or pan. May be made ahead up to this point and refrigerated tightly covered up to 24 hours.

- Bake until crisp and brown on the underside and light golden brown on top, about 20 minutes. Cut into squares and serve hot.

Serve as a side dish, or with a salad of fresh field greens for a full lunch.

This recipe is an Indian adaptation of the famous Swiss Rösti dish, which originated in Berne, Switzerland. Rösti in Switzerland means "crisp and golden."

CLAPSHOT

Scottish Turnips and Potatoes

Serves 4
Prep/Cook Time: 45 minutes

1   pound (450g) potatoes, peeled
    and cut into 1½ inch (4cm) chunks
1   pound (450g) rutabagas or
    white turnips, peeled and cut into 1½ inch (4cm) chunks
2   tablespoons (30g) butter
Salt and freshly ground black pepper

- Put the potatoes in one pot and the turnips or rutabagas in another and cover both with boiling water. Reduce heat to low, season with salt and simmer covered until the vegetables are tender, about 15 to 20 minutes for potatoes and 20 to 25 minutes for turnips or rutabagas.

- Drain off the water and combine vegetables in one pot. Add butter. Season to taste with salt and pepper. Mash thoroughly and serve warm.

Clapshot is a popular Orkney dish. The Orkney Islands consist of a group of about 90 islands and islets in northern Scotland.

Orkney Islands, Scotland

KRAUTFLECKERL
Cabbage and Noodles with Bacon

Serves 4
Prep/Cook Time: 45 minutes

3   cups (170g) of *fleckerl or rotini noodles
¾ pound (340g) lean bacon slab,
      cut in ¼ inch (.6cm) cubes
1   teaspoon sugar
1   teaspoon paprika
1   teaspoon vinegar
2   large onions, chopped
4   cups (450g) finely shredded cabbage
Salt, pepper and sugar to taste

- In a large pot of boiling water, cook noodles until al dente.

- Sauté bacon until cooked through but not crisp. Remove bacon and reserve 3 to 4 tablespoons fat in the pan.

- Brown sugar in the bacon fat over medium heat. Reduce heat to low and add paprika and vinegar. Add onions and sauté over medium heat until golden.

- Add cabbage and salt and pepper to taste and cook covered until cabbage is tender, about 25 to 30 minutes. Add cooked noodles. Mix well and heat. Toss in cooked bacon, adjust seasonings to taste and serve.

Krautfleckerl is an old Austrian standby which is easy to prepare and actually much loved by children who don't seem to notice that there's a green vegetable in it. It is traditionally served as a meal on its own.

***Fleckerl noodles are twisted noodles similar to rotini noodles, which are more widely available in the United States.**

HORENSO GOMA-AE

Sesame Spinach

Serves 8
Prep/Cook Time: 20 minutes

4   bunches spinach, cleaned
      and large stems removed
2   tablespoons sesame seeds, slightly crushed
1½ tablespoons soy sauce
1   tablespoon sake (rice wine)
1½ tablespoons vegetable oil

- Bring a large pot of water to boil. Put spinach in boiling water for 1 minute.

- Drain and rinse spinach with cold water until spinach is cold. Gently squeeze water out of spinach.

- In small bowl, mix sesame seeds, soy sauce, sake, and vegetable oil. Pour sauce over spinach and toss lightly.

- Arrange spinach attractively on a serving platter. Garnish with toasted sesame seeds. Serve cold, or heat and serve warm.

An excellent side dish with Okonomiyaki or with Japanese Beef Tartare (see index for recipes) and short grain rice. This method of cooking also works for broccoli florets. Koreans have a dish similar to Horenso Goma-ae that uses a little sugar instead of sake.

Spinach Pullao

Indian Style Spinach Rice

Serves 5
Prep/Cook Time: 45 minutes

3 tablespoons (45g) butter
½ teaspoon cumin seeds
1 medium onion, chopped
1 green chile, chopped
2 cloves garlic, minced
1 teaspoon finely chopped ginger
3 cups (210g) fresh cleaned spinach, tightly packed
Salt to taste
3 cups (450g) cooked rice
½ cup (125ml) milk

- Preheat oven to 400°.

- In a large skillet over medium-high heat, melt 2 tablespoons (30g) butter and sauté the cumin seeds until they start to crackle. Add onions and sauté for 1 minute.

- Add chile, garlic, and ginger, and sauté for 1 minute.

- Add spinach and salt, and cook covered over medium heat until spinach is wilted. Add cooked rice, milk, and 1 tablespoon (15g) butter. Mix with a fork and transfer into an ovenproof dish.

- Bake for 15 to 20 minutes.

Serve with plain yogurt and mango chutney. Diced parboiled or grated carrots can also be added to the spinach.

Desserts

TIRAMISU

Serves 8.
Prep/Cook Time: 25 minutes,
plus 2 hours to chill

1⅓ cups (245g) sugar
6   eggs, separated
1   pound (450g) of mascarpone cheese
2   7 ounce (200g) packages of *biscotti Savoiardi
1½ cups (375ml) strong hot Italian coffee or,
          1 cup (250ml) coffee and ½ cup (125ml) Marsala wine or brandy
1-2 teaspoons cocoa powder

- Add sugar to egg yolks and mix well for 3 to 5 minutes until mixture becomes creamy.

- Add egg mixture to mascarpone cheese and mix for 5 to 10 minutes with an electric beater until sugar is completely dissolved.

- In a separate bowl, beat the egg whites until soft peaks form. Fold egg whites into the cheese mixture.

- Pour coffee in a shallow bowl. Quickly dip a biscotti Savoiardi in the coffee and place in the base of a medium glass bowl or 8x10 inch (20x25cm) pan, repeating until the bottom is covered with a layer of biscotti.

- Pour a generous layer of the cheese mixture on top of the biscotti.

- Add another layer of dipped biscuits and top with remaining cheese mixture.

- Sift cocoa powder over the top of the last cheese mixture.

- Refrigerate for two hours or more. Remove from the refrigerator 5 minutes before serving.

Note: Refer to the glossary for information regarding the safe handling of raw eggs.

Variations:

If you can't find Biscotti Savoiardi, you'll be very happy with this dessert using two 3 ounce (85g) packages of the airier American lady fingers, just dip them very quickly so they don't fall apart.

Tiramisu's origins go back to Sienna, where it once was called "Zuppa del Duca," or "The Duke's Soup." The dessert became very popular in Florence in the nineteenth century. Tiramisu literally translates to "pick me up." It may have been named Tiramisu because of the caffeine lift of the coffee, or maybe because it tastes so heavenly.

*Biscotti Savoiardi are Italian lady fingers that are dry and are best for absorbing the coffee and mascarpone for Tiramisu. They are found in the specialty cookie section of many supermarkets.

BREAD PUDDING WITH APPLE BOURBON SAUCE

Serves: 12
Prep/Cook Time: 2 hours,
plus overnight to set

Bread Pudding

1	pound (450g) French bread, 2 or more days old
5	eggs, beaten
2½	cups (585ml) (+/-) heavy cream
14	ounces (396g) condensed milk
½	cup (100g) sugar
½	cup (80g) raisins
2	teaspoons cinnamon
½	teaspoon nutmeg
1	banana (ripe), mashed
2	cups (490g) crushed pineapple
2	tablespoons vanilla
1	cup (240g) butter, softened

Apple Bourbon Sauce

1	cup (200g) sugar
1	teaspoon cream of tartar
3	tablespoons water
1	pint (473ml) heavy cream
1	cup (250ml) milk
1	cup apple juice
2	tablespoons corn starch
4	tablespoons water
2-3	ounces (60-80ml) bourbon
6	tablespoons butter

- Cut bread into ½ inch (1.3cm) chunks and place in a large mixing bowl. Add all remaining bread pudding ingredients, except butter. Mix well, cover and let sit overnight in the refrigerator. Add more cream, if bread is not well moistened.
- Preheat oven to 350°. Spread ½ cup (120g) butter on the bottom of an 8x8 inch (20x20cm) deep-dish casserole. Add bread mixture to pan. Spread remaining butter in small slices on top of bread mixture and cover pan with foil.
- Place the casserole in a larger pan which is filled with boiling water half way up the sides of the casserole. Be careful not to allow the water in the larger pan to get in the bread pudding. Place pans in oven and bake for 1 hour. Remove foil and continue baking until set, about 20 minutes. Pudding should be firm in the middle and light brown.
- Prepare sauce while pudding is in the last 20 minutes of cooking. Heat sugar, cream of tartar, and water in a large saucepan over low heat until golden brown, about 10 to 15 minutes. Do not simmer. Sauce will be bitter. Add cream, milk, and apple juice stirring constantly until smooth. Then bring to a boil. Reduce heat. In a small bowl, mix cornstarch and water into a paste. Stir into sauce. Simmer and stir sauce until thickened. Whisk in bourbon and butter, being careful now not to boil. Serve over warm bread pudding.

Bread puddings are based on a flavored custard cream and stale or dry bread to soak up the custard. The fruit in this pudding makes it particularly interesting. It would also go well with a caramel sauce. Using a brioche or challah instead of French bread gives a slightly different flavor and texture.

U S A

CRÈME CARAMEL

Serves 8
Prep/Cook Time: 1 hour,
plus 4 hours to chill

The beauty of Crème Caramel lies in the bottom of the pan, and is revealed when the pan is inverted. The golden top presents itself and the caramel sauce beautifully puddles around the custard on the serving platter. Crème Caramel is referred to in French as crème renversée. It is similar to Flan de Queso from Mexico and Bavarian Cream (see index for recipes).

Caramel Sauce

- ½ cup (100g) sugar
- 2½ tablespoons water from tap
- 2 tablespoons cold water

Custard

- 5 eggs
- 3¼ cups (810ml) milk
- 1 teaspoon vanilla
- ⅓ cup (65g) sugar

- Preheat oven to 350°.

- Place sugar in a small heavy saucepan. Cover with tap water. Do not stir, but tilt pan occasionally to ensure even cooking. Cook on high heat until bubbles appear, then reduce heat to medium. When the caramel sauce begins to turn brown, watch carefully to ensure it doesn't burn. Remove from heat as soon as it reaches a deep brown, about 8 to 10 minutes. While stirring with a wooden spoon, add 2 tablespoons cold water and continue stirring. When boiling dies down, pour the caramel sauce in a 7 to 8 inch (18 to 20cm) round soufflé dish and swirl to coat bottom.

- Prepare Custard: Place milk in the same pan used for caramel sauce and slowly heat to a boil.

- In a large bowl, whisk eggs. Mix vanilla and sugar into eggs. When the milk reaches a boil, gradually whisk milk into the egg mixture.

- Pour custard into caramel lined soufflé dish and place dish in a larger ovenproof dish or pan. Fill larger pan with warm water until water reaches half way up sides of soufflé dish. Bake 40 minutes in center of oven.

- Remove from oven and let cool. Refrigerate for at least 4 hours or up to 2 days. Just before serving unmold by running a rubber spatula around the edge of the soufflé dish and inverting onto a platter large enough to hold the caramel sauce that puddles around the sides.

Belgium

FLAN DE QUESO
Creamy Mexican Flan

Serves 10 to 12.
Prep/Cook Time:
1 hour 30 minutes,
plus 1 hour to chill

2   12 ounce (354g) cans evaporated milk
2   14 ounce (396ml) cans
        sweetened condensed milk
8   egg yolks
2   eggs
1   tablespoon vanilla extract
½   cup (100g) granulated sugar
1   tablespoon water

- Preheat oven to 375°.

- In a large bowl, mix together both milks, egg yolks, and eggs until well blended. Add vanilla and blend. Set aside.

- In a heavy small-sized pan, mix the sugar and water and heat on medium-high heat until dissolved. Continue heating, stirring constantly with a wooden spoon until a light caramel colored syrup forms.

- Pour sugar syrup into a 9 to 10 inch (22 to 25 cm) round cake pan or ovenproof dish. Immediately tilt pan quickly to cover the bottom evenly before syrup hardens.

- Pour milk mixture carefully into the cake pan over the syrup. Place pan in a larger pan and pour boiling water in the larger pan to reach about half way up the sides of the flan pan.

- Cover the cake mold with aluminum foil very tightly so water does not seep in. Place both pans in the oven and bake for one hour. The center of the custard should be soft, but not liquid. Check flan with a knife to determine when custard is sufficiently set.

- Place flan pan on a rack to cool. Turn over onto a rimmed platter, so that syrup is contained, and place in refrigerator for at least one hour to gel.

- Serve flan by the slice at room temperature with a spoonful of syrup as topping.

Flan de Queso is very rich and creamy and should be served in small portions. Garnish with raspberries for added color, if desired.

Cook's Tip
You will have better luck turning out custard such as this flan if you bake it in a metal container. The metal cools more quickly than glass and will release more easily.

MOUSSE AU CHOCOLAT
Classic French Chocolate Mousse

Serves 4
Prep/Cook Time: 15 minutes,
plus 3 hours to chill

A small amount of pepper actually enhances the flavor of chocolate and is an old practice. A Spanish recipe found from 1631 for a Pot of Chocolate called for 2 peppercorns per 100 cocoa beans.

6   eggs, separated
⅛   teaspoon salt
7   ounces (200g) sweet dark chocolate
½   cup (120ml) heavy cream
3-4 tablespoons sugar
Chocolate shavings for garnish

- Using an electric mixer beat egg whites with dash of salt until stiff but not dry.

- Melt chocolate over double boiler or in microwave. Place egg yolks in a large bowl and beat melted chocolate quickly into egg yolks.

- Fold a small amount of egg whites into chocolate mixture. Then fold remaining egg whites carefully into chocolate mixture, until no clumps of white remain, but be careful not to fold too much and deflate whipped whites.

- Pour into a single serving dish or 4 individual serving dishes. Chill at least 3 hours.

- Before serving mousse, whip cream, gradually adding sugar as cream thickens, until firm peaks form. Place a dollop of whipped cream on the mousse(s), and top with chocolate shavings.

Note:

Refer to the glossary for information regarding the safe handling of raw eggs.

Variation:

For a wicked, creamy chocolate mousse with a secret ingredient and a hint of coffee and bourbon, add 2 tablespoons melted butter, 2 tablespoons strong coffee, 3 tablespoons bourbon, and ⅛ teaspoon ground white pepper to the melted chocolate. Fold the sweetened whipped cream in after the beaten egg whites instead putting a dollop on top. Serve chilled topped with chocolate shavings. Let your guests have fun guessing the secret ingredient (pepper).

Gelatina de Cajeta

Mexican Caramel Milk Pudding
with Warm Walnut Sauce

Serves 10
Prep/Cook Time: 20 minutes,
plus 3 hours to chill

Pudding

1	cinnamon stick

Peel of 1 orange, in large strands, not grated

4	cups (1 liter) milk
2	10.9 ounce (310 grams) bottles or cans *cajeta
3	envelopes of unflavored gelatin
½	cup (125ml) warm water

Walnut Sauce

1	10.9 ounce (310 grams) bottle or can cajeta
½	cup (125ml) warm milk
1	cup (120g) coarsely chopped walnuts

- Combine cinnamon stick and orange peel with 4 cups (1 liter) milk. In a 2 quart heavy saucepan, scald over medium heat, about 10 minutes. Add 2 bottles of cajeta and mix well. Dissolve gelatin in warm water and blend well into the milk mixture.

- Strain the milk mixture, discarding cinnamon stick and orange peel, into a greased mold and refrigerate 3 hours or until firm.

- Place the mold in warm water for about 30 seconds and then turn the mold out onto a platter.

- Blend 1 bottle of cajeta with ½ cup (125ml) of warm milk. Stir nuts into sauce and pour on the gelatina at time of serving.

Variation:

Pecans or other nuts on hand may be substituted for the walnuts in the sauce.

Gelatina de Cajeta has a texture similar to flan, but is made without eggs and the cajeta adds a distinctive taste of goat's milk for those who enjoy the flavor.

*Cajeta can be found in most international or Latin markets and is also sold made with cow's milk for those who do not care for the taste of goat's milk. Cajeta is used in Mexico and in some South American countries in desserts or as a topping for ice cream or fruit.

Pastel de Tres Leches
Three Milk Cake

Serves 12
Prep/Cook Time: 45 minutes

Tres Leches
means "three
milks" in Spanish.
Tres Leches cake
is a deliciously
rich dessert that
has been served
for generations
in Cuba and
Central American
countries.
The cake is very
wet and very rich.

6	eggs
1	teaspoon vanilla
1	cup (200g) sugar
1	cup (140g) flour
1	teaspoon baking powder
1	cup (235ml) whipping cream
1	12 ounce (354ml) can evaporated milk
1	14 ounce (396g) can sweetened condensed milk

• Preheat oven to 350°. Spray 9x13 inch (23x33cm) pan with cooking spray.

• Separate eggs. With an electric beater, beat whites until stiff peaks form. Add vanilla. Slowly beat in sugar and then yolks.

• Mix together flour and baking powder. Slowly beat into egg mixture.

• Pour batter in prepared pan. Bake for 20 to 30 minutes, or until cake is golden on top.

• While the cake is baking, whip the cream for one minute in a medium to large bowl with an electric beater. Blend in evaporated milk and condensed milk.

• When the cake comes out of the oven, immediately pour the milk mixture in a slow steady stream over the top and around the sides of cake as it pulls away from the pan. The idea is to drench the cake, which is very light, with the milks. Refrigerate overnight and serve directly from the pan in 1¼ inch (3cm) square slices. The slices will have absorbed most of the milk mixture, but will still be very wet.

226

Cuba / Central America

ROTE GRÜTZE

Red Fruit Pudding

3   10 ounce (280g) packages frozen fruit,
        such as raspberries, strawberries, blackberries
3   tablespoons sugar
Juice of ¾ lemon
3   cups (750ml) cherry or black current juice
½   cup (50g) cornstarch
Handful of fresh blueberries of raspberries, optional
2   cups (500ml) Southern Custard Sauce, (see index for recipe)

• Put all frozen fruit in a large pot. Add sugar, lemon juice and 2 cups (500ml) of fruit juice. Heat on medium-high heat until liquid begins to boil. Add fresh berries if using.

• Mix cornstarch with remaining 1 cup (250ml) fruit juice. Gently stir into berry mixture. Keep stirring until mixture thickens. Refrigerate in a large serving bowl until cooled down, about 3 hours.

• Serve Southern Custard Sauce in a glass decanter. Pour fruit pudding on top and serve.

Variation:

Blueberries and red currants can be added to the raspberries, strawberries and blackberries, although the mixture should be heavily balanced towards the red fruits. Also fresh fruit can be used instead of frozen.

Rote Grütze comes from northern Germany. It can be eaten on top of ice cream or pancakes. The recipe is very quick and doubles easily.

Shortcut Tip:
Instead of preparing the Southern Custard Sauce, use a packaged custard sauce, which is made by mixing a powder with milk.

BAYERISCHE CRÈME

Bavarian Cream

Bavarian cream is much like a vanilla mousse, but it contains gelatin.

The French name of bavarois was given to this dish by French chefs while in the service of the royal family in Bavaria.

1	tablespoon unflavored gelatin
¼	cup (60ml) water
1	cup (250ml) milk
½	cup (100g) sugar
⅛	teaspoon salt
1	teaspoon vanilla
1	cup (235ml) heavy cream
4	egg yolks
1	tablespoon Amaretto
2	tablespoons chocolate sprinkles, or semi sweet chocolate shavings

- In a measuring cup or small bowl stir gelatin into water. Set aside.
- Scald milk in a saucepan with ¼ cup (50g) of sugar, salt, and vanilla while stirring.
- Whip cream until soft peaks form and set aside.
- Beat egg yolks and ¼ cup (50g) sugar and combine with milk mixture. Cook over medium-low heat until mixture begins to thicken. Do not let mixture boil.
- Remove from heat and mix in gelatin.
- Place saucepan with milk mixture in a large bowl filled with ice to cool.
- As soon as the mixture cools, but before it begins to set, add Amaretto and fold in whipped cream.
- Pour into 4 individual serving dishes and chill in refrigerator for at least 30 minutes. Garnish with chocolate sprinkles, or shavings and serve.

Rijstpap or Riz au Lait

Rice Pudding

Serves 8.
Prep/Cook Time: 1 hour,
plus 3 hours to chill

1½ cups (300g) short grain rice
7 cups (1.75 liters) milk
½ tablespoon (8g) butter
⅛ teaspoon salt
1 vanilla pod or 1 teaspoon vanilla extract
⅔ cup (125g) sugar
2 eggs, separated
Light brown sugar

- Bring rice, milk, butter, salt, and vanilla to a boil on medium-low heat, stirring occasionally.

- Reduce heat to low and cook approximately 30 minutes. When rice is nearly cooked, add sugar and continue to cook, stirring often, until rice is completely cooked.

- Let it cool down until warm, not hot, stirring occasionally.

- Add the egg yolks, one at a time, stirring well.

- In a separate bowl, beat the egg whites until stiff but not dry and fold into the rice mixture.

- Chill at least 3 hours. Serve cold with brown sugar sprinkled on top according to taste.

Note:

Refer to glossary for information regarding the safe handling of raw eggs.

This luscious rice pudding is very popular throughout Belgium, particularly in the northern Dutch speaking area, Flanders, where it originated. In Flanders this dessert is known as rijstpap, but in other areas of Belgium it is known as riz au lait.

Belgium has three official languages. Dutch is spoken in Flanders, the northern area; French is spoken in Wallonia, the southern area; and German is spoken in a small southeastern area of Belgium.

APFELKUCHEN
Apple and Cream Shortcake with Almonds

Serves: 10
Prep/Cook Time:
1 hour 45 minutes

A tradition in Germany is to spend a weekend afternoon with friends and family walking in the woods. Afterwards, everyone gathers for cake and coffee. This cake is most popular in the fall months when the apples are fresh.

Shortcake

2	cups (285g) flour
½	cup (100g) sugar
1	egg
10½	tablespoons (160g) butter, at room temperature

Apple and Cream Filling

6-7	firm apples, Granny Smith, Braeburn, Fiji
	Juice of 1 lemon
10½	tablespoons (160g) butter, at room temperature
½	cup (100g) sugar
1	egg
	Peel of 1 lemon, grated
¾	cup (105g) flour
1	cup (235ml) whipping cream
½	cup (50g) slivered almonds

- Mix together all shortcake ingredients with a mixer and knead until the dough is a smooth consistency. Refrigerate for 30 minutes.

- Roll ⅔ of the dough to fit the bottom of a 10 inch (25cm) springform cake pan and place it in the bottom of the pan. Roll the remaining dough in a long strip to fit 1 inch (2.5cm) up the side of the pan all the way around. Refrigerate the shortcake while preparing the filling.

- Peel, core and cut apples in quarters. Sprinkle with lemon juice. Place in a tight circle pattern on the dough in the bottom of the pan.

- Preheat oven to 350°.

- With electric beater, beat butter, sugar, egg, and lemon peel for filling until foamy. Add flour, mix only until blended.

- Whip the cream until stiff and fold into the batter. Pour evenly over the apples and sprinkle with almond slivers.

- Bake for 1 hour or until golden. Let cool in the pan. Serve with vanilla ice cream or whipped cream.

Germany

BLITZKUCHEN

German Lightning Cake

Serves 6
Prep/Cook Time: 30 minutes

T o p p i n g

¼   cup (50g) sugar
4   tablespoons (60g) butter, cut into small pieces
⅓   cup (40g) chopped pecans, or other nuts

C a k e

½   cup (120g) salted butter, at room temperature
½   cup (120g) unsalted butter, at room temperature
¾   cup (150g) sugar
1   teaspoon vanilla
4   eggs
2   cups (285g) flour
1   teaspoon baking powder

- Preheat oven to 400°. Grease a 9x13 inch (23x33cm) pan.

- To prepare topping, cut sugar into butter pieces with a fork. Mix in nuts.

- In a large bowl, beat together butter and sugar. Mix in vanilla extract and eggs.

- In a medium bowl, combine flour and baking powder. Stir into the egg and sugar mixture.

- Pour mixture into greased pan and sprinkle with topping.

- Place cake on the middle rack of oven and bake 15 to 20 minutes until done.

Blitz means "lightning" in German. This cake is easy and lightning fast to make.

Cook's Tip:
Baking powder loses its effectiveness over time. If you have some on hand of unknown age, a quick way to see if it will still do the job is to put ½ teaspoon of baking powder into ¼ cup (60ml) of hot tap water. If the water bubbles, the baking powder is still fresh enough to use.

WORLD'S UGLIEST CAKE

Chocolate Meringue Mousse Cake

Serves 12
Prep/Cook Time:
1 hour 45 minutes,
plus 4 hours to chill

This divine dessert should have a free form rather than a set look. If you're artistic decorating the top, it'll be beautiful, if not, it might live up to its name. Either way, you will love this cake.

Meringue

5	egg whites
1/8	teaspoon cream of tartar
3/4	cup (150g) granulated sugar
1¾	cups (200g) powdered sugar
1/3	cup (40g) unsweetened cocoa powder

Mousse

13	ounces (365g) semi-sweet chocolate
7	egg whites
1/4	teaspoon cream of tartar
3	cups (750ml) heavy cream, well chilled
1½	teaspoons vanilla

- In a large bowl, beat 5 egg whites with cream of tartar until they hold soft peaks. Beat in granulated sugar, 2 tablespoons at a time, beating until all sugar is incorporated and the meringue holds very stiff peaks. Sift powdered sugar and cocoa powder together and fold into meringue.

- Preheat oven to 200°. Using an inverted 8 inch (20cm) square pan as a guide, trace three 8 to 8½ inch (20 to 21cm) squares onto sheets of parchment paper and set them on 3 cookie sheets. Spread meringue evenly among the squares taking out to the traced edges.

- Bake meringues about 1 hour. Turn off the oven, open the door and let meringues sit in the oven for 5 minutes. Take the baking sheets from the oven and let cool. Remove the parchment paper when cool.

- In a double boiler set over hot water, melt semi-sweet chocolate. Let cool to lukewarm.

- In a large bowl, beat 7 egg whites with cream of tartar until stiff peaks form.

- In a separate bowl, beat cream with vanilla until stiff peaks form. Gently fold chocolate into the egg whites and then gently fold in the cream.

- Put 1 meringue on a cake platter and spread it thickly with 1/3 of the chocolate mousse. Top the mousse with the second meringue and repeat with second layer of mousse. Top with the last meringue. Transfer the remaining mousse to a pastry bag fitted with a decorative tip and decorate the top of the cake. Chill lightly covered for 4 hours to 48 hours.

U S A

CHOCOLATE TORTILLA CAKE WITH SOUR CREAM FROSTING

Serves 10
Prep/Cook Time: 20 minutes,
plus 24 hours to refrigerate

5   tablespoons powdered sugar
20   ounces (590ml) sour cream
1   12 ounce (355ml) bag semi-sweet chocolate chips, melted and cooled
5   8 inch (20cm) flour tortillas
1   pint (225g) fresh strawberries, halved, optional

- In a small bowl, mix 3 tablespoons powdered sugar and 10 ounces (295ml) of sour cream until smooth for sour cream frosting. Set aside.

- In a medium bowl combine remaining sour cream and powdered sugar. Beat in cooled melted chocolate until smooth. Make sure the chocolate is cool so it won't clump.

- Place 1 tortilla on a serving plate. Spoon ¼ of the chocolate mixture in the center of the tortilla, spreading evenly until ¼ inch (.6cm) from the edge. Cover with the next tortilla and repeat with chocolate mixture. Layer remaining tortillas in the same manner, ending with a plain tortilla on top.

- Frost the top and sides of the tortilla layers by pouring sour cream frosting on top and working outward, making sure entire surface is covered. Avoid getting any chocolate in the frosting. Wipe off any frosting that drops on the serving plate.

- Refrigerate, covered for 24 hours. While still chilled, cut into thin wedges using a very sharp knife. Serve chilled, garnished with strawberry halves if desired.

This is a pretty and rich dessert that compliments a spicy meal. It is best served in thin slices

Chocolate Trivia:

The word chocolate comes from the Aztec word xocolatl, *meaning bitter water. The Spanish explorer Cortes introduced this fabulous find, chocolate, to Europe in 1519. For almost 300 years after its introduction into Europe, chocolate was thought of as a drink. Only in the nineteenth century was it to be mass-produced in block form for eating. West Africa is now the main producer of Chocolate.*

U S A

ENGLISH BUTTER CAKE

Serves 10
Prep/Cook Time: 1 hour

1½ cups (360g) butter, softened
3   cups (600g) sugar
6   eggs
1   tablespoon baking powder
2   teaspoons salt
3¾ cups (500g) flour
1½ cups (375ml) milk

- Preheat oven to 350°. Grease and flour a Bundt or tube pan or three 9 inch (23cm) round cake pans.

- In a large bowl, cream butter with sugar. Add eggs, one at a time.

- Combine baking powder, salt, and flour in a medium bowl.

- Add flour mixture and milk to butter mixture in an alternating fashion.

- Pour batter into prepared pan(s) and bake until done, about 45 minutes for a Bundt or tube pan or 35 minutes for layer cake pans. Remove when the cake pulls away from the sides of the pan and springs back when touched.

Layer this moist cake with Lemon Curd (see index for recipe) or with sweetened whipped cream and sliced strawberries. Serve with a cup of Earl Grey or Darjeeling tea. As it holds its shape well, English Butter Cake is also perfect for cutting into shapes and decorating for a child's birthday party or a holiday such as Valentine's Day.

England

HERSHEY BAR CAKE

Serves 10
Prep/Cook Time: 2 hours

6   ounces (170g) Hershey's chocolate candy bars
2½   cups (355g) flour
½   teaspoon baking soda
¼   teaspoon salt
1   cup (240g) unsalted butter
2   cups (400g) sugar
4   eggs
1   cup (250ml) buttermilk
2   teaspoons vanilla
1   5½ ounce (154g) can chocolate syrup
1   cup (115g) chopped pecans

• Preheat oven to 300°. Coat tube pan with cooking oil spray.

• Melt chocolate bars over double boiler or in microwave.

• Sift flour with baking soda and salt.

• In a mixing bowl, cream butter and sugar until light and fluffy. Beat in eggs one at a time. Stir in melted chocolate, buttermilk, vanilla, flour mixture, and syrup. Stir in pecans.

• Pour into prepared tube pan and bake in center of oven for 1½ hours or until a toothpick inserted in the center comes out clean.

In the late 1800s, chocolate was expensive and made in fancy designs meant for candy boxes. Milton Hershey adopted modern methods, and in 1900 began mass producing simple chocolate bars in Lancaster, Pennsylvania, at prices the public could afford. Any good quality chocolate will work equally well in this cake.

U S A

TANT MARTAS SOCKERKAKA
Aunt Marta's Sugar Cake

Serves 12
Prep/Cook Time: 1 hour

1¼ cups (240g) granulated white sugar
1¼ cups (175g) unbleached flour
2   teaspoons baking powder
10 tablespoons (150g) butter
⅔   cup (150ml) water
2   eggs
1   teaspoon vanilla
Powdered sugar for sifting on top

- Preheat oven to 350°. Grease and flour an 8 inch (20cm) spring form pan.

- Sift together sugar, flour, and baking powder in a large bowl.

- In a saucepan, melt butter over low heat. Add water and quickly bring to a boil. Remove from heat and let cool 2 to 4 minutes.

- Mix liquid mixture into the dry ingredients. Blend in eggs and vanilla. Pour into prepared pan and bake for 30 to 40 minutes or until cake is golden and toothpick comes out clean.

- Sift powdered sugar over cake while it is still warm.

This is a light, simple cake that Swedes enjoy at a coffee break or for dessert. Fresh berries and Crème Chantilly are a nice accompaniment.

Crème Chantilly

1 cup (235ml) heavy whipping cream
1 tablespoon powdered sugar
½ teaspoon vanilla

Whip cream until soft peaks form. Sprinkle powdered sugar into cream and whip again until peaks are just becoming stiff.

LEMON GLAZED CAKE

Makes 1 loaf
Prep/Cook Time:
1 hour 10 minutes

Cake

6	tablespoons (75g) shortening, at room temperature
1	cup (200g) sugar
2	eggs, at room temperature
1½	cups (215g) flour
2	teaspoons baking powder
¼	teaspoon salt
½	cup (125ml) milk, at room temperature
	Zest of 1 lemon
½	cup (65g) chopped walnuts, chopped, optional

Lemon Glaze

1	cup (115g) powdered sugar
4	tablespoons lemon juice

- Preheat oven to 350° and butter a 9 inch (23cm) loaf pan.

- Combine flour, baking powder, and salt.

- Cream shortening and sugar in a large bowl. Beat in eggs one at a time until well combined.

- Alternately add flour mixture and milk, mixing just to combine after each addition. Stir in lemon zest and nuts if desired.

- Pour batter into loaf pan and bake 50 to 60 minutes or until a toothpick inserted into the center comes out clean.

- About 5 minutes before loaf is finished baking, prepare the glaze. Beat lemon juice and powdered sugar in a small bowl.

- Remove lemon loaf from the oven and make a few holes in the top using a skewer. Drizzle glaze over the top and let the glaze soak in. Serve warm or cold.

Cook's Tip:

After pouring cake batter in the pan, lift the pan about 5 inches (12cm) above the counter and drop it gently. This will dislodge the air bubbles in the batter, which would otherwise bake into the finished cake as holes. Don't do this with angel food or other chiffon cakes.

England

TORTA DI RISO DELLA NONNA
Grandma's Rice Cake

Serves 12
Prep/Cook Time:
1 hour 45 minutes

This is a traditional cake from the Bologna region of Italy. It has a delicate and interesting flavor and is usually prepared in the winter months. This cake is also often made with finely diced candied fruits added with the crushed almonds, making an Italian fruitcake.

1   quart (946ml) whole milk
⅔   cup (135g) short grain rice
1   cup (200g) sugar
Peel of 1 large lemon in large pieces
⅓   cup (50g) almonds
4   eggs, slightly beaten
2   teaspoons vanilla

- Place milk, rice, sugar, and lemon peel in a 2 quart (2 liter) saucepan that has a lid. Turn stove to medium and heat uncovered until milk begins to simmer. Reduce heat to low, cover, and cook 30 minutes or until rice is cooked, stirring occasionally. Remove from heat and let rest until all liquid is absorbed and rice is cool. Remove lemon peel.

- Preheat oven to 325°. Butter a round or square 9 inch (23cm) baking pan.

- Chop almonds finely in food processor or crush with a rolling pin.

- Stir eggs into rice. Add almonds and vanilla and mix well.

- Pour batter into greased pan and bake for 1 hour or until cake just begins to turn golden. Cool and serve at room temperature or cold. Traditionally served cut into 1½ by 2 inch (4 by 5cm) lozenges (diamonds).

KAISERSCHMARRN
The Kaiser's Pancakes

Serves 6
Prep/Cook Time: 30 minutes
plus 30 minutes to soak raisins

2 tablespoons raisins
4 tablespoons rum
4 egg yolks
¼ cup (50g) sugar
⅛ teaspoon salt
2 cups (500ml) milk
⅛ teaspoon vanilla
1 cup (140g) flour
5 egg whites
¼ cup (60g) butter
Powdered sugar for garnish

- Soak raisins in rum for ½ hour.

- Beat egg yolks, sugar, and salt until creamy. Add milk and vanilla, mixing well. Gradually mix in flour.

- Drain rum from raisins and discard. Fold raisins into pancake batter.

- Beat egg whites until stiff peaks form and fold into the batter.

- Melt one tablespoon butter over low heat in a heavy skillet. Pour in ½ batter and cook 4 minutes over low heat until bottom is golden brown. Turn and brown other side. Remove from pan and repeat with remaining batter.

- Tear pancakes with a fork into 6 to 8 pieces each.

- Melt remaining butter over medium heat in skillet and fry pieces well, turning frequently. Pile on a serving plate and dust with powdered sugar. Serve immediately.

Kaiserschmarrn was a favorite dish of Kaiser Franz Joseph of Austria and hence receives its name, Kaiserschmarrn, which roughly translates to "Kaiser's mess," because the pancakes are torn up. In Austria it is usually eaten as a dessert or second course after a light meal, but would make a nice addition to an American brunch.

BUTTER TARTS

Serves 12
Prep/Cook Time: 45 minutes

Pastry

1¾   cups (245g) flour, sifted
⅛   teaspoon salt
½   cup (120g) margarine, chilled
1   tablespoon very cold water

Butter Tart Filling

⅓   cup (80g) soft butter
1   cup (200g) brown sugar
1   egg, beaten
2   tablespoons milk
1   teaspoon vanilla
½   cup (80g) raisins

- Sift flour and salt together in a medium mixing bowl. Cut chilled margarine into flour mixture until little balls form. Add water and, using a fork, mix just until pastry forms a ball. If needed, add more cold water 1 tablespoon at a time until ball forms.

- Roll dough out on a floured board. Cut circles about 3½ inches (9cm) in diameter to line a nonstick shallow muffin pan. The dough should just line each muffin cup with no pastry above the side of the cup.

- Preheat oven to 450°.

- To make filling, beat butter and brown sugar together until fluffy. Add egg, milk, and vanilla, and continue beating until well mixed.

- Place a few raisins in each cup. Pour enough filling in each cup to cover bottom, but do not fill more than half full.

- Bake for 10 to 15 minutes until the filling bubbles. Tarts should be carefully watched to ensure that batter boils to the edge but does not boil over.

- Cool tarts completely before removing from muffin pan, and serve at room temperature.

This is a version of sugar pie, which is a traditional Canadian dessert.

Cook's Tip:

Proper oven temperature is very important for baking. An oven's thermostat can often malfunction and the temperature might be off by several degrees and turn out unwelcome results. An oven thermometer can be purchased at most grocery stores or hardware stores to check oven temperature if there are any doubts as to its accuracy.

AMANDINE AUX POIRES
Almond Pear Tart

Serves 8
Prep/Cook Time:
1 hour 30 minutes

Pastry

2	cups (285g)	flour
3	tablespoons	sugar
½	teaspoon	salt
9	tablespoons (135g)	unsalted butter
1	egg, beaten	
3	tablespoons	water

Pear and Almond Filling

1	15 ounce (420g) can pear halves	
¾	cup (60g)	ground almonds
⅓	cup (65g)	sugar
1⅔	cups (400ml)	cream
¼	cup (60ml)	milk
¼	cup (60ml)	rum
Powdered sugar for garnish		

- Mix dry ingredients for pastry in a bowl and cut in butter using two knives or a pastry blender. Mix in egg and water and form into a ball. Flatten ball slightly and wrap in plastic wrap. Chill 30 minutes or longer.

- Preheat oven to 375°.

- Drain pears and cut each half into 2 lengthwise pieces.

- Roll out dough until large enough to press into a 12 inch (30cm) tart pan to form a shell. Prick the crust with a fork all over.

- Distribute pear quarters evenly over tart shell.

- Mix remainder of filling ingredients and pour into the tart shell.

- Bake for until set, about 45 minutes. Sprinkle with powdered sugar. Serve immediately or refrigerate and serve the next day.

Almonds are native to Asia, and were introduced to Europe via Arab traders in the 6th century. Almonds have been widely used in Europe for sweets and stews since the Middle Ages.

French dessert tarts are like open faced pies where you can see all the filling. Because of this, decoratively arranging the pears on the shell can make a particularly pretty dessert without much extra work.

Brandy Tipsy Tart

Brandy Tipsy Tart is best made one to two days in advance so the flavors can blend. Serve with ice cream or whipping cream.

Pastry

3	tablespoons (45g) unsalted butter, at room temperature
1	cup (200g) sugar
1	egg, well beaten
1	cup (150g) finely chopped walnuts
1½	cups (210g) finely chopped dates
1	teaspoon baking soda
1	cup (240ml) boiling water
1½	cups (215g) flour
¼	teaspoon baking powder
½	teaspoon salt

Sauce

1¼	cups (250g) sugar
2	teaspoons vanilla
2	teaspoons (30g) butter
¾	cup (185ml) brandy
¾	cup (185ml) water

- Preheat oven to 325°. Grease two 9 inch (23cm) pie plates

- Using an electric mixer, cream butter and sugar until mixture is pale yellow and fluffy. Add egg.

- Combine nuts, dates, and baking soda in a bowl and pour boiling water over mixture. Add to the creamed butter mixture.

- Sift flour, baking powder, and salt and fold into the butter mixture.

- Divide between two prepared pie plates and bake for 30 to 35 minutes. Remove from oven and cool. While the pastry is cooling, prepare sauce.

- Mix all sauce ingredients in a small pan and heat to a boil over medium heat. Boil gently for 7 minutes.

- Make small slits in cooled pastry and pour sauce over it, letting the syrup soak in.

CHOCOLATE MOUSSE PIE

Serves 8
Prep/Cook Time: 45 minutes,
plus 4 hours to chill

Sugar for dusting pie pan
8   *ounces (225g) semi-sweet chocolate*
¼   *cup (60ml) water, less one teaspoon*
8   *large eggs, separated*
1   *teaspoon orange liqueur or strong espresso coffee*
⅔   *cup (125g) sugar*
1½ *cups (350ml) whipped topping,*

- Preheat oven to 350°. Oil a 9 inch (23cm) pie pan and dust with sugar.

- In a saucepan over low heat, melt chocolate in water, stirring until smooth. Remove from heat and cool slightly. Beat in egg yolks and liqueur or espresso.

- In a large mixing bowl, beat egg whites until foamy. Gradually beat in sugar until stiff peaks form. Stir one quarter of the whites into the chocolate mixture.

- Fold chocolate mixture into the remaining whites.

- Pour four cups of the chocolate mixture into the prepared pie pan. Chill the remaining mixture.

- Bake for 20 to 25 minutes or until just set. Cool slightly and then chill for one hour. The center will fall, forming a pie shell.

- Spoon chilled chocolate mixture into chilled shell. Chill at least 3 hours or overnight. Serve with whipped topping.

Note:

Refer to the glossary for information regarding the safe handling of raw eggs.

This makes an excellent dessert that is perfect for the Jewish holiday of Passover, as it has no flour.

Cook's Tip:
Bring egg whites to room temperature before beating for the most volume.

KEY LIME PIE

Serves 8
Prep/Cook Time: 25 minutes,
plus 3 hours 30 minutes to chill

Graham Cracker Crust

1½ cups (150g) graham cracker crumbs
¼ cup (50g) sugar
6 tablespoons (90-105g) butter, melted

Key Lime Filling

1 14 ounce (390g) can sweetened condensed milk
3 large egg yolks
½ cup (125ml) *key lime juice
Grated zest of 1 lime
Lime slices for garnish, optional

- Mix all crust ingredients together. Press in bottom and sides of an 8 inch (20cm) pie pan. Chill for 30 minutes.

- Preheat oven to 350°.

- Combine milk, egg yolks, lime juice, and zest. Blend until smooth. Pour filling into chilled graham cracker crust.

- Bake for 10 minutes. Remove from oven and let cool. Refrigerate for at least 3 hours, and serve.

Variations:

The crust for this key lime pie is nice and thick. A 6 ounce (175g) ready-made pie crust may be used when time is short. Double the filling recipe if a 9 ounce (250g) ready-made crust is used.

A key lime is smaller and tarter than the larger and more common Persian lime. Key limes are native to Florida, but are now grown many places including Mexico. The juice can often be found bottled in most large supermarkets, if fresh key limes are not available. The juice of either lime may be used for this pie, but the juice of the key lime is tarter.

USA

PÂTE MOLLE
Warm Apple Pastry

Serves 6
Prep/Cook Time: 45 minutes

Cake

5	tablespoons flour
1	teaspoon baking powder
⅛	teaspoon salt
3	tablespoons sugar
3	tablespoons milk
3	tablespoons vegetable oil
1	egg, lightly beaten
2	large granny smith apples, peeled and cored

Sauce

5	tablespoons (75g) unsalted butter
1	egg, lightly beaten
3	tablespoons sugar

- Preheat oven to 375°. Grease a 9 inch (23cm) glass or ceramic pie dish with butter. Do not use cooking spray.

- In a large bowl, mix all cake ingredients except apples and pour into pie dish.

- Cut apples in thin slices and place in a circular pattern on top of batter. Bake 15 minutes.

- While baking, prepare sauce. Melt butter in a pan. Remove from heat and mix in egg and sugar, blending well.

- Pour sauce over apples and continue baking another 15 minutes until golden brown. Serve warm.

Pâte (paht), without the accent over the e, is a general French term for pastry dough, bread dough, batters, and sweet pastes. The word Pâté (pah TAY), with the accent over the e, is applied to a dish consisting of a pastry case filled with meat, fish, vegetables or fruit, which is baked in the oven and served hot or cold.

SOUTHERN PEACH AND BLUEBERRY COBBLER

Serves 4
Prep/Cook Time:
1 hour 15 minutes

This is an uncomplicated, simply delicious dessert. It is best served hot and bubbly from the oven.

Most every good Southern cook will have at least one cobbler recipe handed down from their grandmother.

¼   cup (60g) butter
⅔   cup (125g) sugar, plus ¾ tablespoon sugar
2   cups (450g) fresh peaches, peeled and sliced
½   cup (70g) flour
⅛   teaspoon salt
1¼   teaspoons baking powder
½   cup (125ml) milk
½-¾   cup (55-80g) fresh blueberries

• Preheat oven to 350° Place butter in an 8 inch (20cm) glass baking pan. Place baking pan in oven until butter is melted.

• Sprinkle ¾ tablespoon sugar over sliced peaches.

• Combine ⅔ cup (125g) of the sugar and remaining dry ingredients and mix in milk. Pour batter over melted butter in baking dish.

• Scatter peaches over batter. Scatter blueberries over peaches.

• Bake 1 hour and serve warm with Southern Custard Sauce (see index for recipe), vanilla ice cream, or fresh whipped cream.

Variations:

Substituting frozen peaches and blueberries for the fresh ones works very well with this recipe. This cobbler is also excellent with pitted cherries or using either blueberries or peaches alone.

U S A

TARTE AUX MYRTILLES
Blueberry Tart

Serves 8
Prep/Cook Time: 1 hour

Tart Crust

1¼ cups (175g) flour
⅛ teaspoon salt
2 tablespoons sugar
7 tablespoons (105g) unsalted butter, softened
3 tablespoons water

Filling

1 pound (450g) fresh blueberries
2 eggs
1 cup (235ml) crème fraîche or heavy cream
   (see index for recipe or purchase information)
¾ cup (150g) sugar
2 tablespoons flour

• Preheat oven to 350°. Butter a 10 inch (25cm) tart pan with removable bottom.

• In a medium bowl mix flour, salt, and sugar. Mix butter into dry ingredients and work with fingers or two knives. When no clumps of butter remain, add water and work into a ball using your hands to knead gently. This entire step can be done in a food processor.

• On a floured board, roll out dough slightly larger than 10 inches (25cm) round. Line prepared pan with dough. Trim edges and prick the dough several times on bottom of pan.

• Spread blueberries evenly on crust.

• Beat eggs and crème fraîche with a fork. Add sugar and beat. Add flour and beat again. Pour mixture on top of blueberries.

• Bake for 30 to 40 minutes or until set. Serve lukewarm.

Strictly translated, myrtilles are actually huckleberries that are native to northern regions of Europe and America. Huckleberries closely resemble, and are often mistaken for, blueberries. Blueberries are the listed ingredient for this recipe as they are easier to find. If huckleberries are available, they are equally delicious.

France

TARTE TATIN
Caramel and Apple Tart

Serves 8
Prep/Cook Time:
1 hour 10 minutes

1   tablespoon (15g) unsalted butter
½   cup (100g) plus 2 teaspoons sugar
¼   cup (60ml) water
6   apples
Zest of 1 orange
Puff pastry for one tart pan
1   cup (140g) flour

- Preheat oven to 350°. Place ½ (8g) tablespoon of butter, sliced in small pieces, in bottom of a 9 to 10 inch (23 to 25cm) deep dish tart pan or ovenproof deep skillet.

- Melt ½ cup (100g) sugar and water in a small pan over high heat stirring constantly until mixture turns from butterscotch to deep amber, 10 to 12 minutes. When caramel sauce is amber, pour it in the bottom of tart pan or skillet.

- Peel, core, and quarter apples lengthwise. Arrange a ring of apple quarters against the sides of the pan, standing the apples on the thin edge of their cut side so as to fit as many as possible. Fill in the center with remaining apple quarters.

- Cut ½ tablespoon (7g) butter in small pieces and place on top of apples. Grate orange zest on top and sprinkle with 2 teaspoons sugar.

- Sprinkle 1 sheet puff pastry with flour and roll out 1 inch (2.5cm) wider than tart pan. Place pastry over apples and tuck the overhand pastry under the apples in the pan and discard any extra.

- Bake until the crust is deep golden, about 40 minutes. Remove from oven, loosen edges, place a serving dish on top of the baking dish, and turn tart upside down. Remove the baking dish and return any apples that stick to the tart pan. Serve warm with vanilla ice cream or Crème Chantilly (see index for recipe).

Tarte Tatin was a specialty of the Tatin sisters, who ran a hotel restaurant in Lamotte-Beuvron at the beginning of the twentieth century. The tarte was cooked over the fire in a metal pan that allowed the apple mixture to caramelize. Traditionally this is made with a crust such as the one used for the Tarte aux Myrtilles (see index for recipe), but a puff pastry crust makes preparation quick and easy.

WORLD'S BEST FUDGE PIE

Serves 6
Prep/Cook Time: 45 minutes

½   cup (120g) unsalted butter,
       at room temperature
1   cup (200g) sugar
2   ounces (55g) unsweetened chocolate, melted and cooled slightly
2   eggs, separated and at room temperature
⅓   cup (50g) flour
1½ teaspoons vanilla
⅛   teaspoon salt
1½ cups (350ml) whipped cream, slightly sweetened
⅓   cup (65g) fresh raspberries, optional

- Preheat oven to 325°. Grease a 9 inch (23cm) glass, not metal, pie dish with butter. Do not use oil or cooking spray.

- In a large bowl cream butter and sugar. Add chocolate and beat well. Beat in egg yolks and gently stir in flour and vanilla just to combine.

- In a separate bowl whip egg whites and salt until stiff but not dry. Fold into chocolate mixture. Spread in buttered pie dish.

- May be made to this point up to 1 hour ahead.

- Bake 30 minutes. Do not overcook; center should be slightly gooey and sides crisp. Serve warm from the oven with whipped cream and garnish with raspberries, if desired.

This is an easy dessert that never fails and is elegant enough to serve at a dinner party. As it has no baking powder, it can be made before guests arrive and popped in the oven before sitting down to dinner, and taken hot out of the oven just in time for dessert.

Cook's Tip:

For the most volume in cream, beat it when it is very cold. In fact, pop the bowl and beaters in the freezer for a few minutes before whipping the cream.

U S A

249

LINZERTORTE WITH MARZIPAN

Serves 8
Prep/Cook Time:
1 hour 20 minutes,
plus 1 hour to chill dough

The Linzertorte takes its name from the town of Linz, Austria. There are many wonderful Austrian tarts and cakes such as this and the Malakoff Tart (see index for recipe). These are usually eaten in the afternoon with coffee rather than as dessert.

Crust

1½	cups (215g) flour
1	cup (115g) powdered sugar
1	cup (150g) almonds, toasted
1	teaspoon grated lemon peel
¼	teaspoon ground cinnamon
⅛	teaspoon ground cloves
¾	cup (180g) unsalted butter, cut into pieces and softened
2	large egg yolks
1	teaspoon vanilla

Marzipan and Raspberry Filling

1	8 ounce (225g) can of almond paste
3	tablespoons (45g) soft butter
½	cup (100g) sugar
1	egg
¼	cup (35g) flour
1¼	cups (400g) raspberry jam

Powdered sugar for dusting
1½ cups (350ml) fresh whipped cream, lightly sweetened

- Blend flour, powdered sugar, almonds, lemon peel, cinnamon and cloves in food processor until nuts are finely ground. Add butter and process until coarse meal forms. Add egg yolks and vanilla. Process until mixture forms a moist clump. Process in 1 to 3 teaspoons cold water as needed for a manageable dough. Divide dough in half. Flatten each half into a disk and wrap separately in plastic wrap. Refrigerate 1 hour.
- Preheat oven to 350°.
- Roll 1 dough disk between two sheets of plastic wrap to an 11 inch (28cm) round. Remove top plastic wrap and transfer dough side down into 9 inch (23cm) tart pan with removable bottom. Remove top plastic wrap and press dough to fit tart pan. Trim edges.
- Place almond paste, butter, sugar, egg, and flour in food processor and process until well blended. Spread filling over the dough in tart pan. Spread raspberry jam on top of Marzipan filling.
- Roll remaining dough between two sheets of plastic wrap to 10 inch (25cm) round and place in freezer for 3 minutes. Remove chilled dough to a cutting board.
- Cutting through plastic wrap and dough, make 8 to 10 strips. Remove plastic wrap from one side of strips. Form a lattice by arranging half of strips, dough side down, atop jam spacing evenly. Remove plastic wrap from top of strips placed on jam. Repeat with remaining strips on angles to create a lattice. Press ends of strips to edges of crust. If strips break, squeeze together with fingertips and a little water.
- Bake until crust is golden, about 50 minutes. Dust with powdered sugar. Serve warm or at room temperature with whipped cream.

Austria

Malakoff-Torte

Serves 16
Prep/Cook Time: 1 hour,
plus 2 hours to chill

1   cup (250ml) milk
2   egg yolks
¼   cup (50g) sugar
½   teaspoon vanilla
1   ¼ ounce (7g) envelope granulated gelatin, or
            3 sheets of gelatin soaked in ½ cup (125ml) water, and then drained
½   cup water
2   cups (473ml) heavy cream, whipped to soft peaks
1   tablespoon, plus ⅓ cup (85ml) rum
1   cup (250ml) water
40-45 lady fingers, enough to fill a 10 inch (25cm) springform pan
1   cup (100g) sliced almonds or finely chopped hazelnuts

- Fill the bottom of a double boiler with water, bring to a simmer. Mix milk, egg yolks, sugar and vanilla in the top of double boiler and cook until the mixture thickens, being careful not to let it reach a boil.

- Add gelatin to milk mixture and stir until cool. Just before mixture starts to jell, fold in half of the whipped cream and 1 tablespoon rum.

- Combine remaining ⅓ cup (85ml) rum and water in a shallow pan. Dip ladyfingers quickly in the mixture, so they don't get too soggy, and line the bottom of a 10 inch (25cm) springform pan with them.

- Spread ⅓ of the cream and gelatin filling over the ladyfingers, and repeat with two more layers. Chill tightly covered in the refrigerator for 2 hours.

- Take off the springform ring and cover the entire cake with remaining whipped cream. Decorate with nuts around the tops or sides of the cake and serve.

This is a very traditional Austrian torte. The ratio of rum to water for dipping the lady fingers can be adjusted up or down according to your preference for the taste of rum.

SOWHAN

Honey Almond or Pistachio Brittle

Makes 16 pieces
Prep/Cook Time: 15 to 20 minutes

1	tablespoon hot water
1	cup (200g) granulated sugar
2	tablespoons honey
3	tablespoons (45g) unsalted butter
1/2	cup (50g) slivered almonds or pistachio nuts
1/8-1/4	teaspoon saffron
1/8	cup (20g) almonds or pistachio nuts

• Over medium-low heat melt sugar slowly in a small heavy skillet.

• Reduce heat to low and add honey, butter, and slivered nuts to sugar, stirring gently.

• Pound or mash saffron into fine pieces, and dissolve in 1 tablespoon hot water.

• Add dissolved saffron to sugar mixture, mixing gently but quickly.

• Remove from heat.

• Drop by tablespoon on ungreased cookie sheet.

• Working quickly, press several pieces of remaining nuts on each piece and let cool.

• Gently remove from cookie sheet to prevent breaking. Store in cool, dry place in airtight container.

Almonds are a sign of fertility in many cultures which is probably why candied almonds of one sort or another are often served at wedding celebrations.

Sowhan is served in Iran at celebrations for weddings and the Persian New Year, which is the first day of spring.

Iran

ANZAC BISCUITS
Oatmeal Coconut Cookies

Makes 3 dozen cookies
Prep/Cook Time: 30 minutes

½   cup (120g) butter
1   tablespoon Lyles golden syrup, or
        mixture of half corn and half maple syrups
1   cup (100g) rolled oats (oatmeal)
¾   cup (75g) desiccated (dry) coconut, shredded or flaked
1   cup (140g) flour
1   cup (200g) light brown sugar, or
        ½ cup (100g) brown sugar and ½ cup (100g) white sugar
1½ teaspoons baking soda
2   tablespoons boiling water

- Preheat oven to 300°.

- Melt butter and golden syrup over low heat. Place all dry ingredients, except baking soda, in a large bowl.

- Stir baking soda into boiling water, and add to butter and syrup mixture.

- Combine liquid with dry ingredients and blend well.

- Drop by rounded teaspoons or form teaspoons of dough into rolls and place on cookie sheet spaced well apart. Bake for 15 to 18 minutes until golden. Cool on a rack.

The secret with these wonderfully crispy cookies is desiccated coconut. The normal coconut found in American supermarkets has water added. Dry coconut can often be found in the international section of large supermarkets or is available in international markets.

ANZAC biscuits received their name during World War I from the Australian and New Zealand Army Corps (ANZAC). They were sent by loving mums and wives to the troops fighting on the Gallipoli Peninsula. ANZAC Day is commemorated every year in Australia and New Zealand on April 25th.

LAMINGTONS

Makes 20 lamingtons
Prep/Cook Time:
1 hour 45 minutes,
plus 24 hours to age cake

Cake

9	tablespoons (135g) butter
¾	cup (150g) sugar
1	teaspoon vanilla
2	eggs, slightly beaten
2	cups (285g) flour
1	teaspoon salt
3	teaspoons baking powder
½	cup (125ml) milk

Icing

3¾	cups (430g) powdered sugar
3	tablespoons cocoa
½	teaspoon (3g) butter
¼	teaspoon vanilla
6	tablespoons (+/–) boiling water
3	cups (300g) unsweetened desiccated coconut

- Preheat oven to 350°. Butter a lamington or lasagna pan, about 7x11 inches (18x28cm).

- Cream butter, sugar, and vanilla until light and fluffy. Gradually beat in the eggs one at a time.

- Sift flour with salt and baking powder and fold alternately with milk into creamed butter and sugar, beginning and ending with flour. Beat until smooth, but do not over beat as tunnels may form in the cake during baking.

- Pour batter into greased pan. Lightly smooth top and bake for 25 to 30 minutes or until toothpick inserted comes out clean. Cool on a wire rack and store for one day, as fresh cake will crumble.

- The next day cut cake into 2 inch (5cm) squares, about 20 in all.

- Mix powdered sugar, cocoa, butter, and vanilla in a large bowl. Add boiling water and stir until smooth and shiny. Mixture should be thin enough to coat the squares but not runny. It may be necessary to test on one square and add more water as needed.

- Pour coconut into a separate bowl.

- Dip each cake square in icing, using two forks to hold the cake. Let excess icing drip off into bowl. Roll coated square in coconut until all sides are covered. Place on a rack to set.

Lamingtons first appeared in Australian cookbooks around 1909. They were supposedly first made by an enterprising cook looking to use a stale sponge cake, and were named after Lord Lamington, Governor of Queensland from 1895 to 1901. Australian school children have Lamington Drives to raise money and most homes will have a pack or two in the freezer. The cake may be frozen until ready for use and iced lamingtons also freeze well.

LIME COOKIES

Makes 2½ dozen cookies
Prep/Cook Time: 45 minutes,
plus 30 minutes to chill

Sugar Topping

- ⅓ cup (65g) sugar
- ¼ teaspoon cinnamon
- ¼ teaspoon nutmeg

Cookies

- ¾ cup (180g) butter, softened
- 1 cup (200g) sugar
- Grated zest of 2 limes
- Juice of 1 lime
- 2 cups (285g) flour
- 1 teaspoon baking powder
- ¼ teaspoon salt
- ¼ teaspoon cinnamon
- ¼ teaspoon nutmeg

- Mix topping ingredients in a small, shallow bowl. Set aside.

- In a medium bowl cream together butter and sugar until smooth. Add lime zest and juice.

- Sift together flour, baking powder, salt, cinnamon, and nutmeg. Combine with butter mixture. Refrigerate dough covered for 30 minutes.

- Preheat oven to 350°.

- Roll dough into 1 inch (2.5cm) balls.

- Place balls on a greased cookie sheet. Flatten with bottom of a glass dipped in the sugar topping. Bake for 13 to 16 minutes until just barely starting to turn golden. Remove from cookie sheet immediately and cool on racks.

This recipe doubles well.

Lime Trivia:

In the mid-nineteenth century, British seamen were nicknamed limeys because lime juice from the West Indies was added to their daily rum ration to prevent scurvy.

U S A

GLACE AU GRAND MARNIER

Grand Marnier Ice Cream

Serves 8
Prep/Cook Time: 30 minutes,
plus 10 hours to freeze

Glace au Grand Marnier does not freeze hard, but remains a creamy consistency and should be served immediately upon removing from the freezer, as the high alcohol content will cause quick melting.

Cointreau may be substituted for the Grand Marnier with an equally delicious result.

5   eggs, separated
½   cup (60g) powdered sugar
⅓   cup (85ml) Grand Marnier
1¼ cups (300ml) heavy whipping cream
½   cup (100g) granulated sugar

• In a large mixing bowl, beat egg yolks with powdered sugar until pale yellow and fluffy. Add Grand Marnier.

• Combine cream and ¼ cup (50g) of the granulated sugar in a separate bowl. Whip until peaks form. Add to egg yolk mixture.

• Beat egg whites in a separate bowl, slowly adding remainder of the granulated sugar as egg whites start to foam. Beat until peaks form and hold. Fold into egg yolk mixture.

• Place into a container and freeze for at least 10 hours. Serve in chilled dishes.

Note:

Refer to the glossary for information regarding the safe handling of raw eggs.

ISRAELI ORANGE SORBET

Serves 6
Prep/Cook Time: 20 minutes,
plus 11 hours to chill

1   cup (200g) sugar
1   cup (250ml) water
Grated zest of 3 oranges
Grated zest of 1 lemon
Juice of 1 lemon
2   cups (500ml) freshly squeezed orange juice, strained
Fresh mint for garnish
3   tablespoons *Sabra, or other orange flavored liqueur, optional

- In a small saucepan combine sugar, water, orange zest, and lemon zest. Slowly bring to a boil stirring until sugar dissolves. Cook 5 minutes. Remove from heat and let cool.

- Cover tightly and refrigerate 3 to 4 hours or overnight.

- Remove from refrigerator and combine with lemon and orange juice. Place in a metal bowl and freeze 3 to 4 hours until semi-soft.

- In a food processor with a metal blade, process until creamy, 30 to 45 seconds.

- Return to metal bowl and freeze another 1½ hours. Scrape into food processor again and process until light and creamy, 30 to 40 seconds.

- Freeze 3 to 4 hours until completely firm.

- Soften 5 minutes at room temperature before scooping into individual serving glasses. Garnish with mint leaves and, if desired, a few tablespoons of Sabra.

This recipe also works well in an ice cream maker following manufacturer's directions.

*Sabra is a chocolate-orange flavored liqueur made in Israel that makes this sorbet very special.

Sorbet, a French term, is distinguished from sherbet by the fact that sorbet never includes milk or cream.

Israel

SOUTHERN CUSTARD SAUCE

Makes 5½ cups
Prep/Cook Time: 30 minutes

1   cup (200g) sugar
1   quart (950ml) milk
⅛   teaspoon salt
4   eggs
1   tablespoon vanilla

- In a 2 quart (2 liter) saucepan, blend sugar, milk, and salt. Heat over medium heat until hot, but not boiling.

- In a large bowl, beat eggs until light and very frothy. Whisk hot milk mixture very slowly into eggs, continuing to whisk constantly until all milk is blended into eggs.

- Pour egg and milk mixture back into the saucepan, and heat over low heat. Stir constantly, until the custard coats a spoon, being careful not to let boil. The color of the mixture should be a pale yellow. Put custard through a strainer if necessary to remove any lumps.

- Pour custard into a bowl, add vanilla, and stir. Cover with wax paper until custard cools. Serve warm or cold.

Custard sauce is excellent served alone or over cake with fresh berries or bananas and whipped cream. It is a tradition in many homes in the southern United States for mothers to serve this type sauce as a special treat to their children when they are sick. Serve with Rote Grütze or Southern Peach and Blueberry Cobbler (see index for recipes).

U S A

Seasonings, Condiments
& the Rest

Punjabi Garam Masala

Makes ¾ cup
Prep/Cook Time: 15 minutes

¼   cup (25g) cumin seeds
¼   cup (25g) coriander seeds
1½ tablespoons cardamom seeds,
       removed from pods
2   whole cinnamon sticks, about 3 inches (8cm) long
1½ teaspoons whole cloves
3   tablespoons black peppercorns
4   bay leaves, broken up
½   teaspoon ground mace

• Heat a medium heavy skillet for 2 minutes over medium-high heat.

• Combine all spices except mace and put into hot skillet. Dry roast spices, stirring constantly until they have turned several shades darker and exude a spicy aroma, about 10 minutes.

• Transfer to a bowl, and let cool completely.

• Grind cooled spices to a powder using a blender, spice mill, or coffee grinder.

• Add mace and store in an airtight container for up to 3 months.

Garam Masala is a basic spice blend used in Northern India. This is a traditional recipe from the Punjab. Other versions use fennel or fenugreek. It is less spicy than the curry powders of Southern India. It is used in Lentil Dahl, Minced Turkey with Mint, and Aloo Merich Sabzi (see index for recipes).

Garam Masala can also be purchased in most international or Indian markets and in the international or gourmet section of some supermarkets.

West Indian Seasoning

Makes ¾ cup seasoning
Prep/Cook Time: 15 minutes

½   cup (150g) kosher salt
6   cloves garlic, finely minced
½   teaspoon dried parsley
2   teaspoons ground black pepper
½   habanero chile, diced

• Combine ingredients in a shallow bowl or place in a glass jar, and shake until combined. Store refrigerated in a tightly sealed glass jar for weeks. Use to season meat, poultry or fish for grilling or broiling.

This delicious seasoning has been used for generations to season fish, poultry, pork or beef in the West Indies. It is prepared with the habanero chile, a distinctively flavored, extremely hot pepper that is native to the West Indies. Hands should be washed immediately after handling the chile or gloves should be worn. Red pepper flakes or cayenne pepper can be substituted if the habanero chile is not available.

MINT CILANTRO CHUTNEY

3½ cups (105g) fresh cilantro
2   cups (60g) fresh mint
1   cup (140g) coarsely chopped green onions
1   2 inch (5cm) cube ginger, peeled
3   cloves garlic
¼   cup (40g) blanched almonds
½   cup (125ml) fresh lime juice
4   Thai chiles or finger hot chiles

• Place all ingredients in a food processor and blend to a paste. Add water if needed to reach a smooth paste.

Serve with Spicy Lamb Kebabs or Tandoori Chicken Kebabs (see index for recipes). Any extra chutney may be frozen for later use.

Chutney is a Sanskrit word meaning "for licking". It is to be served on the side with a meal and often provides a contrasting flavor to the rest of the meal. Most people are familiar with the sweetish cooked chutneys such as Mango Chutney, but Mint Cilantro Chutney is in the form of a chopped herb sauce.

NUOC CHAM
Dipping Sauce

Makes sauce for 50 spring rolls
Prep/Cook Time: 10 minutes

½   cup (125ml) nuoc mam (fish sauce)
¼   cup (60ml) white vinegar
½   cup (125ml) water
Juice of ½ lemon
½   teaspoon crushed hot red pepper sauce or more to taste
1   tablespoon sugar
2   carrots, finely shredded
1   clove garlic, finely minced
½   *daikon radish, finely shredded

• Combine all liquids and sugar in a large mouth jar. Put lid on jar and shake until sugar is dissolved. Add carrot, garlic, and daikon, put lid on jar and shake to blend. Serve or store for later use tightly sealed in the refrigerator.

Nuoc Cham is to the Vietnamese what ketchup is to the Americans. It's in most all Vietnamese kitchens. It keeps indefinitely refrigerated and is the sauce for Bun Xao Thit Bo (Beef with Fine Rice Noodles) and Vietnamese Spring Rolls (see index for recipes.)

*Daikon is a Japanese white radish. It is milder than the smaller red radish and can be very easily grated.

CONFITURE D'OIGNON

Onion Jam

Serves 12
Prep/Cook Time:
1 hour 30 minutes,
plus 1 hour to chill

1   tablespoon (15g) unsalted butter
2   pounds (900g) onions, peeled and sliced
3/4 cup (90g) powdered sugar
1/4 cup (60ml) red wine vinegar
3/4 cup (185ml) red wine

• Melt butter in skillet over medium-low heat.

• Add onions and cook slowly for 5 minutes, not allowing onions to brown.

• Add powdered sugar and cook uncovered 30 minutes on very low heat until onions are very soft.

• Add vinegar and wine and cook uncovered 30 minutes more on very low heat.

• Remove from heat and let cool to room temperature. Cover and chill at least 1 hour before serving. This jam may be stored tightly covered in the refrigerator for up to 7 days.

Confiture d'Oignon is excellent served cold with a homemade pâté such as the Country Herb Pâté or Veal and Ham Pie (see index for recipes).

SUGAR BACON, BASIL AND TOMATO SANDWICHES

Serves 6
Prep/Cook Time: 20 minutes

Basil Mayonnaise

2	cups (60g) packed basil leaves
1	large whole egg
1	egg yolk
4	teaspoons fresh lemon juice
1	cup (250ml) olive, safflower or canola oil

Sugar Bacon and Tomato Sandwich

½	cup (100g) (+/-) sugar
18	lean bacon slices
	White sugar to coat bacon
2	vine ripe tomatoes, peeled and sliced
12	bakery fresh white bread slices
	Basil leaves

- Place basil leaves, eggs and lemon juice in a food processor and process until leaves are finely chopped and ingredients are well mixed.

- Slowly pour in oil while processing until the mixture has thickened.

- Place in an airtight container and store until ready to use.

- Pour sugar on a paper towel and coat both sides of each bacon slice with sugar. Discard any excess sugar. Microwave bacon until cooked, being careful not to burn.

- Spread bread slices generously with basil mayonnaise, and assemble each sandwich with a layer of bacon, tomato, and basil leaves.

Note:

Refer to the glossary for information regarding the safe handling of raw eggs.

The mayonnaise will keep in the refrigerator for up to 3 weeks. The sandwiches are best served immediately, but if made ahead should be kept refrigerated until ready to serve.

U S A

265

Swiss Cheese Fondue

Serves 4
Prep/Cooking Time: 25 minutes

1½ tablespoons kirsch
1½ tablespoons cornstarch
1   clove garlic, peeled and halved
1½ cups (375ml) dry white wine
3   cups (360g) grated *Emmentaler cheese
3   cups (360g) grated **Gruyère cheese
Freshly ground pepper
Freshly grated nutmeg
1   loaf of French bread, cut into bite sized cubes

- In a small bowl, combine kirsch and cornstarch. Stir to a paste and set aside.

- Rub the inside of an earthenware fondue dish or a heavy duty 2 quart (2 liter) pan with garlic, discarding garlic afterwards. Pour wine into fondue dish and bring it almost to a boil on stovetop.

- While stirring continually with a wooden spoon, add grated cheese. Just before the mixture reaches the boiling point, stir in the cornstarch and kirsch paste. Make more cornstarch paste with water if needed to make the sauce creamy and thick enough to coat the bread well. Continue to stir, adding pepper and a little grated nutmeg to taste.

- Transfer the fondue pot to an alcohol burner, which can be regulated to keep fondue at the simmering point. Serve the bread separately.

- Each diner, sitting around the table, can dip the bread into the fondue using a long handled fork. Make sure to stir the fondue regularly with the bread so that the cheese does not burn.

Cheese fondue is a traditional dish in German speaking Switzerland and the French region of Savoie.

**Emmentaler cheese is named for Switzerland's Emmental valley in the Canton of Bern. It is a cow's milk cheese that is hard and has many holes.*

***Gruyère cheese comes from the Gruyère valley in the Swiss Canton of Fribourg. It is also a cow's milk cheese with a firm but pliable texture and a nutty sweet flavor.*

LEMON CURD

Makes 12 -16 ounces
(340-450g)
Prep/Cook Time: 20 minutes

3   medium lemons with unblemished skins
½   cup (120g) unsalted butter
3   large eggs
1   egg yolk
1   cup (200g) sugar

• Grate the peel of the 3 lemons, and extract the juice, straining seeds.

• In a medium microwave-safe bowl, melt butter in microwave, being careful not to burn.

• In a separate bowl, beat eggs and egg yolk together.

• Add the sugar, beaten eggs, lemon peel and juice to the melted butter. Whisk gently.

• Cook mixture on high in a microwave for 2 to 3 minutes, whisking at least once a minute or pour into a double boiler and cook while stirring until thickened. Be careful not to overheat mixture because it will curdle.

• Pour into clean, dry, warm jam jar, cover and refrigerate.

Lemon Curd is an old English specialty. It is delicious with English Butter Cake or Dumbbread (see index for recipes), or your favorite pancakes, toast or croissants. Some like to strain out the lemon peel at the end of cooking for a smoother lemon curd. It keeps in the refrigerator for up to 2 weeks.

Cook's Tip:

Grate only the outermost colored part of citrus fruit for the zest. The white part is bitter.

England

COOKING WITHOUT BORDERS

2890 North Fulton Drive
Atlanta, GA 30305
404-841-3845
www.aischool.org

Please send me _____ copies of *Cooking without Borders* @ $19.95 each _____

Postage and Handling   @ $3.50 each _____

Georgia residents add 7% sales tax.   @ $1.40 each _____

Total _____

Name _____

Address_____

City_____ State_____ Zip_____

Make checks payable to *Cooking without Borders*

- -

COOKING WITHOUT BORDERS

2890 North Fulton Drive
Atlanta, GA 30305
404-841-3845
www.aischool.org

Please send me _____ copies of *Cooking without Borders* @ $19.95 each _____

Postage and Handling   @ $3.50 each _____

Georgia residents add 7% sales tax.   @ $1.40 each _____

Total _____

Name _____

Address_____

City_____ State_____ Zip_____

Make checks payable to *Cooking without Borders*